Text Classics

ROBIN BOYD is arguably Australia's most influential architect. He was born in Melbourne in 1919 in to one of the nation's great creative families, which included the painter Penleigh Boyd, novelist Martin Boyd and artist Arthur Boyd. Joan Lindsay, author of *Picnic at Hanging Rock*, was his cousin.

From the late 1940s Boyd wrote extensively about the importance of design in inexpensive housing. He was an idealist who believed that good design would improve the quality of people's lives, a tireless public educator and an outspoken social commentator. In 1952 he published *Australia's Home*, the first substantial survey of the country's domestic architecture. His masterwork, *The Australian Ugliness*, was first published in 1960 and the title has since entered the Australian lexicon. In all, Boyd wrote twelve books.

Boyd's architectural practice was prolific, and he worked with other leading architects, including Roy Grounds and Frederick Romberg. In his comparatively short career, he designed more than two hundred buildings of many kinds: houses, blocks of flats, motels and churches. He designed the now-demolished Australian pavilion for Expo 67 in Montreal.

Robin Boyd died in 1971, when he was fifty-two. In 2005 the Robin Boyd Foundation was established to celebrate his legacy and to promote debate about Australian design and society.

CHRISTOS TSIOLKAS is the author of four novels: *Loaded* (made into the film *Head On*), *The Jesus Man*, *Dead Europe* and the award-winning bestseller *The Slap*, which has been made into a television series for the ABC.

JOHN DENTON is a Director of Denton Corker Marshall, a proudly Australian international architecture and urban design practice with offices in Melbourne, London and Jakarta.

PHILIP GOAD is Professor and Chair of Architecture, and Director of the Melbourne School of Design, at the University of Melbourne.

GEOFFREY LONDON is the Professor of Architecture at the University of Western Australia and the Victorian Government Architect, having previously been the Western Australian Government Architect.

ALSO BY THIS AUTHOR

Victorian Modern
Australia's Home
Kenzo Tange
The Walls Around Us
The New Architecture
The Puzzle of Architecture
The Book of Melbourne and Canberra
New Directions in Japanese Architecture
Living in Australia (with Mark Strizic)
The Great Great Australian Dream
Artificial Australia (Boyer Lectures, 1967)

The Australian Ugliness
Robin Boyd

Text Publishing Melbourne Australia

Copyright Agency
Cultural Fund

Proudly supported by Copyright Agency's Cultural Fund.

textclassics.com.au
textpublishing.com.au

The Text Publishing Company
Swann House
22 William Street
Melbourne Victoria 3000
Australia

Copyright © Robin Boyd Foundation 2010
Foreword copyright © Christos Tsiolkas 2010
Afterword copyright © John Denton, Philip Goad & Geoffrey London 2010

Every effort has been made to trace copyright holders and obtain permission for the use of copyright material. The publisher apologises for any errors or omissions and would be grateful if notified of any corrections that should be incorporated in future reprints or editions of this book.

All rights reserved. Without limiting the rights under copyright above, no part of this publication shall be reproduced, stored in or introduced into a retrieval system, or transmitted in any form or by any means (electronic, mechanical, photocopying, recording or otherwise), without the prior permission of both the copyright owner and the publisher of this book.

First published in 1960 by F. W. Cheshire, Melbourne
First published by The Text Publishing Company in 2010
This edition published in 2012
Reprinted 2015

Designed by W H Chong
Typeset by J&M Typesetting

Printed and bound in Australia by Griffin Press, an Accredited ISO AS/NZS 14001:2004 Environmental Management System printer

Primary print ISBN: 9781921922442
Ebook ISBN: 9781921921995

This book is printed on paper certified against the Forest Stewardship Council® Standards. Griffin Press holds FSC chain-of-custody certification SGS-COC-005088. FSC promotes environmentally responsible, socially beneficial and economically viable management of the world's forests.

'It is taken for granted that Australia is ugly…'
ANTHONY TROLLOPE

CONTENTS

FOREWORD

Christos Tsiolkas

A few years ago I was sitting in a friend's apartment in Barcelona. She was living on a small street off the Parc de la Ciutadella, near the Arc de Triomf, walking distance from the tourist mecca of the Barri Gòtic. It seemed full of old-world character, with rows of ramshackle working-class apartments that housed the city's immigrant population. Every evening we would hear music outside on the street: the frenetic beating of drums; the call and response of English- and Spanish-language hip-hop; the chanting of the Call to Prayer. Music, motion, life lived on the streets—everything missing, I said, from our cities back home. My friend, an expat, nodded her head in agreement at my criticisms of Australian suburbia. But a Catalan colleague of hers who had joined us for a drink rolled her eyes in frustration at our whingeing. 'You haven't seen *our* suburbs,' she challenged me. 'You've come in straight off the Metro and think that this is the heartbeat of the city. Well, ninety per cent of people in Barcelona don't live here. They live in the suburbs, as I do, and the suburbs are ugly as sin. Let me take you *there*.'

She did take me there. And she was right; the suburbs of Barcelona—wave after wave of ugly grey concrete towers that begin where the boundaries of the tourist maps end—*are* ugly. But they are not ugly in the way our Australian cities can be ugly, in the way that our suburbs and towns are ugly. Europeans and Australians do not breathe the same air, walk the same earth, see with the same light. Robin Boyd's *The Australian Ugliness* reminds me that not only our landscape but also our history is unique, and that both have been crucial in creating this space called Australia. It is one of the remarkable joys of reading Boyd's classic study of the Australian approach to shaping our environment that we are presented with a social history that explains *us to ourselves*. With pithy dry wit, with an exuberant passion for his subject, Boyd dissected the progress of architecture and urban design on the Australian continent. Fifty years after the book's publication Boyd's observations still resonate, still make sense of Australian sensibility and culture. In the devastating third chapter, 'Anglophiles and Austericans', Boyd begins to essay a description of the Australian character by observing that it is 'Cruel but kind'. Then he proceeds to distil all my ambivalence, all my hatred and love for something called Australia and a people called Australians into one deadly accurate paragraph:

> Cruel but kind—a precise description of one element
> in the pervasive ambivalence of the national character.
> Here also are vitality, energy, strength, and optimism
> in one's own ability, yet indolence, carelessness, the
> 'she'll do, mate' attitude to the job to be done. Here is
> insistence on the freedom of the individual, yet
> resigned acceptance of social restrictions and censor-
> ship narrower than in almost any other democratic
> country in the world. Here is love of justice and devo-
> tion to law and order, yet the persistent habit of crowds
> to stone the umpire and trip the policeman in the
> course of duty. Here is preoccupation with material

things—note, for example, the hospitals: better for a
broken leg than a mental deviation—yet impatience
with polish and precision in material things. The
Australian is forcefully loquacious, until the moment
of expressing any emotion. He is aggressively committed to equality and equal opportunity for all men,
except for black Australians. He has high assurance in
anything he does combined with a gnawing lack of
confidence in anything he thinks.

He got us. *He still gets us.* Boyd understands that like all peoples we
are contradictory; he also understands what many subsequent social
commentators and historians have forgotten, that we are responsible
for ourselves. *The Australian Ugliness* offers the reality of Australia
once the excuses and justifications and squabbles over history are
stripped away. This book is written with precision and clarity. Half a
century hasn't diluted the potency of the brew. Reading it is
cleansing.

Of course, many things have changed since the first publication
of *The Australian Ugliness.* Some of Boyd's beliefs about aesthetics
and form were to be very quickly challenged, firstly by the rise of the
Pop artists who celebrated the kinetic energy of mass culture, and
then by the ascendancy of postmodern theories of architecture and art
that destabilised traditional notions of the beautiful and of the functional. Boyd may have been just too good an architect, too fine an
aesthete, to give himself over to the undisciplined energy and chemical
rush of the 'new world'. I don't share his suspicions of the grandiose,
the gaudy, or of suburbia for that matter; and I possibly prize the vital
over the sublime, desire the vigour of the 'ugly' over the lassitude of
the 'beautiful'. (In my home town of Melbourne, for example, I am
glad for the paean to both consumerism and wog aspiration that is the

new Doncaster Shoppingtown—and I'd also give a nod to the new Epping Plaza—and I admire the boldness and anti-gentility of Southbank and Federation Square.) *The Australian Ugliness* was written on the eve of the sixties. The wogs, the war, the drugs, notions of the beautiful and the correct and the proper—so much seemed about to change.

Plus ça change, plus c'est pareil. Boyd was not clairvoyant but he was remarkably prescient. He foresaw how, within a generation, migrants to Australia would take on the pioneer-settler ethos of the new world and recreate themselves anew, cast from an Australian consumerist mould. His criticisms of 'arboraphobia' and of the denial of the continent's dryness in the planning of our towns and cities must ring more powerfully now than when the book was first published. In the twenty-first century, which has seen the rise of a vapid empty nationalism that feeds off our insecurities and cultural cringe (*What do you think of Melbourne, Mr Cruise? What do you think of our argument, Mr Hitchens?*), a book like this one reminds us that no, this isn't the best of all possible worlds. We can, we must, do much better.

For there is finally no excuse for the unrelenting ugliness, the dismal depleted landscape that confronts us as we drive from the airport into the city. The endless freeways that devour the greenery are partly at fault, as is the slipshod history of urban Australian design. But as the woman in Barcelona reminded me, the failures and blind spots of suburbia are now not only confined to the new world. The suburbs—a new-world legacy—foster the aspirations of people across the globe. Boyd's book, his arguments, arose from a specifically Australian context but carries warnings and admonishments and questions for anyone interested in built environments, in the histories of society and place. I recognise myself and I recognise my world in this book, all the ugliness and all the beauty.

THE AUSTRALIAN UGLINESS
ROBIN BOYD

INTRODUCTION

The ugliness I mean is skin deep. If the visitor to Australia fails to notice it immediately, fails to respond to the surfeit of colour, the love of advertisements, the dreadful language, the ladylike euphemisms outside public lavatory doors, the technical competence but the almost uncanny misjudgement in floral arrangements, or if he thinks that things of this sort are too trivial to dwell on, then he is unlikely to enjoy modern Australia. For the things that make Australian people, society and culture in some way different from others in the modern world are only skin deep. But skin is as important as its admirers like to make it, and Australians make much of it. This is a country of many colourful, patterned, plastic veneers, of brick-veneer villas, and the White Australia Policy.

Under the veneer, practically all the impulses that lead to the culture of Australia are familiar in other prosperous parts of the world. Abstract art, prefabrication, mass-production and perverted Functionalist ethics provide the moulds that shape things in Australia, as they do wherever English-speaking people build communities. The extroverted flair of the Latin countries and the introverted refinement of Scandinavia are not to be expected. The chief characteristic is inconsistency; good and bad muddled together, sophistication and schoolboyishness, toughness and genteelness, all strongly marked and clearly isolated, but so cut up and mixed up that no one can be quite sure which in the long run predominates. Much the same can be said about the collective qualities of the Australian people. The national character is as cut up and mixed up as can be. Yet undoubtedly a distinctive quality does exist and is to some extent recognized by visitors immediately they arrive. Naturally, then, the visitor is inclined to look expectantly for more evidence or confirmation of it in the streets and homes and in all the popular arts and crafts. He is often disappointed, not because there is no Australian character in building and display and product-design but because it is so confused and so subtle that all but the historian or an intense student are likely to lose patience in the search. The climate of design is something like an uninhibited California. It is diametrically opposed to that of Sweden, where the average exhibited taste is cultivated and there are few who rise above or sink below. In Australia the artificial background of life is all highs and lows. A modernistic folly in multi-coloured brickwork may sit next door to a prim Georgian mansionette on one side and a sensitive work of architectural exploration on the other.

If, with the utmost patience, one can penetrate the superficialities and can extract the elements of a consistent Australian school of design, one finds it is not definable in conventional artistic or architectural jargon, but is bound up with the collective character of the Australian people. It is not, as might be expected, a result of uniformity of the climate or the geography. Contrary to the established impression, Australia is not all blazing sun. The populous coastal crescent is mostly mild, and often freezing. The centre is a furnace, but few visitors to the cities complain of the heat. Most have occasion to complain of unheated rooms. Neither is the terrain monotonous nor the larder of building materials limited. An Australian town may be on a lake, a mountainside, a river, or may spread along behind a white ocean beach. After the first clumsy convict settlements, the whole world's building products have been available most of the time and have been used at least as freely as in any country.

The elusive quality in Australian design which can be called typical, and can be recognized if transported abroad, is not a fundamental original quality. It would be better to call it a thin but well-established Australian veneer on international Western culture. This veneer and its concomitant tastes are the substance of everything peculiar in Australian living practices and artistic habits. Which came first, the veneer or the habits, has never been firmly established. One may ask, for instance, are the sex-segregated public drinking habits maintained because the hotels have no pleasant facilities for women, or do the hotels have hideous facilities for women deliberately: part of the old cult of masculinity? Both veneer and habits have strong effects on the aesthetic pattern which runs from sky-scraper to plastic doyley; certainly they have a stronger effect than the direct geographic or climatic influences. But this book will make no attempt to separate chronologically the chicken of human character and the egg of habit. It is simply intended as, firstly, a portrait of Australia with the background in the foreground and, secondly, a glance at the artistic philosophy which permitted this background to be so shallow and unsatisfying.

The recorded history of the visual Australian background has terrible gaps, but a few standard works of reference provide the essential information for anyone wishing to investigate the historical aspects which are cursorily referred to in these pages. On the old colonial work of the first fifty years, the book is *The Early Australian Architects and Their Work*, by Morton Herman (Angus and Robertson, 1954). The nineteenth century in New South Wales is covered by the same author in *The Architecture of Victorian Sydney* (Angus and Robertson, 1956). The cast iron age, with natural emphasis on Victoria, is described with beautiful illustrations in E. Graeme Robertson's

Victorian Heritage (Georgian House, 1960). Much of the charm of Tasmania's past is recorded by Michael Sharland in *Stones of a Century* (Oldham, Beddome and Meredith, Hobart, 1952). South Australia still waits for a local inhabitant sufficiently enthusiastic about his native State to undertake the work. Western Australia and Queensland have nothing within stiff covers but the institutes of architects in each State have published illustrated collections of notable buildings.

I am indebted to the above books for references in the text, and to Professor C. M. H. Clark's *Select Documents in Australian History* (Angus and Robertson, 1950) for the quotations from early visitors to Australia. Parts of Chapter Three, starting with the passage on Austerica, were first published in the Literary Supplement of *The Age*, Melbourne, in 1957, and parts of Chapter Four first appeared in the *Sydney Morning Herald*. The quotations from Ruskin are taken from *The Stones of Venice* and *Seven Lamps of Architecture*, those from Sir Geoffrey Scott are in *The Architecture of Humanism*, Rudolf Wittkower's is from *Architectural Principles in the Age of Humanism*, Le Corbusier's is from Chapter Two of *The Modulor*, and Piet Mondrian's is from *Plastic Art*. The mathematical 'melody' in Chartres Cathedral is described by Ernest Levy in an MIT Humanities booklet, and A. S. G. Butler's comments are taken from *The Substance of Architecture*. Finally, the quotations from William Hogarth and Horatio Greenough are from two classic statements from opposite sides of the interminable debate. Hogarth's *The Analysis of Beauty*, edited by Professor Joseph Burke (Oxford, 1955), first published in 1753, details the rococo-aesthetic approach, and Greenough's *Form and Functions*, edited by Harold A. Small (University of California, 1947), first published a century later in 1852–3, states the rational-functionalist argument.

*

I warn you now: this whole thing is old hat. It was old hat when it was first published seven years ago and it is old hat now, but for different reasons. Its initial staleness was due to the fact that various English architects had discovered the ugliness of the technological age years earlier and had been writing about it and drawing it in the *Architectural Review* and elsewhere. It is old-fashioned now because the war against ugliness has become a cause which has wide support, especially among artistic conservatives, and when any cause gets as respectable as that it draws reaction out of the shadows to gibe at it. At this moment (but the situation may well change again in no time) urban, technological and mass squalor is in: ugliness au go go. It is, some say, a sort of Pop Art. For example, when a few architects in New South Wales published the latest broadside against non-design in 1966, called *Australian Outrage*, the critic Max Harris called them old fogies and found the photographs ravishing. 'Vulgarism,' he wrote in *The Australian*, 'is the very life force and dynamic of an affluent urban free-enterprise society…We have to incorporate outrage into our aesthetic. We can't stem the irresistible cultural tide, but we can change our aesthetic.'

This can be an acceptable proposition, in a certain half-light. Some of the early Functionalists around the turn of the century were truly anti-aesthetic and argued that honesty to the function was all that mattered. There was really no ugliness anywhere; just eyes which refused to break old habits. If we could all just switch over our aesthetic awareness in tune with the twentieth century, we would realize that the modern world of wires and poles, service stations and soft drink signs, cut-outs, whirlers, flags, fairy lights and mutilated trees, is a beautifully vital place, while real ugliness—first sensed in an unpruned tree—reaches a screaming crescendo in an open, virgin landscape. If Functionalism is a sound principle, then what could make more powerful visual sustenance than the service wires on their crooked poles and the jig-saw puzzles of advertising signs serving so truly the function of making suburban dollars?

If that argument appeals to you, please read no further. The argument which follows is that the ugliness in the streets of almost every city in the modern world is not art of any sort and is really not very pop either. It is as functional but as artistically heedless as an anthill and as accidental as a rubbish dump. No matter how one photographs it, draws it, looks at it, or describes it, it remains physically an awful mess. In any case negative, careless ugliness is not the worst thing. What really must concern us more is the positive, atrocious prettiness of bad design. The disease of Featurism, which sweeps Australia in epidemic proportions, is hardly less virulent and threatening anywhere that modern technology and commerce are in coalition. In describing the horrible Australian symptoms of this distressing international complaint, the one thing I have intended to prove is this: that every object made by man has its own integrity; that it should be an honest thing, made with an understanding of all its functions and with a sense of order. To learn how to make things like that is the main problem and duty of professional designers of all sorts; but this is a social problem too. To learn to appreciate sound design when it does appear is part of the essential artistic education of everybody; so it seems to me.

When most objects are truly and sensitively functional, this technological age will be civilized and as beautiful in its own way as the nicer streets of classical Greece.

The problem is universal, but the justification I claim for having written this book, after English writers had tackled the subject fairly thoroughly, is that I concentrate on the Australian aspect of it. For this reason, when it was first published some Australian critics said it was unpatriotic. Quite a number said it was also unfair because the ugliness of which I complained was not Australian but international. On the other hand, it was curious to note that among those who accepted the book were some who were not really interested in aesthetic or even visual considerations. They welcomed it simply because it was critical, and not very much criticism of Australia by Australians was being published then. Yet the smugness with which the majority of Australians appeared to regard their own country was building up a fierce reactionary distaste in a minority. Australians who did not see eye to eye with the conservatives in matters of cream-brick veneer and plastic flowers and censorship were inclined to blame the social establishment for everything else they found imperfect about this country, including any bush fires or droughts, and the flies, and the slowness of growth that must accompany under-population. This diffuse distaste has since found some healthy relief in a growing volume of criticism and satire. The pressure is reduced and it seems to be allowed now that one can criticize specific aspects of the land without condemning the whole. In fact, the more criticism that appears, the more acceptable and lovable Australia becomes to more people. Even an ineffectual vocal antagonism to complacency restores a semblance of civilized balance. In this spirit I feel obliged to reaffirm that the Australian ugliness is not only unique in several ways, but is also worse than most other countries' kinds.

That is not to deny that other countries have hideous aspects. The USA has become painfully conscious of 'the mess that is man-made America' (see page 39) since John F. Kennedy's occupation of the White House. He was the first President of the USA since Thomas Jefferson to be actively interested in planning and architecture, and Lyndon B. Johnson has carried on the campaign he began. An essential element of Johnson's Great Society is the cleaning up of the visual squalor that surrounds all American cities and permeates some. The American Institute of Architects lately has become almost obsessed with the desire to tidy up the urban background against which its members usually have to work. Among fairly recent books on the subject is a devastating photographic attack on the ugliest aspects of the urban scene, and on the devastation of the beautiful American landscape. It is the work of Peter Blake and is called 'God's Own Junkyard'. Its pictures tell something of the same old story that can be found in the following pages, but with an American accent. Whereas Australia throws old mattresses over the back fence, America piles old cars or even airplanes yards high between the highway and the view.

The British ugliness possibly has more in common with the Australian. For one thing, a great deal of its mess is second-hand American, as Australia's is, which makes it intellectually as well as visually offensive. The mind boggles at the stupidity of copying the trash which America itself is trying to eliminate. However, the opposition is strong in England. In fact the fight against the outrage of modern development began there and carries on aggressively in the face of continuing tree destruction, pole erection and the primary screams of billboards. As for national scores in the degree of bad conscious design, I think that Britain and Australia have in common more of it than most other countries. There is bad design in the USA of course, but probably not as much, proportionately, as in Britain and Australia. The bad American architect tends to be a little more adventurous, which gives a certain liveliness to his vulgarity. His British and Australian colleagues are inclined to be ineffably dreary at heart, and are conscious of this, so that they dress up the drabness with party trappings more desperately gay than the American ever uses. Yet in England, unlike America and Australia, there is always something of genuine beauty around the corner, a medieval church or a glimpse of field, hedge and honest stonework, even if it is hemmed in by rival service stations and haunted by the wiry ghosts of electricity and telephones.

So I think it is only fair and honest to admit that among the

English-speaking nations with which Australia likes to compare herself she is very high on the list of conspicuous ugliness. And then, as everyone recognizes, English-speaking nations top the world list. A consistent vandalistic disregard for the community's appearance runs through them all.

Most Australians are proud of their cities; proud of the very fact that they exist when the rest of the world clearly thinks of it all as a sheep run, and proud also of their appearance. For each city has some good things and these make the images that linger in the mind of a lover. Thus the Sydneysider pictures his city from the Harbour or the Bridge, its new white offices piling up against the sky they are trying to scrape. He does not see nor recognize the shabby acres of rust and dust and cracked plaster and lurid signs in the older inner suburbs. The Melburnian thinks of his city as Alexandra Avenue where it skirts the river and the shady top end of Collins Street, which are indeed two of the most civilized pieces of urbanity in the world. He dismisses as irrelevant to this vision the nervy miscellany of the main commercial artery, Swanston Street, not to mention the interminable depression of the flat, by-passed inner suburbs. Most Australian children grow up on lots of steak, sugar, and depressing deformities of nature and architecture. Unlike the British child they are seldom exposed to the repose of pre-Featurist centuries. Unlike the American they seldom if ever experience the thrill of the twentieth-century idiom when it is in sole charge of an area large enough to constitute an environment. So the Australian child grows up ignorant, innocent, of the meaning of architectural integrity.

The Australian ugliness is never stagnant. Even in the seven years since first publication there have been new developments. For instance, a new kind of amenity has come to harass the holiday areas: the chair-lift. One of these now seems to run to the top of practically every beauty-spot, following a wide swath sliced through whatever forest is in the way. Wrecked trees lie where they fell in a mass of mud and twisted branches below, but one is invited to ignore these and admire the view beyond. This follows an old rule: as nature gets visually lovelier, man's habits grow visually viler. I regret that through ignorance I neglected to mention in earlier editions the tourist slums of pastel-tinted fibrous-cement and fairy lights which have been made, with the approval of the Queensland Government, on some of the once-idyllic coral islands of the Great Barrier Reef.

And then the most brutish form of vandalism, the slaughter of wildlife, is increasing, and getting uglier in its execution. Plastic flowers, which seemed only a passing joke in 1959, are now a universal menace. Something of the tragic artistic vacuum which is at the core of the Australian ugliness is symbolized in the cheap, vivid, unearthly colours of the imitation annuals blooming in plastic imitation cut-glass vases on Australian mantelpieces. The difference between these thin flowers and the abundant plastic monsteras and philodendrons of a Hilton hotel foyer indicates the difference between the Australian and the American uglinesses.

Another difference is symbolized in the product that is advertised as Australia's Own Car, General Motors' locally produced Holden. In this new printing of the book I owe that car a conciliatory word, since the 1967 model is so immeasurably improved from the awkward thing that was the current model in 1960, shown on page 15. Yet that thing was such an unspeakably crude example of cynical (or perhaps ignorant) commercial design that I think there is historical justification for not revising the rather harsh opinions of it written at the time. Even now it is not necessary to alter the observation that General Motors, in conformity with the best practices of Austericanism, always cunningly continues to keep their colonial model two years behind Detroit's fashion lead. No blame attaches to General Motors for this. They are not in the business to elevate

Australian taste or her cultural independence. No one in his right mind could expect a popular Australian car at the point of sale to be anything but a pale copy of Detroit style, unadventurous and unoriginal even when of better design. On the other hand, there is every reason to expect that soon after it reaches the street it will be adorned with a remarkable collection of entirely original Australian accessories, including plastic draft deflectors, bobbles or a fringe round the rear window, football-striped cushions on the back shelf, red reflecting sticky-tape on the bumper bar, and a variety of comical yellow transfers on the windows, including one showing a curvacious Aboriginal lass above the caption 'Genuine Australian Body'.

Revised 1968

PART ONE

1

THE DESCENT INTO CHAOS

Outside the little oval window the grey void is gradually smudged across the middle with deep tan like a nicotine stain. The smudge grows lighter, becomes an appalling orange, then lemon. Streaks of pink break free from it and float into the grey above. Having thus set for itself a suitably pompous background, the sun now rises. Its golden light strikes the underside of the plane, which for a few minutes longer remains the only other solid object in the colour-streaked void. The interior of the plane rustles and stumbles into life, and pink eyes stare out for the first glimpse of Australia. The sun has used only the top half of the universe for its performance. The bowl below the horizon is still filled with an even, empty greyness. Then a broken line appears near the rim of the bowl, as if drawn hesitantly in pencil, and below this line the grey is lighter. The travellers from the north perceive that the pencil line is sketching the junction between a quiet ocean and a silent continent—that above the line up to the horizon is land and that this land is for all practical purposes as flat as the water. Soon the plane begins to descend and some details grow clear. Darwin appears as a little peninsula with a spatter of white roofs, and the pre-dominant colouring of the land emerges from the grey. It is a dusty combination of ochres and puces.

Any visitor arriving by air from the north looks down on thousands of square miles of this colouring before he reaches the eastern coast and a touch of green. From Darwin to the region of Bourke in central New South Wales he crosses over country which is burnt brown and patchy, like a tender sunburnt skin, with sections of darker brown and blood red and blisters of lighter ochre. The palest suggestion of an olive tint is as near to green as this northern landscape goes. It is not treeless; the shadows of trees can be seen, but they are dry eucalypts, spare, blue-grey, with their thin, gentle leaves hanging limply, vertically, with no real intention of providing shade or a good display to aerial travellers.

Unlike most countries, this red backland of Australia looks from the air satisfyingly like its own maps. Most of the trees cling to the wildly vermiculated creek beds and mark them as firm dark crayon lines. Near the rare settlements a white road darts zigzagging in long straight draftsmanly lines. Every element stands out clearly: a tiny black square of water, a spidery track, twenty or so buildings at a station headquarters, their iron roofs dazzling white.

This is the Australian Never-Never, the back of beyond; hard, raw, barren and blazing. Yet it is not malevolent in appearance. There is something deceptively soft about its water-colour tints of pinks and umbers. And it is a subtle desert, insinuating itself into the background of Australian life, even to the life of the factory worker in a southern city or the sports-car enthusiast who never leaves the bitumen. Its presence cannot be forgotten for long by the inhabitants of its fertile fringe. It colours all folk-lore and the borrowed Aboriginal mythology, and in a more direct and entirely unmystical way, two or three times every summer, it starts a wind of oven intensity which stirs the net curtains of the most elegant drawing-rooms in the most secluded Georgian retreats of Vaucluse or Toorak.

On the northern edge of this great red heart, on the far side of this back country of Australia, the white man has scrabbled on the surface and made a foothold at Darwin, an outpost of southern Australian culture. This the visitor who arrives by air sees first in a reception lounge inserted into a hangar at the airport. He sees numerous primary colours in paintwork and brilliant plastic chair coverings, richly polished wood trimmings, spun light fittings of bright copper preserved in lacquer, black wrought iron vases shaped like birds screwed to the wall at eye-level and holding bright little bunches of pink and orange flower-heads.

The springs are deep beneath the washable plastic upholstery. The air is cool, conditioned. After his quick but sticky leap across the equator the visitor finds crisp white tablecloths again, and marmalade in sturdy plated dishes, and showers, hot water, piles of snowy towels surrounded by square yards of glazed ceramic tiles. Here is a good introduction to Australian ways, and it is a cheerful and compact example of the visual style which rules everywhere that man has made his mark on this continent: the style of Featurism.

Featurism is not simply a decorative technique; it starts in concepts and extends upwards through the parts to the numerous trimmings. It may be defined as the subordination of the essential whole and the accentuation of selected separate features. Featurism is by no means confined to Australia or to the twentieth century, but it flourishes more than ever at this place and time. Perhaps the explanation is that man, sensing that the vastness of the landscape will mock any object that his handful of fellows can make here, avoids anything that might be considered a challenge to nature. The greater and fiercer the natural background, the prettier and pettier the artificial foreground: this way there are no unflattering comparisons, no loss of face.

Or perhaps it is simply that man makes his immediate surround-ings petty in an attempt to counteract the overwhelming scale of the continent, as man always in building has sought maximum counterac-tion to natural extremes—of cold or heat, of all the other discomforts of open air. It is unusual, however, for counteraction to apply in the artistic approach. Throughout the history of architecture there have been buildings which gently lay down with nature and buildings which proudly stood up in contrast. 'Two distinct trends,' as Sigfried Giedion wrote in *Space, Time and Architecture*: 'Since the beginning of civilization there have been cities planned according to regular schemes and cities which have grown up organically like trees. The ancient Greeks put their mathematically proportioned temples on the top of rocky acropolises, outlined against their southern skies.' On the other hand Frank Lloyd Wright sometimes nestled his houses so closely into the folds of the earth 'that they seem to grow into nature and out of it'. Neither of these two constantly recurrent ways of approaching nature is necessarily superior. 'The artist has the right of choice.' But Featurism is a third and the most common approach to nature which Giedion didn't mention, because it is seldom adopted by respectable architects. It is neither sympathetic nor challenging, but evasive, a nervous architectural chattering avoiding any mention of the landscape.

Featurism is not directly related to taste, style or fashion. The features selected for prominence may be elegant, in good taste according to the current arbiters, or they may be coarse and vulgar. Featurism may be practised in Classical or Contemporary style, in the most up-to-date or the dowdiest of old-fashioned manners. It may be found in architecture or in the planning of cities or the design of magazines, espresso bars, neon signs, motorcars, gardens, crockery, kitchenware, and everywhere between. It is the evasion of the bold, realistic, self-evident, straight-forward, honest answer to all questions of design and appearance in man's artificial environment.

To hide the truth of man-made objects the Featurist can adopt one or both of two techniques: cloak and camouflage. Each has its special uses. Cloaking changes the appearance of materials, and camouflage changes their apparent shapes. Cloaking of common materials with more exotic finishes has always been a favoured practice in Australia. After technology arrived in 1867, in the form of the first wood veneer saw, the practice of sticking a film of imported wood over the plain native boards gradually grew to be routine in furniture manufacture. Now wood veneering is accepted in the most ethical circles of armchairs, and modern technology is continuously offering new, richer veneer temptations. It can provide superbly coloured and grained images of marble and timber photographically printed on to any cheap base, gold more brilliant than any alchemist dreamed in rolls of plastic. These things are well received in Australia. A faint stigma that once attached to the idea of veneering is gone. Brick-veneer construction—a single thickness of brickwork instead of weather-boards on a timber house—is the standard technique for middle-income housing, at least in Victoria. Veneering has become entirely respectable.

Nevertheless, simple veneering has its limitations; it allows the real shape of the object to show through. To disguise reality more completely it is necessary for the Featurist to resort to camouflage, utilising almost the same technique as the services use in wartime. Introducing several different arbitrary colours and shapes, he breaks up the whole thing into a number of smaller things. A Featurist city has little or no consistency of atmospheric quality and plenty of numbers on the guide map directing the visitor to features of interest: the Classical town halls, the Gothic cathedrals, the English gardens. Non-Featurist towns are rare. The description must be confined to unspoilt peasant villages, of which Australia has none, or to towns built specially, and completed in one drive, for a specific purpose. Of these Australia has very, very few, and in most of them Featurism has overtaken the original concept, and advertising, overt or oblique, rules the environment. Some streets in any city manage to grow naturally, cohesively and non-Featuristically: streets of warehouses and whole-sale commercial enterprises, streets of economically matched houses, and streets where no one cares. But the Featurist street is the fighting retail street where each new building is determined to be arresting, or the street in the competitive suburb where every house feels obliged to suggest a high degree of success—or if not success then certainly superior taste. If there are mean motives suggested here Featurism can also develop in a city on the crest of high ideals—when public buildings, churches, museums, and others naturally inclined to be outstanding, can sometimes shatter the inherent unity of their sur-roundings by their conscientiousness and self-consciousness.

All this is the involuntary Featurism of competitive societies. The more interesting sort, the psychopathological sort, is the voluntary, deliberate Featurism practised without economic or political stimulus. The building which is featured in the commercial street is itself broken into features: a spiral stairway featured behind a huge feature window, the firm's name featured on a feature panel, the initial of the name featured in an exotic letter-face. The house which is featured in the suburban *cul-de-sac* is itself a gift box of features: the living-room thrust forward as a feature of the facade, a wide picture window as a feature of the projecting wall, a pretty statuette as a feature in the picture window, a feature wall of vertical boards inside the fea-tured living-room, a wrought iron bracket holding a pink ceramic wall vase as a feature on the feature wall, a nice red flower as a feature in the vase.

The problem of design which occupies a few serious-minded

planners, architects, industrial designers, and graphic artists in other practical fields is to find order in a confusion of functional require-ments and conflicting economic demands, to blend separate parts into a whole, single, unified concept. The Featurist, on the contrary, delib-erately and proudly destroys any unified entity which comes into his hands by isolating parts, breaking up simple planes, interrupting straight lines, and applying gratuitous extra items wherever he fears the eye may be tempted to rest.

Voluntarily or involuntarily, Featurism dogs Australia even when she sets out with good intentions of avoiding it. Consider firstly the case history of the national capital. If ever there was a city planned to be above Featurism, to be grandly whole and united, it was Canberra, the national capital, founded in 1910 as a compromise to solve inter-state jealousies. A beautiful valley rolling between the hills of southern New South Wales was selected, and in 1911 an international competi-tion was called for a town-plan. The contest was organized on such parsimonious lines that the British and Australian institutes of archi-tects black-listed it. Nevertheless a hundred and thirty-seven entries were submitted and two distinguished foreigners won prizes: Eliel Saarinen, second, and the less famous but already well-known Walter Burley Griffin, first, with a prize of £1,750. The results met with a familiar mixture of sceptical and panegyrical comment, rising indeed as high as: 'The City Beautiful…The Pride of Time.'

Griffin had been with Frank Lloyd Wright some four years when he entered the competition with his future wife, another Taliesin member, Marion Mahony. Their drawings showed a town of interlocking circles and hexagons set on a triangle of three main grand avenues—the whole spread wide on the ground and filled in the centre like a lemon tart with a system of three ornamental 'water basins' fed from the wandering little Molonglo River. The Government acted cautiously. It appointed a board to report on the results of the competition, and the board duly decided that Griffin's plan was impractical. It prepared one of its own, and began forthwith to put this into effect. The new design was so terrible that professional opinion, which hitherto had been hesitant about Griffin, now swung solidly behind him. Patrick Abercrombie wrote in the English *Town Planning Review* that the board's planners were evidently 'utterly untrained in the elements of architectural composition…Indeed the whole layout is entirely outside the pale of serious criticism…It is the work of an amateur who has yet to learn the elementary principles.' The Sydney magazine *Building* began a campaign to 'Save Canberra'. It organized a petition which nearly three hundred architects throughout the country signed within a matter of days. Eventually, after a change of Government in June 1913, Griffin was invited to Australia, the departmental board was abolished and Griffin was appointed Federal Capital Director of design and construction. For seven years then he laboured to put his plan on the ground, opposed continuously by the bureaucratic heads whose plan had been turned down. He suffered maddening frustrations. Plans he required would mysteriously go astray. His own drawings would disappear from files; some were discovered more than thirty years later. He kept himself sane by opening an architectural office in Melbourne, but finally bureaucracy beat him. At the end of 1920, when all he had been able to accomplish was the construction of some of the main avenues and roads, the position of Capital Director was abolished and Griffin's services were dispensed with finally.

Nevertheless the official intention was still to preserve the broad lines of his plan. Several inroads were made, and there were many attempts to scrap it before an official revision—a compromise intended to make the Griffin spirit practical—was gazetted and thus sanctified by Parliament. It was, however, no more than a map, a system of roads. It lacked the lakes and it lacked any sign of the co-ordinated, horizontally stressed, monumental architectural scheme which Griffin had outlined in his prize-winning plans and had later developed in sketches and in his mind. The Canberra in which the mid-century Australian motorist lost himself, in which a pedestrian was confounded as in a Victorian maze, had all the practical disadvantages of Griffin's idea without one of the artistic advantages which motivated him.

Canberra's fathers, including Griffin, had conceived the thing as a governmental and administrative monument. They never contemplated commercial, much less industrial, activities. Griffin saw it as a Capital Splendid, imposing and impressive from the start with grand perspectives and great flights of steps reflected in placid lakes, all set on axial lines between the natural features of the site. Perhaps his concept was too swaggering and ambitious from the start, as many asserted. In any case it never had the opportunity to prove itself. The suburban areas were not strong elements of Griffin's plan, but these, characteristically of Australia, grew most rapidly. By the time of the Second World War they were Spanishy, shaded and cosy. Then wooden wartime cottages occupied acres of treeless ground on the less favoured side of town, and afterwards new suburbs grew almost as undisciplined as in any other Australian city. Canberra reached its nadir about 1954. A rule which required roads to be made before houses were constructed was about all that now remained of the early idealism. The centre was still dry and empty, Parliament House was still the 'provisional' 1927 building next door to the permanent site, and as ill-assorted a group of offices, banks and commercial buildings as ever were built—blue tiles, bacon-striped stone, yellow porcelain, concrete grilles, aluminium—began to disgrace the once-sleepy, arcaded Civic Centre. There were no effective building regulations. The airport reception building was a wooden shed.

The renaissance of Canberra began in 1955 when Parliament set up a Senate Committee of Enquiry under Senator J. A. McCallum. The committee recommended that a new central authority should control all planning, construction, and development. In 1957 the English planner Sir William Holford was invited to visit to recommend modifications to Griffin's plan, and in 1958 John Overall, chief architect of the Federal Works Department, was appointed as National Capital Development Commissioner. It was evident that Parliament, which for thirty years had been divided and doubtful whether the whole experiment of a bush capital should not be abandoned, had finally decided it was there to stay and was concerned at the state it was in. The new Commission reintroduced a measure of control on private buildings and planned an ambitious series of public buildings. A population of 75,000 was expected by 1968 and the total building programme ran into many millions of pounds. Work began on the water basins. At this stage—late, but perhaps not too late—Canberra returned to the principle of planning.

It was already much too late, however, to return to the principle of wholeness. If the Griffin road system struck difficulties, the Griffin architectural system was never even considered seriously. To most eyes unaccustomed to the Chicago School and the Frank Lloyd Wright idiom Griffin's stratified sweeps of shadowy terraces, sudden blank walls and romantic towers, were merely hideous. To anyone who liked the appearance they were plainly idealistic. Griffin was not asked to build a single building (he was busy in Melbourne anyway by the time construction began in Canberra) and the idea of architectural unity floundered. It was not, however, submerged immediately. At first there were tentative efforts to shape the buildings with some sort of consistency in the architectural approach. 'Provisional' Parliament House still stands as a clean white stucco building of surprising clarity and strength, designed by Government architects at the height of Griffin's influence in the mid-twenties. It has a simple monumental concept of steps and portico, but undoubtedly because it was considered only temporary it was not pompous in scale and it was not over-ornamented. Nor was it ever popular. Its only decoration was designed with a draughtsman's set-square and compasses. Between the blue sky and the pink blossoms of its gardens in springtime it is a picture postcard, inspired, without doubt, by someone's recollection of the Lincoln Memorial. The Hotel Canberra is also successfully watered-down Griffin. It is a series of roughcast pavilion blocks, now painted pink, strung on a figure-eight plan around two courtyard gardens. A little later, in the shopping blocks at Civic Centre and housing estates nearby, the Griffin mould was dropped, but another was picked up: a sort of Colonial Mediterranean of stucco and arcades, a reserved Spanish Mission. Soon after this all idea of unity was forsaken. Every new structure featured a new style. The last big building before the Commission took charge, the Government Administrative office block of 1957, was made in the tradition of permanent governmental buildings anywhere in the world: a stolid, austere monumentality which has found favour with Fascist, Communist, and Australian bureaucracy. About the same time Featurism laid its sticky fingers on the remains of the early attempt at unity. The long arcaded facades of the shopping blocks at Civic Centre began to break up into stripes of different colours as shopkeepers decided to feature their own arches.

But the best Featurism and the main tourist attraction of Canberra is the number of official buildings designed and erected by foreign or other Commonwealth countries. Most of the diplomatic visitors have felt obliged to feature themselves for reasons of public relations or propaganda, to display as much as possible of their own national architectural character. The American Embassy set the example about 1940 with the magnificent propagandist splendour of its group designed, unfortunately, shortly before a change of policy in the State Department transformed American official export design. It was conceived as a little Williamsburg, and is in the pure Norman Rockwell style, splendid but cosy, imposing but friendly. Three separate scrubbed red and white Retired Colonel's homesteads stand in a billowing expanse of lawn set with three or four kindly old eucalypts manfully doing their best to look deciduous. Other nations had no intention of letting the USA get away with this coup and they embarked on projects apparently calculated to make Canberra the architectural equivalent of a full-dress diplomatic levee. Unfortunately the falsity of the costumes becomes so apparent in the bright light that the effect is more like a fancy-dress party. The British High Commissioner's island office block near Parliament House is Whitehall Export Modern and is clearly made of stern stuff, capable of keeping a stiff upper lip in the southern hemisphere. It is symmetrical, bleached and negative. The High Commissioner's Residence, on the other hand, is asymmetrical and suitably informal for the colonies. Both were created in London by the Ministry of Works. Advance scouts reconnoitred from the ministry for some time before these buildings were designed, combing Australia for data and for materials worthy of the conceptions. The scouts sent back reports of conditions and samples, but it is evident from the size and orientation of the windows that the package containing Canberra climate leaked while passing through the tropics. All other nations took a similar stand against recognition of the benign nature of Canberra's weather. Even the Swedish Legation, which is the best of the earlier international bunch and in 1935 won the Sulman Award for public buildings, seems to have been designed with a Scandinavian dread of some pitiless antipodean sun. It was planned in Sweden by E. H. G. Lundquist and supervised by the Sydney firm of Peddle, Thorp and Walker. Being low, long and white, it is vaguely reminiscent of an Old Colonial homestead and by this association seems happiest of all the foreign elements in the broad Australian garden. But it is a disappointing export from the home of mature modern architecture. The Embassies of West Germany and Malaya, built in 1958 and 1959, and Japan, built in 1961, belong to the conventional modern school with strong, and only semi-self-conscious suggestions of their respective national architectural characters. The French Embassy, finished in 1959 to the design of Jean Demaret, in Paris, Architect for Civil Monuments and National Palaces, was more consciously Nationalist and frankly Featurist; it is a sort of ranch-style Petit Trianon. Some other foreign embassies, notably the Dutch, are less Nationalist and more Featurist, but the prize example on both counts is the South African building, done in Old Dutch Farmhouse-Colonial, looking like an inaccurately drawn cardboard backdrop for the finale of a musical comedy about Cecil Rhodes. Thus bureaucratic architecture from all nations finally reduced Canberra's architectural mood to farce.

Furthermore, within the failure of Canberra as a city there was another significant failure to achieve a distinguished environment, another attempt at a unified and comparatively non-Featurist design which started with high ideals and lost the way: the Australian National University, established in 1947 to supplement the various State universities. It is a complex consisting of four research schools— for non-clinical medicine, physical sciences, social studies and Pacific studies—and it sits on more than two hundred acres of lightly wooded, undulating land. A ridge down the centre coincides with one of the axial lines of Griffin's original plan, and Brian Lewis, the Dean of Architecture at Melbourne University who was first entrusted with the design, planned the focus of the university on this ridge. At the top he intended to place the tall, blank block of the library, and in front of that a court. Then he planned arms, slightly spread, extending forward on either side of a series of terraces stepping down the ridge. The open axis thus formed was several hundred yards long on dry land, and at the lower end it waded into the future lake and thus extended itself indefinitely. The strict symmetry and formality of this central scheme was allowed to relax on either side and behind the dominating library tower, where small buildings strung themselves bead-wise along the contours.

Professor Lewis's proposed architectural treatment was also relaxed, and generally domestic in quality. Beyond the symmetrical central axis there was no formal unity, but a balance of comparatively small-scale units. He deliberately broke each bigger element of the university into a number of articulated sections, allowing each to be self-governing in form, but he avoided contemporary cliches with as much aversion as he did advanced engineering. He used load-bearing brick walls, tiles and other humble materials to coax vernacular building techniques into a harmonious and easy-going environment. Unfortunately, as in Griffin's case with Canberra as a whole, the university never developed far enough under the original designer to allow the expected quality to take substance. The informal elements remote from the central axis were built first, and without the one thing that linked them: the dominating little-Versailles in their midst. Waiting for years without any real hope of the future lake, they looked merely undisciplined instead of easy-going.

University House, a residential block, social centre and place for formal university functions, was built first and is Professor Lewis's main contribution. It is a big building of flats and bedrooms, a refectory, meeting rooms and offices. The residential section is in a U of three-storey wings yawning to the south, and the rest of the accommodation is in a low wing curved like a hand over the yawn. The hand and the mouth are separate elements, and in this way the design develops: it is Featurism, but of a calm and cultivated kind. The glazed wall on the inner side of the curved front wing looks over a veranda and the long pool, which is a tranquil feature of the courtyard. The refectory is a very tall room, taking the full height of the three residential storeys, and even their roof space, making a big starkly ribbed volume, impressively austere, without as yet the mural intended some day to be featured on the end wall.

The physics block is utilitarian, but impressively so, as these things always are, inside the research laboratory beneath the beaded high-tension towers. About the time it was completed the university began to drift away from the policy of one architect and homogeneity. The John Curtin School of Medical Research, opened in 1958, follows the H-shaped plan set down in the original plan. Its symmetrical facade and central portico avoid, however, even the informality which loosely binds the early university buildings together. After the Curtin School the later buildings of the National University forsook all thought of creating a symbol of the national intellectual centre, forsook all idea of unity, and even of harmony. As in any other Australian university each new project had its own architect, its own brickwork, its own colour-scheme, its own theory, concept, style. Like any ordinary Australian building each new one of the National University knew no higher discipline above the one which someone had arbitrarily selected for it in an isolated moment of conception.

Isolated is the operative word. Absurdly proud, alone in a vacuum, each new Australian building sets out to create an isolated, competitive grain of beauty, like a rose carried on the wind, unconnected with the living bush, like a hank of seaweed drifting in the tide of fashion.

On the higher planes of creative architecture, the buildings are isolated from one another by their lack of a co-ordinating current of artistic philosophy. But now there follows an important secondary consequence of the Featurist approach: on the lower echelons the buildings try to isolate themselves from Australia itself by denuding the ground around them so that they may be better set apart and savoured separately for all the pleasures they offer the eye.

Many sensitive Australians are uncomfortably aware of the root-less nature of their artificial environment. Nevertheless Featurism is frequently perpetrated as much by the artistic section of the community as by the commercialisers, as much by sentimentalists as by the crass and uncaring. As the suburbs grow outwards, as the holiday resorts round the beaches and on the hills fill with campers and week-enders, the continuous process of denudation accelerates. It is the same non-pattern of unrelated snippets of blight whether the countryside which is being overtaken happens to be beautiful or barren. Nature's features of beauty—the waterways, glades, hills, headlands—are not so familiar in the neighbourhood of Australian cities that one would expect them to be treated with contempt, yet the process of their development is this:

Long before civilization reaches out to the beautiful region a few non-conformists find it, love it, and make sympathetic, uncomfortable homes among, and possibly of, the trees. Often these pioneers are art-ists, some complete with canvas and some content to talk about it. Then comes the first wave of domestication. The people are still com-paratively non-conformist, artistic and sympathetic, but they have families and want a house and garden of reasonable conventional form. Like the pioneers, they were attracted to the area by its natural beauty, but unlike the pioneers they do not realize—simply because they never analyse it—what makes the beauty. They are not wanton, but in the course of solving the practical problems of making a com-fortable shelter, several trees may have to go. This minimizes the danger of roots in the drains. Then the wandering creek may have to be filled in to reduce the mosquito menace. The newcomers are not without artistic soul, and please do not think they are without taste or aesthetic education. They are as sophisticated in these ways as most readers of Herbert Read or the *Ladies' Home Journal*. Frequently they commission one of the more imaginative architects, even if his fees mean abandoning the idea of an extra bedroom and some clever architectural device means postponing the acquisition of a dishwasher and central heating. Each newcomer builds an attractive house, an original house, a nice feature on the landscape. After several of these have been built, each tugging at nature in a different direction, the earlier settlers look about in dismay and pronounce the area spoiled. About this time the subdividers arrive, and behind them the main wave of suburbia. Then all the remaining native trees come crashing down before the bulldozers, and soon rows of cottages and raw paling fences create a new landscape. The time required for this metamorphosis varies from place to place, but once any man sets his eyes on any pretty place in Australia the inexorable process of uglification begins. It is inevitable because, even while the intentions of the early settlers towards the landscape are honourable, every one of them has different intentions. They condemn one another for spoiling the landscape, but in fact none is to blame individually while all are to blame collectively. It is not lack of imagination or sensitivity or originality which causes the spoliation, but an over-abundance of these qualities without the co-ordinating discipline of traditional craft technique and, more important of course, without a common artistic aim. Behind the tidy gardens of English annuals and feature shrubs in the vanquished beauty-spot each house is a little cluster of Featurist elements. Many of the occupants know that their neighbours have spoiled the area, and hate them and Australia for their Featurism. Yet when they themselves build again, even when they redecorate, they will be drawn back to Featurism as to a drug, hating themselves for it and knowing inside, even as they apply the Peony Blush paint to the wrought iron, how terrible it will all look tomorrow morning.

The visitor who arrives first by air, not from the north at Darwin, but from across the Pacific at Sydney, sees man-made Australia at its very best. He sees indeed an outstandingly beautiful city; none in the world looks better from the air. The interminable stretch of coastline is intricately eroded by the ocean in this place. Dark blue water within the harbour is clutched by dozens of green fingers encrusted with brown roofs, and in a central patch the grey and white teeth of a crowded commercial centre rise into the hazy air. Even the famous bridge is an insignificant incident in such homogeneous magnificence.

Sydney is all Australian. It is the oldest and biggest city, and proud of being the biggest. It has the tallest buildings, the brightest lights, the best and closest beaches with the burliest lifesavers, the fiercest colours on the fastest taxis with the toughest drivers, the brightest benches in the patchiest parks, the busiest traffic. Sydney has the only facilities for night-life worth mentioning, the highest standard in popular entertainment, the smartest and the tawdriest elements of the Australian pattern.

Her three principal contributions to the visible background of Australian life are her early colonial architecture, her harbour bridge and her contemporary hotel bars. The first of these—the good plain vernacular and the sensitive cultivated building from the protracted end of the Georgian era—she has destroyed so industriously as to relieve us of consideration of it at this point. The second, opened in 1932, is still the world's largest suspended-deck arch bridge and is still the most spectacular single man-made object in the land. It is the image of Australia adopted by airlines' advertisers and by Hollywood to establish the Australian locale in a three-second shot. It is a typical Australian big government project in that it was designed outside Australia, as even today the bridges being built over Canberra's proposed lakes were designed in England. It is also characteristic of Australia in that its design is a spectacular example of Featurist irrationality. The giant arch of trussed steel, the suspension rods, and the wide, thin deck they support make up the whole bridge. But they were not enough. The stone pylons at each end of the arch were raised as towers above the deck almost to the soffit of the arch. Most people at the time it was built appreciated that the pylons were redundant features, but the stonework was welcome as a necessary addition to make the steel presentable. The steel itself was understood to be necessarily ugly; it needed camouflage. The pylon towers reversed the natural shape of the arch by transferring the emphasis from the centre to each end, where everyone who was used to suspension bridges expected to see high pylons. The silhouette now became vaguely, cosily reminiscent also of the Tower Bridge in London. The pylon features thus successfully destroyed the visual reality of the steel bridge, while relieving Sydney of the expense of covering the whole arch with stone veneer. They were a triumph of disruptive patterning.

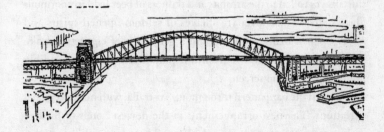

Sydney's third main visual contribution, the contemporary bar lounges, are a product of only the last two or three years and their influence throughout the rest of the country has not yet taken full effect. In these constructions Sydney has given vivid architectural expression for the first time in the twentieth century to Australia's phenomenal beer consumption and gregariousness. Other popular Australian mass activities have not yet produced distinctive architectural types, nor are they of a kind likely to produce new forms. Watching Australian football may have distinctive qualities as an experience: consuming two twenty-six-ounce cans of beer per hour while hemmed in to the bleachers by eighty thousand roaring rain-coated fans. But the stadia required for this activity are much the same as sports stadia the world over. Again, the distinctive habit of having night-club performers entertain two or three thousand people at a time has not yet produced its own building type. Sydney's new beer palaces, on the other hand, are unique.

The ordinary Sydney male drinking bars are not very different from those of any other Australian city. Late on any long summer afternoon, with the temperature and relative humidity both in the high eighties, hundreds of cream-tiled and stainless steel trimmed bars roar behind their street doors with the combined racket of glass-ware, beer dispensers, electric apparatus and amiable oaths. Below the solid jam of red male faces there is a jungle of brown arms, white shirtsleeves rolled to the armpits and slathers of beer held in enormous glasses; above face level are shelves of seldom-opened spirits and never-opened exotic liqueurs and a grey mist of cigarette smoke swirled by a mammoth chromium-plated fan past an inaudibly mouthing television screen.

This is the bar pattern throughout Australia, with minor regional variations. The new arrangements in the newest hotels of Sydney make a first attempt to civilize the beast. They start with the revolu-tionary concepts of providing for both sexes and for fresh air. The space set aside in the hotel is usually a very big room, the size of a nineteenth-century ball-room but with no more than a few square feet of free floor area. All the rest is occupied by small, square, metal-legged, plastic-topped tables and a great number of oddly proportioned metal chairs: of normal height but with plastic seats hardly wider than a hand's span. The big room usually opens through a glass wall on one side to a terrace, perhaps twice as expansive as the room, which is similarly packed with little tables and midget chairs. A muffled Dixieland rhythm from a four-piece band in one corner of the big room manages to rise at times a decibel or two above the level of the conversation of the brilliantly coloured throng perched on the pinhead chairs round the tables of beer glasses. Always there is a television set in view and in some cases, as at the hotel in Sylvania, a southern suburb, the bar terrace extends to take in also a view of a swimming pool.

The total facility is not exactly describable, in international parlance, as a beer garden, and it is certainly not a night-club. But it is somewhere between the two and the unvarying decorative style heightens the ambivalent atmosphere. The usual colouring is in saturated primaries. The usual materials are split stone veneer, chromium-plated steel, anodised aluminium, sprayed vermiculite plaster, crocodile-patterned hardboard and striated plywood, not to mention the customary plastics. Every element is separated from the next by a dramatic change in tone and texture and is divided within itself by violent contrasts of colour introduced in stripes, wiggles, or random squares.

Sydney is a summer city, tensed for action round an outdoor life. Every year, when the thermometer drops, winter comes as a bitter unexpected turn of fate. Now the wind thrashes rain among the pinhead chairs on the terraces and against the window-walls, and the drinkers in the unheated ball-rooms huddle closer in their woollens around the icy beer glasses on the plastic tables. Somehow it is a part of the architectural style to put two-tone crocodiled surfacing on the wallboards before comfort in the unseen air.

Sydney is the unconstituted capital of Australian popular culture. It is larger than Melbourne, older than Hobart and prettier than Perth, and it has by nature and by acquisition most of the things that visitors remark as typically Australian. Sydney is indeed the most proudly Australian of all cities, and the frankest admirer of American ideas. Sydney is alive, impatient to be even bigger and to short-cut ways to be smarter. It is a shop window city. It has more new houses and television sets with fewer new sewerage mains. It has more illustrated advertising painted on higher walls, more moving neon signs, the oldest rows of narrow terrace houses curving over twisting hills in the most picturesque slums. And in such modern palaces of amusement as the musical bar lounges, Sydney carries the contemporary style of the country to its highest intensity.

The Australian ugliness is bigger and better here, but in substance Sydney is only a sharper example of the general Australian townscape. There is beauty to be discovered here, in two categories, natural and artistic, but the trouble is that it must be discovered. The fine things, from the glimpses of magnificent landscape to the rare good buildings, old and new, are all but suffocated by the ugliness. The ugliness also falls into two categories: accepted and unintentional. Australia's accepted, recognized ugliness is no more than the normal blight which afflicts growing communities, especially rich, young, industrialized, growing communities. Part of it is the blight of age: the old buildings, the slum houses, the leaning fences, hoardings, structures of all kinds that were not very good in the first place and have long since outlived their prime, but are left behind to decay as development moves away to new fields. Another part is the blight of expediency: trees uprooted to save diverting a few yards of drain, the ill-considered and uncoordinated assortment of posts, hydrants, bins, transformers, benches, guards, traffic signs, tram standards, a hundred other necessary public appliances, and neons, placards, stickers, posters, slogans—all bundled together like an incompetently rolled swag with loops and tangles of overhead wires. This kind of mess, as made by any progressive community, sometimes is done unconsciously, without thought or care. But often it is done consciously, with a little regret, but with resignation to what seem to be the ines-capable facts of industrial life. The mess is accepted without pleasure or complacency, yet without sufficient distaste to kindle a reaction. It is unfortunate, but it is not tragic.

Unintentional ugliness, on the other hand, has an element of tragedy, because it comes from better visual intentions. It is the ugli-ness that starts in a spark of revolt against the depressing litter of the artificial environment and ends in an over-dressed, over-coloured, overbearing display of features.

The Australian ugliness has distinctive qualities, but in substance it is the same as the thing that has been called: 'the mess that is man-made America.' These were the words of the London magazine *Architectural Review* when it devoted an issue in December 1950 to a devastatingly illustrated attack on American urban and suburban culture. If a means of arresting this visual blight could not be found soon, the *Review* said, 'the USA might conceivably go down in history as one of the greatest might-have-beens of all time.' These comments were not warmly welcomed in the USA. 'One should expect a man breaking in a wild bronco to spoil some grass,' wrote the New York magazine *Architectural Forum* in reply. Pained reaction to the English criticism reached from the architectural journals to the literary papers. Visually educated Americans had long been conscious of the mess, and they resented the *Review*'s implication that it took someone from the cultural side of the Atlantic to notice it. Nevertheless, the outside criticism seemed to spur more self-examination, and the better maga-zines sometimes now are almost as outspoken as the English visitors were. And meanwhile the *Review* discovered that something just as bad was happening at home in England: a world of universal low-density mess was creeping over the once-lovely English landscape. *Outrage*, written by Ian Nairn, in June 1955 issued 'a prophecy of doom'—the doom of an England reduced to a universal mean and middle state, with none of the real advantages of town or country and the disadvantages of both. Nairn pictured: '…an even spread of fake rusticity, wire fences, traffic roundabouts, gratuitous notice-boards, car parks, and Things in Fields. It is a morbid condition which spreads both ways from suburbia, out into the country and back into the devitalized hearts of towns, so that the most sublime backgrounds…are now to be seen only over a foreground of casual and unconsidered equipment, litter, and lettered admonitions.'

The mess of the nineteenth and twentieth centuries is no respecter of a country's age, but then in countries older than Australia other centuries still contribute something to the scene. Nowhere yet is it as extensive as in Australia.

Like Sydney, all Australian towns and villages look their best in the longest view—from high in the sky—when the details of the mess are lost and the spaciousness and extent of the private domestic life can be appreciated best. The love of home can be seen in the great speckled carpets spread wide round every commercial centre. The carpet is coloured, somewhat patchily, a dusty olive in Perth, Adelaide and Melbourne: the mixture of terra cotta roofs and greenery in the gardens, and silvery-grey in the north and inland where most of the roofs are corrugated iron or fibrous-cement. By night the carpets are black velvet sprinkled wider with brilliant jewel lights than any other cities in the world with comparable numbers of people.

From the distance there is continuity, unity and the promise of comfort in the mushroom roofs and the bright background of tended green. But as the plane circles lower near the airport it is apparent that the green of the average suburb is a horizontal veneer no higher than the reach of a diligent gardener's snippers: lawn, compact shrubs, annuals, nothing high enough to threaten with shade the pink terrazzo of the sun porch. And as the plane drops closer and lower still one can glimpse occasionally under the eaves of the mushroom roofs and see the battle of the colours and the decorative iron skirmishes. Still the sandblasted koala bears and the yacht-race scenes on the entrance hall windows are not visible. They are not seen until one has landed and is driving through the suburban streets, by which time it is difficult to avoid noticing also the featured columns supporting the corners of the entrance porches and the plasticized silky-oak featured front doors inside the feature porches, and the black plastic silhouette cockatoos featured on the feature doors.

Featurism has low surface tension. It has the quality of penetrating ever further into the artificial make up. Ten years ago all park benches were dark green (sympathetic) or white (challenging). Then they too began to be featured in contemporary colours: a featured red bench, a blue bench. A little later the separate planks or battens of each bench were featured; red, blue, green, yellow alternating. This technique began about 1950 (as far as one is prepared to track it down) in the sudden light-hearted suggestion of a councillor of Prahran, Victoria, who convinced his fellow councillors that this would restore some much-needed gaiety to the drab green foliage of the parks and playgrounds. Within a few months almost every other council in the suburbs of Melbourne had followed Prahran's lead, and later the multi-coloured paint spread throughout the country. It happened at about the same time that garden pergolas, which had been traditionally monochromatic, began to change many colours, each beam of the pergola featured in a different hot pastel hue. Later the most popular treatment for pergolas, trellises, fences, beer-garden screens and other similar garden adornments was to make them in a squared grid and to feature the inside edges of each square in a different primary.

Colour, this most striking single element in the modern Australian scene, is a comparatively new feature. It is a product of the last half of the 1950 decade, the do-it-yourself era, chemical advances, and the keen competition of the largely British-owned paint companies. Heavy advertising has encouraged the idea of happy family painting bees using lots of different pigments on walls and ceilings, and to pick out features. Ordinary colour-cards grew from six to sixty hues in this period. Multi-colouring brightens the creative task of redecorating for the amateur, and ensures the opening of a profitable number of partly required tins of paint. Again, pigment is relished by the pressing and printing machines which produce many modern surfacing materials. But, irrespective of practical and economic influences, strident colour is a direct popular cultural expression of easy living. It is a reflection of the money in the modern pocket, just as equally intense, but heavier, richer colours in wallpaper and gilded plaster reflected the last boom of the 1880 decade. Between the booms pigment was mainly something to hide dirt marks. A drab series of duochrome fashions reflected the comparatively flat progression of the country through the first half of this century. About 1900 the two acceptable colours were brown and cheese. After the First World War they were sometimes green and grey. Cream and green predominated on all paint colour-cards from the Depression to the war, although the theme was sometimes varied late in this period by the more daring cream and cherry or cream and sky blue in kitchens and entrance porches. Even the rakish jazz-moderne of the pre-war milk bar and picture palace was never a painted style. It indulged in colour only in the neon tubes.

The cream Australia policy lasted for some twenty years, trailing off slowly after the Second World War. For the whole of that time cream was used habitually where other nations would have used white. Most kitchen equipment was not procurable in white enamel. As late as 1955 English manufacturers of stoves and other household appliances and sanitary-ware made special cream models for export to Australia. But by this time cream was losing ground to white or light grey as the neutral base colour, and green was being replaced

gradually by a rainbow. Suddenly colour was triumphantly elevated
as a feature in its own right alongside vertical boarding and split stone
veneer. Now standard household equipment came white, but some
manufacturers began making coloured refrigerators and washing
machines. Then, as the once-black cars in the streets outside adopted
two-tone and three-tone styling, household equipment dropped its
reticence. Many manufacturers offered two-tone equipment and
others provided interchangeable feature panels on the front of appliances where one's favourite fashion shade could be enshrined, easily
to be changed tomorrow when it begins to pall.

Meanwhile, in the commercial streets, where Featurism thrives
in the knowledge of its economic justification, the diversion of attention from wholes to parts grew steadily more agitated. Lettering and
illustrations, crying for attention to the wares of each little shop, grew
from fairly discreet sign writing to huge placards and cut-outs. Hardly
a section of external wall in the shopping streets was left without commercial announcements as Australians grew after the middle of the
twentieth century into the most vigorous and undisciplined advertisers in the world.

Australians now were more prepared even than Americans to
allow anyone with something to sell to take control of the appearance
of their country. Nothing like the Fifth Avenue Association, or the
Hawaiian ladies' organization, or the American Government's control
of advertisements on its freeways, could happen in Australia. The
typical Australian small, prosperous town is all but smothered with
advertising and in extreme examples of holiday towns like Surfers'
Paradise, Queensland, or Belgrave, Victoria, the buildings disappear
beneath the combined burden of a thousand ornamental alphabets,
coloured drawings and cut-outs added to their own architectural features. And meanwhile again the industrial areas keep developing their
own separate Featurist style: the featured administration block thrust

forward towards the street in front of the plain businesslike works, the featured painting of snow-gums on the feature wall in the featured lobby of the featured administration wing.

And look more closely. Follow the successful Featurist with his neatly creased jacket-sleeves and his four-button cuffs when he leaves the office in his two-tone Holden (light pink with plum feature panel) and goes home to have tea in the feature room: the room he calls the sun-room: the one that he used to call the back parlour, the one the American now calls the family-room.

The room's main feature is not really the feature wall in the yellow vertical v-jointed *Pinus Insignus* boards, nor the featured fireplace faced with autumnal stone veneer, nor the vinyl tiled floor in marbled grey with feature tiles of red and yellow let in at random, nor the lettuce-green Dunlopillo convertible day-bed set before the Queensland Maple television receiver, nor any of the housewifely features hung on the walls; nor the floor-stand ash-tray in chromium and antique ivory, nor even the glass aquarium on the wrought iron stand under the window. The real feature of the room is the tea-table, groaning with all kinds of good foods set in a plastic dream. The table top features hard laminated plastic in a pattern of pinks resembling the Aurora Australis. The tablemats are a lacework of soft plastic, the red roses in the central bowl are a softer plastic, the pepper and salt shakers are the hardest of all. And, soft or hard, all this plastic is featured in the most vivid primary pillar-box red, butter yellow, sky blue, pea green, innocent of any idea of secondary or tertiary tints, and all strikingly prominent against the pale, hot pastel tints of the flat plastic paint on the walls; all vibrating like a chromatrope beneath the economical brilliance of the fluorescent tubes on the ceiling. The main feature of the feature window is immediately apparent: the venetian blinds featured in a pastel tint. But look again and discover that this is more than one tint; every slat of the blinds is a different pastel hue.

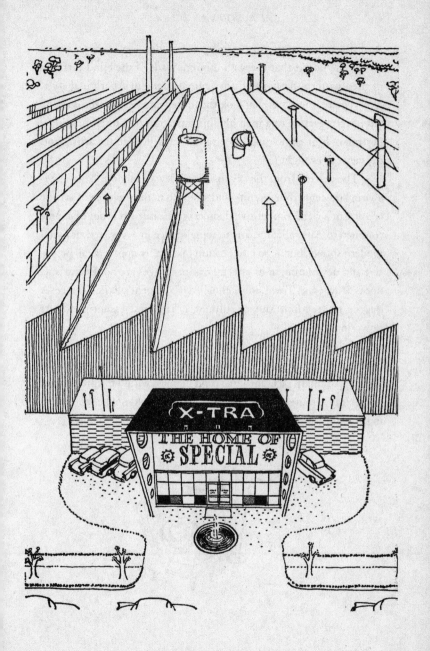

And if you look more closely still you may discover, if this is a very up-to-date house, that every aluminium blade of the blind carries a printed pattern, perhaps of tiny animals done in Aboriginal style. Everywhere, the closer you look the more features you see, as in the old novelty picture of a man holding a portrait of himself holding a portrait of himself holding a portrait of himself, until the artist's and the viewer's eyesight fail.

The descent from the sky to a close view of modern Australia is a visual descent from serenity and strength to the violence of artistic conflict in a rich, competitive democracy. Featurism is not of course confined to Australia; it exists to some degree in every free and vital modern society, but in no other country is it more apparent, all pervasive and devastating in its effect. Peasant villages are not Featuristic, nor is Stuyvesant Town nor Stalinallee nor Regent's Park Terrace. A degree of freedom and unruliness is the first essential for its flowering.

If the devastation seems worst in Sydney, this is only because nature provided so much more to start with and the loss is so much more apparent. In fact, unruliness and ugliness within the precincts of a big, clean, progressive, self-respecting town could not be worse than in her competitive sister city, Melbourne, the capital of Victoria.

2

THE FEATURIST CAPITAL

Melbourne's city plan is a rigid, typical nineteenth century gridiron permitting long wide vistas down every street. And every block down the entire length of every street is cut up into dozens of different buildings, cheek to cheek, some no more than twelve feet six inches wide, few more than fifty feet, some only two storeys, some nowadays over twenty storeys and growing higher. And every facade is a different colour, differently ornamented, and within its two-dimensional limitations a different shape. It is a dressmaker's floor strewn with snippings of style.

Some of these buildings—more every day in this building boom—are described in their company literature as streamlined ultra-modern, and some of them are described in the limited local architectural press with well-deserved praise. Nowadays all the new ones are resolutely modern: some ultra-modern, some sensitive modern. But since even the best is intent on its own private problems, it usually adds to the confusion of the Gothicky, Greekish, or Italianate masonry left over from last century. Few of the plainest new buildings are big enough to create an environment. Usually they aggravate rather than ease the old visual tensions.

Meanwhile, because it is a proud and prosperous city, painting of the old buildings is always in hand. By this means even those which were not especially Featurist when handed down to us by the Victorians are converted to conform with the later twentieth century. Terraces of shops, for example, with which the poorer city streets and the inner-suburban shopping districts are lined, were usually comparatively broad statements beneath the urns which cluttered the skyline. Now each narrow holding within the terrace strip is featured by its separate owner or tenant in a different colour.

The predominance of small properties and the absence of a mutual visual goal has meant that the architectural atmosphere of the total environment has hardly changed during the period between ornamental arch and aluminium louvre. Melbourne's atmosphere is still essentially Victorian: in scale, in intricacy, and in Featurism. Other young cities in other parts of the world certainly are not free of the splintering effect on the street scene of commercial competition, but seldom are others so splintered into such small holdings and seldom is frank, blatant advertising so rampant. But, most important, probably no other city in the world was ever so exclusively and enthusiastically Victorian as the capital of the State of Victoria. Anything other than avid Featurism could hardly have been expected, considering the circumstances of its childhood.

The State of Victoria lived its youth in time and in turn with the queen who gave it her name. It was born, it thrived and subsided gracefully with her reign, growing from an explorer's mud hut to a quite highly civilized community in the half-century that was Victoria's—in the spirit, the letter, and in the image of Victorian taste and Victorian endeavour.

The older colonies in Australia—New South Wales and

Tasmania—were established fifty important years earlier. They grew up between 1790 and 1840 in the manners of the eighteenth century to which their military governors were accustomed. Unstudied late-Georgian dignity thus persevered deep into the nineteenth century, unaffected by the chain of revivals reacting through Europe.

Victoria, too young to have witnessed this one coherent phase of Australia's architectural development, never knew intimately any style. She knew only the wonderful confusion of all styles which was Victorian. The Old Colonial had passed from the minds of the first builders in this new colony at Port Phillip Bay. All at once, with the opening of the new territory, the revivals of the century came crowding in on top of each other. Almost from the beginning every builder indulged in eclecticism unhampered by any local traditions or any special tastes on the part of the bewildered populace. The churches were mainly Gothic; the public buildings leant to Rome. But the houses and offices felt free to dip into history wherever their fancy led them.

The builders who overlooked the Old Colonial details were also oblivious to all lessons on the Australian climate learnt by the older men in New South Wales. In Port Phillip Bay the new settlers found a climate milder than any yet encountered on the new continent. The winter was grey, damp and depressing, but not uncomfortably cold for long periods; never cold enough to take leaves for more than three months from the English trees which they hastily planted. Even the fierce summer sun was accepted philosophically. Despite the lesson of the Old Colonials, verandas were not considered necessary. After some ten summers the need for protection became apparent. A veranda was often added thereafter, but it was separately pitched from light poles and sprang in a galvanized iron buttress to the wall line; it was never an integral part of the Victorian house.

The white man came to Victoria with the nineteenth century (in

1801, the first building, a block-house planted about with ill-fated fruit trees) but a successful foundation was not laid till the eighteen-thirties. In contrast to the older States, this foundation was the work of privately enterprising men under a cloud of official disapproval. Henty, Batman and Fawkner, men of opposed natures, intentions and ideals, pressed across separately from the harshly settled island of Tasmania, bringing fruit trees, seeds, vines, implements, livestock, some labourers, two builders and one architect: Samuel Jackson, of John Pascoe Fawkner's party. Fawkner and Batman each had such strong rival claims to the foundation of Melbourne that some historians, to make peace, have termed the former the 'father' and the latter the 'founder' of Melbourne. Each man was typical of his class in the sharply divided society that developed. Batman, the polite stock-holder, the first of an army of wealthy pastoralists, applied what elegant English features he could to the mud and crackling branches of the wild land. Fawkner was the convict's son, the trader, the self-educated editor of the first newspaper which he stuck in manuscript to the window of his, the first, hotel. He was the fighter, the tough, fierce critic of authority, the forerunner to the radicals who later broke the oligarchical rule that persevered till the middle of the century. He had the spirit that built up trade unionism and wages and cut down working hours to degrees unheard of abroad, the religiously demo-cratic fervour that brought manhood suffrage sixty-one years before it appeared in the United Kingdom, the spirit that led Victoria in 1859 to become the first parliamentary state in the world with a secret ballot at elections, the spirit that discounted experts and suspected artists of all kinds.

Thus the opposing factions were there in strength from the beginning. Those who sought elegance looked for it only in one direction—back across the months of ocean; but those who were required to create the elegance for them with bricks and sticks had no great love of the Old World—for if they had not been deported, they had fled from hunger. The release in architecture for the promoters' nostalgia was thus often frustrated by careless workmanship and the crudest craftsmanship. Not until the eighties, when the sure hands of Italian workmen dwelt lovingly upon the details, and the nineties, when the Australian-born began hunting in their own forests for motives, did craftsmanship reach the stage of competence at which it may be overlooked. Long before this much of the city of Melbourne and most of the provincial cities had been sketched out and roughly filled in.

Before building could begin seriously in the late eighteen-thirties, the raw land had to be cut and sold. The smartest people of Sydney and Tasmania came to pick up huge estates at Government auctions. Everybody of importance stood around the auctioneer's tent on the great sale days, chatting brightly, perspiring gaily under what they believed was the latest London fashion, blowing earthy dust off their cigars and picking little gum twigs out of the French champagne. Between 1837 and 1847 the population rose from 500 to 5,000 and half a million pounds was paid to the Government for land along the Yarra river plains. Building was limited to the town area and the squatters' homesteads of the outer country. The standard house was a single-storied box cottage, recognising only the necessity for immediate shelter. The few Government buildings in brick and local bluestone had more pretensions, and the churches from the first were openly competitive. The first and probably the best was St James's Anglican Cathedral, by Robert Russell, a surveyor-architect who arrived in 1836, when Melbourne was still called Bearbrass.

Thus Melbourne spent a conventional colonial childhood to the age of sixteen. Then suddenly she found the gold, and everything changed. Now she faced the future with supreme self-confidence, determined that from this day on only the world's most elaborate garments would be fine enough. The soil blossomed into golden blooms of all styles of history. Great Renaissance public buildings reared up on every hill as a new constitution was proclaimed and the first Parliament was elected. In 1853 nearly two hundred new buildings arose each month. Spectacular international exhibitions offered self-congratulation on a grand scale. In 1867 Queen Victoria's son, the Duke of Edinburgh, looked in to a quarter-million-pounds entertainment.

The eighties produced revived bursts of spending by the State and the investors. Speculation in land sent Melbourne bounding out across the low hills to the east. New suburbs opened with great mansions—two tall storeys of ball-rooms, banquet halls and galleries, plus a feature tower—set in rolling estates of foreign trees which usually flourished, on this new side of the world, far more quickly than in their native climates. Little houses flocked to the feet of the mansions—poor houses, but finely dressed for the occasion with weather-boards made to look like stone, and cast iron veils on the brims of their galvanized iron hats. Closer to the city, rows of terrace houses grasped all the accommodation that they could from mean slices of land. Big houses squeezed into deep, narrow lots, breaking the single-storey tradition by a second floor and a tower. In the city, office buildings shot up ten and twelve floors until the hydraulic lift power and the city fathers' tolerance ran out. Rich building stones and fine timbers flowed into the port. But not bread alone was imported. Painting collections and musicians were brought from England for the exhibitions. Local groups of painters and musicians formed desperately bohemian clubs. Huge theatres were built.

They were golden years for an architect like Joseph Reed who could catch their spirit. Reed's life ran parallel to the history of the colony. He landed in 1852 in a ship full of diggers headed for the goldfields. Without much money or influence, he prospered in a society which rewarded enterprise. He became rich and powerful as the century grew; and then he collapsed, almost everything lost and his health broken, in the economic debacle of the eighteen-nineties. But after death he left behind more than one grey and hollow baroque mansion, the symbol of temporary luxury which was the principal legacy of most unsuccessful speculators. For he had climbed to success on buildings which will still be standing when we are dead. There is hardly a street in Melbourne in which his work cannot be found. The Town Hall was his, the first section of the Public Library, and several University buildings, including Ormond College and the first Wilson Hall, which was burnt in 1952. The city is still dominated to the north-east by his huge Exhibition Building. In Collins Street alone he did the Independent and Scots' churches, the Bank of Australasia (now the ANZ Bank) on Queen Street corner and the old Bank of NSW, now demolished. The Trades Hall and Wesley Church are his, as well as numerous other churches, public buildings and houses in suburbs and provincial cities.

Joseph Reed won his position by solid work, keen business sense, and the sheer popularity of his architecture. In the young Melbourne which attracted him from England when he was aged about thirty, the appointment of an architect for major works was more often than not the subject of open competition. One story tells that Reed joined a firm of architects and assisted them to win a competition for Parliament House within a fortnight of his arrival. Certainly within two years he had established a private practice and had won a competition for the Public Library. He proceeded to build a substantial practice on his fortune in further competitions, on commissions for large public buildings like the Geelong Town Hall, and on appointments, made on the strength of his other successes, to official positions such as Architect to the University. He built up the first large architectural office in Melbourne. It has also become by far the oldest, for the modern firm of architects and town-planners Bates, Smart and McCutcheon is in direct line of descent from Reed's partnership. David Saunders made a study of Reed's life and methods at the time of his professional centenary, 1952, and described Reed as small, quick, full of energy, his artistic interest centred on music as much as, if not more than, on architecture. He had 'one of the best violin collections in the world', with two Stradivariuses. An employee recalled him as 'an Australian terrier; liable to snap up at you with sudden violence then forget all that he had said and be helpful and kind'. He had his silk handkerchiefs embroidered with the names of his principal Melbourne buildings. He was an excellent draftsman and did many of the finished drawings of his designs.

To judge his work aesthetically by today's standards is out of the question. He was the supreme eclectic, the master Featurist. He worked in almost as many historic styles as he did buildings. Besides several variations of Gothic, he used Italian Renaissance, Romanesque, 'French picturesque chateau styles', and so on. The aims were to absorb the rules of the masters, to discriminate, to borrow gracefully. He was not tempted by individualism or interested in curious cults of romanticism which affected others of the late Victorian era. One may search his various buildings fruitlessly for the characteristic touches which distinguish some architects' work and cut through stylism in any age. He was wonderfully irrelevant and proudly inconsistent.

To select suitably and to reproduce accurately contented him. The general massing of his buildings was strictly according to the rules of the style adopted for that moment. The ornament was faithful, unrefined, impersonal. Much more critical comment on his non-original work could be made on today's standards; and most of the above applies even if his work is judged on the standards of his own day, for his Victorian age was by no means free of architects of creative if usually misdirected individuality.

There was, for instance, his contemporary William Butterfield, the fashionable English architect who found it impossible not to leave his touch over every foot of every church he built. One may imagine that Reed thought little of Butterfield's Gothic Revival, the way he adapted an Italian manner of decoration, consistently colouring his interiors startlingly with tiles and marbles in zebra stripes, checks and chevron shapes. Reed felt no such need to be original, but he respected it in others. Butterfield was commissioned to design Melbourne's St Paul's Cathedral about 1880. He never came to Australia, but sent out streams of plans and instructions. The data sent him could hardly have been carefully prepared. On one of his plans is the note: 'Flinders Lane is assumed to be the East boundary.' Flinders Lane actually was on the north. Under these circumstances it is not surprising that mis-understandings developed between him and the supervising architects. Finally Butterfield resigned, offended, refusing to reconsider. Work stopped on the building. Then Reed was approached, and he accepted an honorary position as 'Cathedral Architect'. His organising ability saw the work through, and he did his best to make it 'as Mr Butterfield intended'.

When all is said Reed's work remains to mock the modern critic, because it still has a generosity and a scale which are proportionately beyond the capacity of today's enterprise. And may it never be said that Reed failed to exploit his opportunities. His thinking was usually almost as big as the commissions he was given. His—and Melbourne's—most spectacular building, the Exhibition, shows up his strongest as well as his weakest qualities. The building marked a first climax in Melbourne's development. It was prepared in 1877 for the 'first International Exhibition in the Southern Hemisphere'. An archi-tectural competition was held and was won, as usual, by Reed, his prize being £300 and the commission. It occupied acres of land on the hill to the north-east of the city and its great dome, standing astride the cross of the plan, was claimed to be not only the biggest but also the most beautiful dome in the world. The main structure is brick, but the interior galleries and ceilings are wood, which was 'grained' to resemble stone. Most of this has been lately repainted grey, with the intent to camouflage the building as a backdrop to the almost continuous trade exhibitions now held there. The cherubs and other airborne, draped figures painted in the pendentives are still intact, however, preserved with reverence by the twentieth-century caretakers. They are ridiculous, of course, and they were recognized as ridiculous even at the time they were done, by critics in the Melbourne press. But despite all the building's tawdry features, it still has a grandeur and magnificence of scale which cannot be experienced in any Australian building of this century. This is not simply the result of overpowering size. Reed knew better than most men how to handle the immense space. Within the style his proportions are confident; the parts are expertly scaled to the whole.

In the Independent Church, Collins Street, in 1867, he introduced the device of Feature Bricks by sprinkling a broken pattern of creams and browns among the common brickwork for perhaps the first time in Australia. Decades later this became one of the ugliest fashions of the Victorian age, and it is still doing well in the suburbs after nearly a century. Reed had just returned from one of his trips to Europe when he entered the competition for the Independent Church. While in Italy he had decided that the Romanesque style was suitable for Melbourne's climate. He prepared an alternative design in 'Gothic'—virtually the same thing with the windows pointed—but the Independent Church authorities preferred the Romanesque one, probably because the novelty of the style seemed to feature better their independence. Reed had a feature for every occasion. He rode on the whim of the day, his work gradually growing through his four decades of practice more confident, coarse and ornamental. He shared the popular distaste for a plain surface. His decoration had the force of habit. It was something required by propriety to clothe a building decently. In his best buildings, like the Independent Church, the form is shapely enough to read through the clothing. In his worst, like the late Eastern Market, the form was inconsequential and negative, and suffocated by urns and frills.

In 1887, in Queen Victoria's colony, the gilded picture was completed with fireworks. The Jubilee of the Queen was celebrated with greater enthusiasm and extravagance than in almost any other part of her Empire. The next four years, marked with rich Victorian detail, was the time that the State of Victoria knew later, through the first half of the twentieth century, as the Boom Period. Future generations will probably know it as the First Boom Period. But even the second boom which started in the late nineteen-fifties has not so far washed away the colour of those days. The Victoria of today still runs in the mould made then. Entire streets in many inner Melbourne suburbs, sometimes entire country towns, still remain as built to the requirements and taste of the eighteen-eighties. When the land gave up the last of its gold and populations dispersed from towns like Bendigo, they left a Victorian pattern strong enough to dominate still the few chromium shop fronts and the slathers of lettering which are all this century has added. No matter what errors in advance planning were committed by the Victorians, their structures were magnificently solid and often their public buildings are adequate for the expected demands of the rest of this century. Nearly every inner-suburban shopping street will be dominated for years yet by a thin Italian Renaissance tower of a town hall built in the eighties. The inner suburbs' residential streets are likely to remain much longer split into narrow slivers of land, wide enough only for a single room and a passage to the rear and covered to two or, rarely, three stories with one unit of a terrace development. The terraces were built two, three, or four at a time, but the units mostly separated into different owners' hands early this century and the problems of collecting them back into one ownership for a sizeable rebuilding has not yet drawn out the bigger investors. The units continue to change hands one at a time, each new owner picking out his own cast iron trimmings in a new feature colour.

Cast iron was the staple decorative element of the boom. Filigree ornamental iron had been imported from England in some quantity since the mid-century. A few houses, such as Corio Villa in Geelong, are standing still as wonderful examples of Victorian ferrous adventure: 'Corio' is a complete English prefabricated iron house of charming intricacy erected in 1855. But in the eighteen-eighties iron was not used as a structure; it was a feature.

The terrace buildings of the time were plain and solid: stucco on brick or bluestone, and the ornament was confined to a perforated skin of iron standing in front of the front verandas. The Australian castings were somewhat coarser and closer in texture than those imported from England earlier in the century. Solid and void were about evenly matched in various floral geometric designs. The balustrades at lower and upper veranda levels offered the broadest scope, but from there the ornamental iron crept up the thin, fluted columns and edged along the upper bressumers, hanging in festoons like pressed wistaria. Sometimes native flora and fauna, or municipal coats of arms appeared suddenly in gaps in the scumble of iron, but the thin columns always remained grotesquely Ionic, with grossly oversized volutes staring like a possum's eyes across the shallow garden strip to the street. Thus a cast iron facade was formed, a lacework screen of iron which threw a pleasant speckled shade on the stucco wall behind.

At the same time there was a certain snobbish reaction to the practice. The richer mansions of the boom eschewed such cut-rate ornament as the sand moulds of the foundries could turn out. For them Italianate was the only accepted costume, and it sometimes inflated even single-storey cottages with extraordinary pretensions until they dripped with plaster encrustations round every marble feature.

The State of Victoria lustily developed Australia's devastating combination of unconcern with essential form and over-concern with features, but the origins were probably older than Victoria. Perhaps they grew invertedly out of the earliest miseries of the penal colonies. At any rate the pattern of Featurism, the concentration on frills and surface effects, was apparent as soon as the first native-born generation became of age to build its own houses, and the number of free immigrants grew to significant proportions. The engrossing desire for conspicuous wealth was noted as a dominant characteristic very early in the nineteenth century. The shame of poverty and convict origins was still a powerful element in a country where many were growing rich and already everyone who was able and willing to work could live in comfort. The Van Diemen's Land *Monthly Magazine*, in November 1835, noted 'incongruities in buildings, furniture, dress and equipage, which we fear cannot fail to strike the observant stranger. This love of display, so inconsistent with the character and situation of settlers in a new country, may indeed have partly originated in each wishing to impress upon his neighbour a due sense of his previous circumstances, and standing in society. But, whatever the cause, the effect is too apparent.'

Was this, then, the origin? The desire of free citizens, practically all of whom had left the old country in some sort of personal cloud or dudgeon, to prove that they had been, back in that veiled past, men of some substance, accustomed to the richer things? But a few decades later, when the convict shame had faded considerably, a new motive for display appeared with gold: those who found it wanted to show off their good luck by throwing enormous parties, having their horses shod with solid gold horseshoes, and raising conspicuously useless features like towers above the roofs of their mansions, belvederes, and temples of love in their artificial lakes. Motives thus came and went, styles came and went; and only Featurism remained unchanged.

In the later part of the boom period the staple Italianate Georgian made way at times for a new popular genre peculiarly suited to Featurism: the Gothic Revival, a rich fruit of the union of ostentation and sentiment.

The Gothic Revival in Australia was a fabric of myths. Firstly, the most persistent myth in architecture: that in the days of the cathedrals the emotional expression of building reached shimmering heights inaccessible to the more materialistic generations of builders before and after. Secondly, the myth that this towering, flowering of architectural art was essentially English and lingered on in the blood of the lowliest Colonial, that it was indeed the only architecture which a truly upstanding patriot could consider. And thirdly of course the perennial myth that an ancient expression could be revived simply by copying the details. Perhaps a devout fervour did run through a medieval construction team, as the first myth holds, inspiring everyone from the tough old mason-architect to his most bucolic hod-carrier: a fiery spirit moulding the clusters of columns and sending them soaring irrepressibly into the dark vaults. Perhaps the ascensional spaces of the cathedrals were a simple, involuntary act of faith. But they were also a trial of strength between man and gravity, an adventure in construction. And this is the spirit, having nothing to do with religious or emotional expression, which marked the best of the Gothic Revival and almost justified its gross extravagance in ornament. But this spirit was rare, and Australia is full of Gothicky churches of crashing structural dullness stuck about with decorative features. Even before Ruskin published his *Seven Lamps* in 1849, most embryonic Australian cities had a cathedral or two with spire and pointed-arch windows roughed into shape in orange brick or timber slats.

Many of the earliest secular buildings, including Francis Greenway's stables at Government House, Sydney, had a comparatively subdued Gothic intonation. The style was never one of the most popular in the chain of domestic fashions. It was always a little bewildering to the builder-designers, but it kept appearing in rather special work by architects, from Edmund Thomas Blacket's Greenoakes Cottage, 1846, at Darling Point, Sydney, to a few fretworked dolls' houses of the late eighteen-eighties. Even in the twentieth century, a symbol of Gothicism, the pointed gable, may be traced, always clinging to the architects' movements a little ahead of the vernacular. Even in small-house suburbs built after the Second World War the last weary skirmishes of the Battle of the Styles were being fought out. Above the walls of cream brick and weather-board, a hipped roof was still symbolic of the Georgian rule of taste, and a low gable of the Gothic, with all passion spent.

The English, Scottish and Australian Bank on the north-east corner of Collins Street and Queen Street, Melbourne, is probably the most distinguished building of the whole Australian Gothic Revival era, not forgetting the cathedrals. Sir George Verdon, a friend of Pugin and a dedicated Gothic-fancier, was general manager of the bank, and William Wardell, a pupil of Pugin and for years the Inspector-General (chief architect) of the Public Works in Victoria, was the architect. These close friends prepared the designs for an unstinted £50,000 building. Although it was probably the most Italian-looking thing in Australia until the espresso bars of the 1950s, it was described at the time, in the *Illustrated Australian News*, 3 October 1883, as 'English of the fourteenth century, of the period generally known as, the "Geometrical decorated".' The directors of the bank deserved congratulation, the *News* felt, for choosing an 'English style of architecture'. When it was finished three years later it turned out to have a restrained Venetian Gothic exterior in red sandstone from Pyrmont, near Sydney, and an interior which was a richly imaginative combination of non-classical features. It is undamaged still.

The reinforced concrete columns of the banking chamber rise to a dazzling ceiling. This was the work of a Scotsman named Wells, who lived on the premises during building and worked under the scrutiny of Verdon and Wardell. In strongest contrast to the stuffy confusion which characterized most Victorian Gothic work, this is light, brilliant, open and coherent. Flying arches spring from the columns. The steel joists supporting the ceiling are exposed, with their lines of rivet-heads picked out in gold. Copper flowers and foliage sprout from the capital of each column. All this is painted in light blue, with many primary accents and enough gold leaf, the modern bank informs, to run an inch-wide ribbon round the equator. The fine mosaic of the floor is preserved, but covered at present. At the rear, diagonally opposite the entrance, the banking chamber opens to the shimmering white Tasmanian limestone 'Cathedral Room', which is part of the next-door building in Collins Street: the old Stock Exchange of 1890, a conventional commercial palace by Collins Street's greatest Goth, William Pitt.

Three blocks west down Collins Street are two of the most elaborate flowers of the period: the Rialto and Olderfleet office blocks. But if these seemed rather over-ornate even to some of their more critical contemporaries, at least the maze of ornament was simply embroidery on a reasonably rational form. On the other hand, the next popular style after Gothic was far less embroidered but discarded all idea of rational form. This was the strange hybrid domestic style of red bricks, turrets, gables, bay windows and pointed spires of terra cotta tiles: every house a brimming bowl of features without leavening. By this time the convict shame was well buried and forgotten and the gold had long since run out. The motivation now seemed to be the desire for respectability, and this was somehow associated with England, 'Home', and solidity in the contorted brickwork of the style spectacularly misnamed 'Queen Anne'.

If the desire to settle down into the Suburban-Puritan society of the twentieth century produced Queen Anne about 1900, the desire to escape this stuffiness led to a violent reaction nearly four decades later. Meanwhile other minor fashions—Californian Bungalow, Spanish Mission, Tudoresque and so on—had all exercised some small influence on shaping a consolidated suburban villa-cottage style. The reaction to all this came gradually after the mid nineteen-thirties in the form of the 'Modernistic', the jazzy 'Moderne', a fidgety sort of iconoclastic, beatnik aberration which obtained, while it lasted, a firmer foothold in Australia than in any other country except France. Houses of the style are common in the white-collar suburbs which built up rapidly in a few years after the Second World War. In the typical application the house has two storeys, which in itself separates it from its neighbours. The external face of the brick-veneer walls is in a special, or many different special, coloured bricks. The most popular colour, known as 'cream', is an undrinkable muddy yellow. The favourite special brick for features, porches or accents around windows, is the manganese brick: a rich, glossy brown. These are ideal for making miniature sky-scraper effects on the top of window openings or to break the skyline of the parapet walls which conceal the roof. The front corners of the house are rounded, and windows sidle around them, draped inside with cream lace festoon blinds. In the centre of each wall the parapet steps up in a little manganese zig-gurat. The entrance porch has been done with the most special care and curves, and is trimmed with wriggles of wrought iron. As can be seen from this brief description, the whole is a combination of two different inspirational themes: the rectilinear aspiration of New York's technology and the graceful femininity of the Parisian furniture emporium. Inside, the houses have cream plaster walls, multi-coloured floral carpets, circular peach mirrors with scalloped edges, genoa velvet lounge suites and walnut-veneer cocktail cabinets supported on bent chromium pipes. A popular feature of the mantelpiece ornaments in this style is a Mephistopheles cast in plaster, very thin, about two feet high, and painted vivid gloss-red. This style, which is as Australian as the Old Colonial or spaghetti on toast, began reluctantly to decline about 1950, when the more formal, straighter version of 'Contemporary' was in ascendancy.

At this time the Australian scene was undergoing another more important change, an injection of something like ten per cent of Continental European stock into its Anglo-Saxon blood. As numerous observers forecast, this transfusion was enormously beneficial to the patient in many fields, such as coffee-making, music, ski-ing and the stocking of delicatessen shops. But, contrary to some prophets, it did not assist in broadening or sharpening the taste as manifest in the suburban street. The experience of people in charge of official and unofficial bureaux of housing information, like the Small Homes Service of the Royal Victorian Institute of Architects, was that Continental migrants sought plans for small houses of the most conventional—Australian conventional—form. At the same time, successful migrants who built expensive houses in the richest suburbs commissioned replicas of the neighbouring modernized-Georgian mansions, and their New Australian architects expertly complied. In short, New Australians reinforced rather than weakened the somewhat smug spirit of suburbia which they discovered, notwithstanding that nothing less like their own traditional urban way of life could be imagined. The desire to belong, it seems, overcame any inherent distaste for the scattered suburban manner of living. Moreover they were prepared to be led by Australians in the matter of domestic architecture, since this was the one field of cultural activity in which the ordinary Australian was more practised than the ordinary European.

Thus various undercover desires, for respectability or for status, have led Australians of many periods to the desire for display in the background of their lives and have ensured a good reception for every passing flamboyant decorative device. But still this does not go far to explain the phenomenon of Featurism.

Well-adjusted people, whether peasants or princes, who are content to appear what they are, scorn display, and are not tempted by Featurism. Visually alert people, whether artistic or sophisticated, may need or want display but are aware that they should avoid it and are adept enough not to sink to it. Only when a community is not entirely well-adjusted and not very alert, when people want consciously or unconsciously to display and know not how best to display, only then is Featurism likely to prosper. Indeed it is then inevitable, because Featurism is the most elementary form of expression historically displayed by peoples emerging from primitive Functionalism. The symbol or the image, the miniature of the new aspiration, is applied to the old thing in the hope that it will tinge the whole old thing with new colour. And, to unalerted eyes, indeed a feature can succeed in suffusing the whole of the thing to which it adheres. The ordinary wigwam becomes an object of awe when a totem is added. The weather-board shed takes on a new aura with a wooden cross attached to the point of the front gable. Anyone without the technical, economic, or artistic means of achieving a desired quality in any article of use or of art naturally and inevitably resorts to the application of symbolic features: a bas-relief high up in the right-hand corner injects culture into a spiritless masonry facade; a single feature wall of expensive Japanese wallpaper imparts an air of luxury to an otherwise economical waiting-room.

Again, all over the world Featurism thrives in the presence of a quality which has always been a tap-root of ugliness in various fields: urgency. Commercial competition in itself need not lead directly to the demolition of a sense of unity and integrity in a city. This develops only when the level of commercial urgency rises high enough to bring the competition above the surface. Car design, for instance, goes through convulsive changes between Functionalism and Featurism. When rivalry in Detroit is keenest, or when British cars struggle hardest to regain some of their lost ground to Continental makers in places like Australia—these are the times of the Featurist styles, of the Cadillac symbols, when the tail fin is invented, and separate features are made of each headlight, taillight, stoplight and turning light. These are the times of the sudden kinks in every straight line, the feature panels of contrasting tone inset in the sides, three-tone paint finishes—all giving the lead in turn to the control panels of washing machines and room-conditioners and kitchen-tidies.

It takes an assured product and a confident advertiser coolly presenting unassailable facts to produce a functional design, a genuine style and a calm advertisement. These are things which are so rare as to be noteworthy whenever they appear in the Australian street, kitchen, magazine, or newspaper. Freedom from anxiety to please, freedom to overestimate the customer's intelligence, are kinds of freedom remote from modern Australia. The worst anxiety is usually at the promotional level, but it soon transfers itself along the line through architect, industrial designer, muralist, interior decorator, typographer—everyone feeling his duty to create a feature, no one unanxious enough to make a plain statement of fact.

PART TWO

3

ANGLOPHILES AND AUSTERICANS

Two things, then, are essential for the generation of the climate in which Featurism thrives. One is the desire to make things seem other than what they are. The second is inadequate facilities for the process of camouflaging.

There can be few other nations which are less certain than Australia as to what they are and where they are. Even in the second half of the twentieth century, a generation of Australians which is not too old to lead in politics and board-rooms still refers to England as 'Home', to the Commonwealth as 'The Empire', and to their own nationality as 'British'. Most Australians, however, consider these terms pleasant enough but no longer realistic. The British lion, it is realized, is preoccupied with its own problems and not much help out here. There is even a trace of superiority in the popular attitude to England. The novelist, the late Nevil Shute, always gathered an eager audience when he discoursed on his favourite topic of the eminence of Australia next century, with a hundred million people and the spiritual leadership of the Commonwealth. But there are other busy people who do not picture Australia ultimately connected with Britain, but who would sign her up tomorrow to economic junior partnership with the United States in a ceremony tumultuously applauded by a million jiving teenagers.

The historical, cultural and economic justifications for both these attitudes are overlaid by a slightly neurotic condition brought about by loneliness. The physical isolation from the West is only partially alleviated by radio and jet travel. Australia still feels cut off from what she thinks of as her own kind of people, and the obvious cure of her loneliness, fraternization with her neighbours in Asia, is not acceptable. The immigration policy remains rigidly opposed to Asians and even its madly offensive, if unofficial, name of 'White Australia Policy' is sacrosanct. Yet there are public men who have virtually dedicated their lives to reminding Australians that they live in warm Asian waters.

Thus Australia is pulled in three ways at once from three remote points of the compass, and with every tug there is inside herself an equal and opposite reaction. Sometimes these forces are expressed openly in the culture. The self-conscious Englishness of the Gothic Revival of last century later expressed itself in a Tudor Olde Englishe look in some shop buildings. And always there was the Georgian, symbol of Good Taste and Breeding, for those most anxious to display their Englishness. On the other hand there was the self-consciously American Californian Bungalow style in houses after the First World War, not to mention here the dominating American influence at the sales-counter level. At the third point of the triangle are the Orientalism advocated by the late Hardy Wilson and the Japanese architectural-decorative style which developed late in the nineteen-fifties. Finally, representing the reactionary pull to all these influences, there are the self-consciously nationalist Australian styles: either New-Old Colonial or Log-Cabin Bushmanist.

Two important things to be noted about all these overt expressions of the subconscious tensions are that they are rare, and that only seldom are they Featurist. All the clear-cut unequivocal geo-cultural styles, including the Australian, have had about equal weight in the total scene, and each was very lightweight. Most of these in their heyday injected something like two per cent of colour into the body of the community culture. Their combined effect, however, was more than the sum of the twos. The overt expressionists were rarely Featurist because they had an idea, however removed from reality, which they wanted to convey, and to some extent they encouraged this one idea to rule the entire building. Their combined effect, on the other hand, merely reduced the uncommitted mass of people to a state of confusion. The simplest escape from this confusion for the ordinary builder and designer was to reject all strong suggestions of style, to carry on with the economic-utilitarian conventions, but to add snippets from one or more, or all, of the passing fashions, and to feature each snippet against an uncontroversial background. The resulting mixture, displayed in the passing fashions of the lounge-room and the shop window, accurately conveyed the uncertainty of the national psyche. The Featurist wants to belong, but where can he? In eighteenth-century England, nineteenth-century Australia, twentieth-century America, or twenty-first-century Asia?

For years Australians have been noted for seeking an answer from visitors. 'What do you think of Australia?' 'How do our cultural achievements stand?' 'Is our work world-class?' Amiable visitors respond by praising the high peaks of development. Less agreeable ones condemn the troughs, and the nation seethes with anger at them. For what was requested of the visitors was not criticism, favourable or unfavourable, of specific efforts, but something more fundamental: an assurance of how the averages stand, how the standards stand in the world scene. If one is not an initiator, if one lives by copying, it is essential to be reassured on such points at regular intervals.

But what has happened to the wild colonial boy, the weathered bushman, and the sentimental bloke that they are reduced to this? The typical Australian of folk-lore was too well-adjusted to worry about others' opinions of him; he knew where and what he was. Visitors built up a picture of him. 'Quick and irascible, but not vindictive,' said J. T. Bigge in 1820, looking at the first native-born generation. 'Unenergetic, vain and boastful, coming too quickly to a weak maturity, too content in mediocrity,' said Anthony Trollope in 1871. 'They have no severe intellectual interests. They aim at little except what money will buy,' wrote J. A. Froude in 1886. 'They have too often the self-sufficiency that is gotten on self-confidence by ignorance,' said Francis Adams in 1893. 'They have in their underside,' he added, 'the taint of cruelty.' Max O'Rell in 1894 agreed, but found Australians also 'the most easy-going, the most sociable…'

Cruel but kind—a precise description of one element in the pervasive ambivalence of the national character. Here also are vitality, energy, strength, and optimism in one's own ability, yet indolence, carelessness, the 'she'll do, mate' attitude to the job to be done. Here is insistence on the freedom of the individual, yet resigned acceptance of social restrictions and censorship narrower than in almost any other democratic country in the world. Here is love of justice and devotion to law and order, yet the persistent habit of crowds to stone the umpire and trip the policeman in the course of duty. Here is preoccupation with material things—note, for example, the hospitals: better for a broken leg than a mental deviation—yet impatience with polish and precision in material things. The Australian is forcefully loquacious, until the moment of expressing any emotion. He is aggressively committed to equality and equal-opportunity for all men, except for black Australians. He has high assurance in anything he does combined with a gnawing lack of confidence in anything he thinks.

Cruel but kind; it is easy to present a picture of romantic repulsiveness in describing Australians. Those who love the country best
are inclined to try to make the inescapable faults sound interesting to
outsiders. Thus Colin MacInnes introduced Sidney Nolan's paintings
of Australia to the London public in 1957: 'The People—the
"Aussies"…have terrible defects: they are cruel, censorious, incurious,
flinty-hearted, and vain as Lucifer at being all these things. But their
virtues! Phenomenally brave, open-hearted, shrewd, humorous,
adventurous, fanatically independent and, most blessed of all, contemptuous of fuss.' Cruel again, but humorous at the same time: yet
in fact Australia's national failings are not as interestingly hateful as
this. Thoughtlessness is closer the mark. The failings are most often
the obtuse failings of adolescence, and as embarrassingly mixed and
uninteresting as any adolescence to outsiders.

In the mixture, the English ingredients are likely to be found as
pure, semi-digested lumps. The essentially English foundations of the
people and buildings are immediately recognized by visitors, especially non-English visitors. They note the dark brown hush of the
conservative clubs in the bigger cities as well as the noisy habits of
humour and slang, not to mention accent, which have distinct
Cockney qualities. They also note the awe in which the Old Country's
aristocracy is still held, the immutable practice of utilising unoccupied
English military gentlemen for Governors, the habit of appointing
Englishmen to key cultural positions like the chairs of universities and
the editorship of the *Sydney Morning Herald*, the way an authoritative
command in an English accent can still make the toughest union man
jump to it. They note that the difference between an English and an
Australian accent is a class distinction, and that a visiting Englishman
cannot really take seriously any intellectual or artistic idea expressed
in the Cockneyesque whine of many highly educated, highly intelligent, but tone deaf Australians. The persistence of mother-country

snobbery was the theme of Ray Lawler's second play, *The Piccadilly Bushman*, following the outstanding success in London of his uncouth Australians and their seventeenth doll. *The Bushman* was judged moderately unsuccessful by Australian audiences, not simply because of certain demerits it had as a play. It was the theme that received the sharpest criticism. Most Australians decline to recognize the patronage in the British and American attitude in such enterprises as *Vogue Australia* or the Holden car, and do not wish to be reminded of the facts that their country is still known abroad as an artistic and intellectual desert, and that they themselves would never be taken seriously without their denying to some extent their Australian upbringing and background, and that highly talented Australians in any of the non-useful fields of art or science have to face a dramatic decision early in their careers. They can stay here in easy-going comfort with their talent and their frustrations both working at half pressure, or they may wrench themselves from their own country in order to develop themselves.

J. D. Pringle, one Englishman who spent five years as Editor of the *Sydney Morning Herald*, described in his book *Australian Accent* how the Englishman expects to feel at home but finds a foreign atmosphere and can never settle down to easy relationships with the Australian: 'All too often the Englishman feels he is resented and the Australian that he is patronized.' 'On the other hand,' he said, 'the Americans, especially the West Coast American, finds nothing frightening or strange…no subtle class system, no sophisticated manners, no intellectual pretensions.' Mr Pringle thus found a curious paradox: 'Australians are strongly pro-British but tend to dislike individual Englishmen, while they like individual Americans but tend to disapprove of the United States.' Yet there have been many visiting Americans who obviously felt that the opposite is true. In fact, until the Second World War any visitor was something of a curiosity and was liable to find anything but the easy-going democratic friendship which Australians claim to display to each other.

Air transport, which cut the time of travel from Europe or America to about one-twentieth—one or two days by air against four weeks on the water—has had more effect on the antipodes than people of the northern hemisphere are likely to realize. A visitor now is less likely to find discourteous curiosity, and, be he British, Continental or American, his accent no longer will raise eyebrows or overmuch impatience.

Australians hope, however, to astonish the visitor. Nothing is enjoyed more than seeing a look of surprise on the face of some new arrival who discovers glass sky-scrapers where he might have expected kangaroos. On the other hand the bush atmosphere is prized chauvinistically by people who would not dream of going beyond the suburbs except in a Jaguar. Much vicarious enjoyment is to be had savouring the beery swashbuckling legends of bushland, and contrasting imagined down-to-earth ways and manners with the effeteness of the English or the pampered artificiality of Americans.

As if to assist the bustling modern visitor in getting a good, quick general impression, many of the more characteristic qualities of Australian cultural and social habits are concentrated at hotels, public eating and drinking places, and in public transport. In the ordinary course of living nowadays it might take a visitor months to meet a satisfying amount of the surly service from maintenance men, civil servants, and so on, for which Australia is known abroad. But the armour of casualness and Diggerism which still clings to many enterprises connected with travel immediately heightens the colour for visitors, while it distracts those who have ambitions to create a conventional tourist trade. As anywhere, taxi-men teach the visitor a lot about their towns, intentionally and unintentionally. In Sydney the convention is for the passenger to sit in the front beside the driver, but he has the alternative of taking the back seat since he has to open the door for himself. In Adelaide, a city retaining some colonial graces, the driver leans across and opens the door to the seat beside him for his fare. In most country hotel dining-rooms the convention is for strangers to be crowded together into one table no matter how many other tables are empty and available. When a special effort at graciousness is being made, as at the Yallourn Hotel, Victoria, the waitress introduces the diners to each other by name so that they may chat uninhibitedly as she stacks them into as few tables as possible. Most people who have occasion to travel Australia's highways retain favourite stories illustrating country hotel service. I recall a hotel in Yass, New South Wales, and a waiter with arms bare to the pits dealing out soup bowls like playing cards round the packed table and responding to my circumspect enquiry about the possibility of a glass of wine with the succinct phrase: 'I think you'll be stiff, mate.' Many of the stories involve table wine—Australia's great social subdivider—and usually centre on the expression of some rotund gourmet on being presented with iced claret or sparkling (sweet) sherry.

It is possible to read into all this reflections of the Australian mythology, of mateship and down-to-earthiness, of the creation of a Diggerdom where all men are equally inferior. But a less complicated explanation of these habits and attitudes is that they ease the strain of the working day by reducing stretching, laundering, and care; and Australians generally have been free enough from want to be able to afford carelessness. Not caring has been a traditional Australian mental luxury stolen from conditions which made physical luxury unlikely. As Max Harris has written, 'The "she'll do", "she'll be right" phenomenon is not indicative of colonial laziness, but an attitude of the hopelessness or uselessness of doing any better. It is to be correlated with the other idea of "you can't win".' But today the picturesque carelessness of the Australian scene is threatened. The horizon of attainable comfort is broadening for everyone and physical luxury is no longer out of the question for any healthy worker. This removes the justification for the philosophy of 'near enough'. Now you *can* win. Now the old contempt for giving service, and contentment with a life of protracted smokeohs, are restrained by the continuous demands of labour-savers and leisure-occupiers run on hire-purchase.

In the main cities a few sky-scraper hotels have been built. Some were designed in the USA, and some are being operated by American hotel machines. In the country the old hotel with a two-storey iron veranda wrapped around reluctance, impatience and primitive plumbing is feeling the cold draught from a new air-conditioned competitor: the motel. The growth of motels through the second boom period was watched by Australian travellers with almost touching faith. But as the business grew it seemed to develop to some extent in the shape of a craze: not exactly like the yo-yo or hula hoop, but at least a little like midget golf. In its approach to the public, in social and aesthetic values, in style, the motel often turned out to be a substantial offspring of the merry-go-round or the juke-box. Even the picture theatre in its heyday never sank to this level; it was merely *outré* in a pompous sort of way. The visitor might wonder at the frenzied appearance of many of the buildings to which he entrusts himself for the night. Why should anything with the serious public duty of housing weary travellers choose to deck itself in a buffoon's costume of patchwork and particoloured trappings? There is, unfortunately, nothing mysterious about it. The raw colours, the checker-board painting of fibro panels, the jaunty skillion roofs and angled props to the eaves, the autumnal stone veneering and all the rest of the catch-penny style are not seen to be anything but normal, gay, smart Contemporary design.

Some of the bad motels make their substantial contribution to

the mess by the Australian roadside in the old spirit of defiant carelessness: red and yellow is good enough as a bright colour-scheme;
she'll be sweet. Some others are done with the new anxious care, but
only a businesslike care for detail, without as yet any knowledge or
any wish to buy knowledge of visual design. The effect in these cases
is as distracted and discordant as the results of carelessness, and rather
more fearful in implication because of the neater and more permanent, self-satisfied finishes. The new careful Australian has as yet no
apparent understanding even of the cynical ways of using design to
serve business. In the case of the American motel, for instance, there
are three precisely shaped and balanced symbols. Outside, on the
highway, there is the eye-arrester, the car-stopper: a monumental
illuminated structure done in the richest carnival style. This is the
symbol of a good time, promising vaguely exciting justification for
jamming on the brakes. Once the driver has stopped, however, the
jazzy tinsel no longer strikes the right note. Now, as he hesitates
before signing the register, his confidence has to be built up. So the
porte-cochère and the office block are made in a firm, undeviating
Functionalist manner. This symbolizes efficiency and good account-
ancy. Then, once he is hooked, he may be allowed to relax, so he is
given something soothing, familiar and cosy. The bedroom wings are
made Colonial Georgian: symbol of gracious living. This sort of
design approaches the limit in exploitation and prostitution of the art
of architecture. But at the same time it is deliberate, studied, ordered,
and for these reasons only is preferable to the often illiterate, always
ill-considered and utterly undisciplined roadside style of Australia,
where the carnival symbolism is the only symbolism, and often is
unconscious at that.

The American flavouring in Australia is today more evenly
assimilated than the pure English elements. It is the American now
who comes from Mecca. The comparative similarities between

Australia and America, socially, historically and in size, are clear. At times like the gold rush period a century ago when many from California transferred to the Australian diggings, and the Second World War when many American soldiers were based in Australia, a strong feeling of identification with the United States has been apparent. Naturally Americanism has been no less pronounced than in other parts of the world, and in the years after the Second World War the American influence in popular arts and superficial character amounted to mesmerism. The west coast of the United States was the model in the minds of many people who were in a position to shape Australian development. What Paris was to the nineteenth-century land baron, Las Vegas was to the knight of commerce and industry in the middle of the twentieth century. Thousands of shops with their sloping windows and signboards, and hundreds of little roadside factories with their tiled faces striped with stainless steel and tiles: acres and acres of the new non-residential expansion round the cities were built in Drive-In Style, a confused austerity recollection of the Californian dream. When this approach extended to the richer parts and the professional level it resulted in manifestations of the Cadillac cult as rich as could be found anywhere in the world. Most new hotel lobbies, office foyers, and places of luxurious entertainment are found to display the special kind of arbitrary lushness best represented by the shapes of that enviable car with its heavy swell of comfort and the almost scientific restraint of its vulgarity. But the essential thing to be noted about American influence in Australia is that, unlike the English, it never survives the ocean crossing intact. The most mesmerized imitators of America always add a trace of Australian accent and subtract a measure of sophistication, tending continuously to transform Australia into a state which can be called Austerica.

Austerica is on no map. It is, as an Austerican advertisement would say, not a place but a way of life. It is found in any country, including parts of America, where an austerity version of the American dream overtakes the indigenous culture. As its name also implies, it is slightly hysterical and it flourishes best of all in Australia, which is already half overtaken by the hysteria. Austerica's chief industry is the imitation of the froth on the top of the American soda-fountain drink. Its religion is 'glamour' and the devotees are psychologically displaced persons who picture heaven as the pool terrace of a Las Vegas hotel. Its high priests are expense-account men who judge the USA on a two-weeks' hop between various Hilton and Statler hotels and return home intoxicated with conceptions of American willingness of labour (judged by the attitude of martini waiters), the average American standard of living (judged by a weekend at the managing director's house on Long Island), and American godliness (judged by a copy of 'Guideposts…an inspirational publication', which is left by the bedside for every one of the hotel guests of Mr Conrad Hilton).

It is inevitable that Australia should be drawn deep into the aura of American influence in this second half of the American century. However, there is a difference between being stimulated by ideas from another country and copying the detailed shape of its thinking, habits and fashions. The former is normal international cultural exchange, and America makes no bones about being in this market. She absorbs ideas from outside with avidity, but she changes and develops them. Australia's method of copying America, on the contrary, is in the second category: the Chinese copy, the parrot's imitation, the little boy mimicking his big brother's actions without fully understanding what he is doing. As this is one of the best ways to kill one's own national identity, Australia today, culturewise (to use a favourite Austerican means of expression), is sinking out of sight into the Pacific.

Austerica thrives in the matted fringe of the entertainment business, as in the fake American accents on the radio and television, the crew-cuts in the Australian magazine illustrations laboriously plagia-rized from American journals, and all the muddled Americana of the clothing fashion world. Advertisements of all kinds, displays, window dressing—all the visual trivia of modern Australia—are dominated by the Austerican outlook, for Austerica's credo is that everything desirable, exciting, luxurious and enviable in the twentieth century is American. Therefore the more one copies America in every visual and aural detail, the better for all concerned. In pursuit of this idea, the good Austerican displays unerring judgement in selecting all the wrong things, all the worst aspects of many-faceted USA. He lives by the law of the American magazine, but not necessarily the best maga-zine, and never the latest copy. For the Austerican has one firm business rule which qualifies his desire to re-create America: he believes that the latest American style is just a little too glamorous for Australia. About two years old is usually just right.

The Austerican is entirely aesthetic, confining himself to visual and aural imitations. When he builds a show-room he copies, not the air-conditioning, but the flashiest ornament he noticed on Wilshire Boulevard. The Austerican has no time for the great socialized enter-prises of the USA, like the multi-billion dollar programme of super-highways which bind together the United States with their meticulous planning, clockwork techniques, continuous planting and their ban on wayside advertisements. He prefers the mad scramble of the commercial strip, with its screaming signs, flashing light, plastic stone and paper brick. The Austerican excels himself in the hotel business. He buys an old pub, paints the entrance hall shocking pink, gives the surly waiters new uniforms and changes the name from The Diggers' Arms to the Waldorf-Vegas. Wherever there are cars you are likely to find Austerica unalloyed. If Austerican aspirations could be epitomized in a single object it would be a mauve two-year-old American convertible with ocelot upholstery and white sidewalls.

After the Second World War American cars were subject to the sternest import restrictions, and they were one thing the Austerican could not hope to imitate. But some used-car lots decorated their hoardings with dollar signs, and one of the most entranced advertising slogans in all Austerica ran across the fence of the 'Reno' car lot in Richmond, Victoria: 'Open up those golden gates—the biggest little used-car lot in the world.'

Perhaps the Holden, General Motors' Australian car, advertised as 'Australia's Own Car', is the best example of Australia's happy acceptance of second-hand Americana. With sales higher than all other makes put together, its body styling keeps straight on the track of its richer American cousins at a measured distance of two models behind, while it indulges the ravenous appetite for multi-coloured effects and disdains labour-saving mechanical innovations such as power braking or steering. 'We're not ready for automatic transmission yet in this country,' explained one car salesman in an Ivy League suit when the 1960 model Holden arrived on an expectant market with its old gear lever intact. 'General Motors are still selling coloured beads to the natives,' remarked one non-buyer. His was a minority report.

Austericans sometimes are frustrated people who imagine that their own country is restricting them and is unappreciative of their talents in mimicry. Some of them float in a dream of residing one day in the land flowing with homogenized milk and maple syrup. They live with a hopeless yearning for the dazzling Hollywood night and the *Life* life.

The genuine wonders of America pale against the American ability in projecting herself overseas in an enviable, desirable image from every angle. If the projection is true for three-quarters of the way, about a quarter of the total perhaps is not in fact as perfect as it seems in the magazine-film-television presentations. One of the great strengths of America is the gentleman's agreement throughout the mass-communications industry to maintain a continuous stream of mutual congratulation. The big companies like to take the minutes of their 'commercials' on television reminding audiences that all they want from life is to continue being one of the essential providers to Americans of the world's best way of life. 'This could happen only in America,' announces the National Association of Manufacturers in its programme showing new industrial processes, 'because we have a free competitive system.' A first principle of the American way is the unhesitating acceptance that American home life and housing are the best in the world. Other well-housed nations like Sweden look at the acres of derelict walk-up apartments surrounding every old American city and hide a polite Scandinavian smile. But Australia, mouth open, blind to the extraordinarily high average of her own standards, swallows the American unofficial propaganda intact. Every intelligent American is, of course, as aware of faults in his own country as all Australians are aware of Australia's shortcomings. Where he differs is that he is only self-critical, not self-destructive. He recognizes faults and difficulties, but he sees them set against a sunny background, an ever-broadening horizon, and unwavering lines on millions of graphs rising firmly and steadily. Although there are numerous differences between the Australian and the American ways of living, the standard of well-being is much the same in each country at every level of occupation and worldly success—provided one balances cheaper swimming pools against more accessible beaches and intangibles like more variety against a more leisurely rat-race. But the Austerican doesn't believe this. The Austerican, like the American, accepts the American National Association of Manufacturers' version. If any American or Austerican is asked to describe a 'Typical American' he is likely to cite a thirty-year-old Ivy League college graduate junior-executive with a pretty wife, two cars (one an

Oldsmobile; the other 'one of the low-priced three'), a Ranch Style house, two children, a Cocker Spaniel, a small swimming pool and some wholesome hobby like 3-D photography. On the other hand, the Australian, even in the prosperity of the nineteen-sixties, retains a backlog of pessimism built up in the first half of the twentieth century when little prospered except the spirit of suburbia. Thus if you ask an Australian to name a 'Typical Australian' he does not take the Australian equivalent of the optimistic American model, but a tradesman living in a Housing Commission estate, treating his harassed wife and sniffling child in an ill-mannered way and bettering himself only by supporting union action for shorter hours. The Australian is inclined to survey his surroundings not only without the American's rose-coloured spectacles but with grey sunglasses that cut out all the highlights.

These respective national attitudes are very relevant to the design of everything which makes up the background culture of the two countries. The unassailable optimism of the American climate breeds confidence in design; the American consumer is extremely pleased with something that looks American. But the Australian customer is by no means attracted to anything that looks at all Australian. This is an essential commercial principle to be borne in mind in any design, especially for the lighter side of life, especially for the leisure trade. For this reason, the capital of Austerica is the capital of Australian holiday resorts: a town called Surfers' Paradise on the Pacific in the south-eastern corner of Queensland, centrally situated on a fifteen-mile stretch of glorious beach with a floating population of some 150,000 holiday-makers.

Surfers, as it is popularly called, is something of a phenomenon. It is one of the few nationally recognized resorts, attracting people from two and three States away. It grew up in the nineteen-fifties around a nondescript little beach hotel which happened to have this

unlikely carnival name: Surfers' Paradise. It is a musical comedy of
modern Australia come to life. It is a fibro-cement paradise under a
rainbow of plastic paint. It has some big hotels, Lennon's and Chevron,
but mostly it is souvenir shops, wooden night-clubs with 'fabulous
floor shows', bikini bars selling floral wisps of bathers and Hawaiian
shirts through windows open to the footpath, ill-lit cabarets, over-
lighted cafes, indoor planting, outdoor denuding, beer gardens, signs,
hoardings, posters, neons, primary colours—purple, green and orange
straight from the brimming pot. The strident signs of the motels are
rivalled by those of the shops of the 'Financiers', 'Subdivision
Specialists' and the eager drive-in banks. By day the illusion is disturbed by a little too much unpaved, dusty, yellow earth between the
roads and the footpath, but it comes into its own in the warm evenings, lit by pulsating neon signs or, where there is nothing to
advertise, simply by festoons of globes. At night it could be any
American tourist town, from the smells of open-air grilling to the
sounds of splashing from numerous flood-lit swimming pools.

Surfers has some impressive natural attractions: magnificent
scenery in the hinterland, the wide, white beach, and a prevailing cool
wind which is almost as effective as San Francisco's ocean breeze on
the other side of the Pacific. Summer and winter the wind blows off
the water from the east, gathering strength nearly every morning
about ten-thirty, taking the hot edge off the dazzling sunlight. But it
blows a low cloud of sand over the beach, driving the local inhabitants
into the township for their coffee and real-estate deals. There, in glass-
fronted offices, the accepted dress is the lightest cotton shorts and
shirt. Waitresses at an espresso bar wear some sort of reduced sarong.
A stockbroker stands on the footpath outside his office-shop on the
yellow Pacific Highway dressed in black bathing trunks, briefcase and
a flapping floral shirt. Everywhere in the streets, shops and cafes,
chocolate-brown limbs bulge out of short sleeves and shorter

trouser-legs. There is a feeling of adventure and excitement, rare enough in Australia. You might call Surfers a sort of cream, or thick skin, skimmed off the top of Australia's mid-century boom. It is rowdy, good-natured, flamboyant, crime-free, healthy, and frankly and happily Austerican. It sets out to be a little Las Vegas. It is proud of being a poor man's Miami. See the names of the motels and guest-houses flashing against the starry black sky: 'The Las Vegas', 'Honolulu', 'Edgewater', 'Beachcomber', 'New Orleans'. Drive down Sunset Boulevard. Read the menus at the 'bar-B-cues' beneath the dusty palms: 'Southern Fried Chicken', 'Chicken in a Basket', 'American-Style Pancakes and Maple Syrup'. Eat at the 'Los Angeles', 'Bar 20', or the 'Chuck Waggon'. Rent a house in 'Florida Gardens' near the district known as Miami.

Or you may wish to buy a block for your dreamhouse on Paradise City, one of the subdivisions of reclaimed land behind the town. Paradise City was opened and offered in 1960 by Bruce Small Enterprises. The four-colour, six-page brochure for this 'sub-tropical haven…as rich in earthly blessing as Man and Nature could devise', told a story of typical modern Australian enterprise which no parody could better. Mr Bruce Small visited Miami, USA, in 1958, the bro-chure reported, and there, 'on the lavish holiday coast fringing the Everglades, he studied the great land reclamation projects in which the area abounded. His imaginative mind was seized with the parallel that existed on Queensland's own Gold Coast—land awaiting devel-opment at the hands of a bold and enterprising builder…Bruce Small was fired with just such enthusiasm that had motivated Australia's first gold pioneer. He, too, sped home to bring his vision to reality…'

Some of the principal propagandists for the happy state of Austerica are self-appointed and acting in an honorary capacity: for instance the journalists of the jabbering centre pages of the news-papers. For years before television came to Australia—it was politically delayed until 1956—the little screen represented high-pitched excitement to Austericans. They used to read in the 'Star-Dust' gossip columns of the dailies and the women's weeklies chatter about the private lives of American and British television 'personalities' who had never been seen or heard in flesh or shadow in Australia. If there seems something of moon-madness in this, it followed a thoroughly familiar pattern. Australians are well conditioned to vicarious delights in the entertainment field. For about two years before *My Fair Lady* was staged in Australia its score was barred by its copyright-holders from radio and television and record shops, although a market existed in illegal tapes and smuggled discs. Notwithstanding that the enjoyment of the stage-show was denied her, the Australian woman was tempted during this trying period with numerous drapers' advertisements for 'My Fair Lady Fashions'. Unlike the gossip journalists, advertisers are propagandists with a clear ulterior motive, continuously exploiting and egging on the Austerican attitude. One model of the Vauxhall, advertised in the *New Yorker* as distinctively British, was advertised in Australia as 'The most American-looking car' on the non-dollar Australian market. Developing the same theme, a sports-trouser manufacturer advertises his 'American-Style' product with the caption, 'The best you can buy with Australian money,' and another Ivy League tailor announces: 'The Slim American Look, backed by a hundred years of British craftsmanship.' But the best, unimpeachably authoritative and almost official mouthpiece of Austerica is, of course, commercial television.

For years Australian leisure has been taken against the steady recorded beat of an all-American hit parade, but till 1956 a high proportion of the entertainment on the evening air was of Australian origin. When television came, the greatest mesmerizer of them all, it neutralized the last insulating effect of the Pacific Ocean for an ever-growing number of steady viewers. Before four years had passed television was dominating the entertainment field and American programmes were dominating television. These were not the sensitive, experimental, or intellectual programmes of the New York studios. They were the half-hour snippets which Hollywood grinds out especially for British and Australian audiences: mostly 'Austerity Westerns', made to a cynical formula for assured popularity. These films crowd the peak viewing hours, and leave Australian material room only in token corners of the programmes.

The television invasion did not happen without letters to the newspapers, or raised voices in Canberra, or talk of quotas, or patient explanations by the television station proprietors of the economic difficulties. But even while the argument proceeded it was understood by everybody that the Australian mass audience was delighting in the Hollywood throwaways. Meanwhile, the better educated section of the community usually was evading television altogether, for a variety of reasons including intellectual snobbery and the odd self-denying puritanism of the country. So the children's watching hours were and still are filled with dusty Californian violence and sudden death, and cryptic conversation loaded with hints of more unspeakable evils out in the tin shed. Who could believe there is anything degrading in these stories? For the victims are always male. Australian censorship, always sensitive in matters of sex, Catholicism, and family life while expansively tolerant of brutality between males, is careful to snip out every scene of women being struck, thus safeguarding the Australian girl's illusions. Then, two or three times a week, Hollywood briefly drops its guns for a view of the Family Room, presenting a picture of enough sweetness and light in toffee-coated human relationships to dissolve any calluses which tender minds might have developed through the earlier torture scenes. The effect of all this is apparently as paralysing to Australia's television performers as it is numbing to the viewers. Whenever youths and girls do get an opportunity to appear in live performances they change sooner or later into cowboy clothes. Singing, one of Australia's most notable native talents, is done silently. As the recorded voices of California's favourite singers roll on along their relentless, changeless hit parade, young Australians occupy the screen, mouthing the words and engaging in desperate soundless antics in a sort of last rite of American worship.

As every producer knows, the mass audience rejects the possibility of any Australian entertainment being entertaining. To most teenagers, the idea of an Australian culture clearly evokes all that is stodgy, shaggy and shudderingly boring, while America represents all that exciting, glamorous, sparkling, neon-lit fun.

So the Austerican influence spreads out from centres like Surfers, on the air and in the movies, magazines, comics, all the time-killers, along the country highways with their rearing motel signs: 'Pan American', 'Bellair', 'San Fernando', flashing to the solid beat from teenage dance spots: 'Campus', 'Embers', 'Ivy Club', rushing in to fill the vacuums in every vacant corner of the Australian mind. The most fearful aspect of Austericanism is that, beneath its stillness and vacuous lack of enterprise, is a terrible kind of smugness, an acceptance of the frankly second-hand and the second-class, a wallowing in the kennel of the cultural under-dog. The Austerican knows he can't do more than imitate feebly the atmosphere he craves. He knows his country is not America, as the over-enthusiastic Anglophile, in his morning suit at a Government House garden party in a temperature of a hundred in the English poplar shade, knows it is not England. They know—all Australians know very well—that here is a country far removed in space and time from both the Old Country and the rich country, with its own separate, special truths, values, realities and strengths.

And what is Australia's essential truth? Something too big and frightening to contemplate, thank you. For the present it is much

wiser and safer not to be too definitive; and why need one be when all
the trimmings anybody could wish for are available for the picking in
the cultural markets overseas?

This is how one turns to Featurism. Not prepared to recognize
where, when, or what he is living, the Australian consciously and
subconsciously directs his artificial environment to be uncommitted,
tentative, temporary, a nondescript economic-functionalist background on which he can hang the features which for the moment
appeal to his wandering, restless eye. Thus he shapes his houses,
industrial areas, towns and cities, often making them carefully, sometimes even beautifully in an indeterminate way, but almost always
noncommittally. He knows that he can change the features tomorrow
if necessary without much trouble. He does not care that the only
thing of any meaning in art, the only creation, ultimately the only
satisfaction in life, lies in understanding himself and making decisions
accordingly.

4

PIONEERS AND ARBORAPHOBES

The failure of Australia to come to terms with herself—worse: her failure to have the least desire to come to terms with herself—can be largely explained in a phrase: the cult of pioneering. The early period of discovery, exploration and taming of the country coloured the national outlook till long after the frontier was pushed back out of sight of the corner window of Mon Repos in Hydrangea Crescent. And when Australia grew a little too long in the tooth to cling any more to the blanket excuse of youth a new pioneering period opened and revived the spirit.

The second period of pioneering, starting about the beginning of the second half of the twentieth century, is less romantic than the first was, since it involves factories and subdivisions instead of sheep, gold and limitless acreages of the bush, but it is no less affecting to the participants. After half a century of coasting Australia is now a pioneer land again, conscious of her enormous potential and of the challenging work waiting to be done. As a pioneer land she has little time for introspective questioning, no patience with conservation, and little or no sentiment for hereditary possessions. As a pioneer, she adds to the indecisive quality of her new culture the devastating extra element of destructiveness. This ranges from spendthriftiness to arrant vandalism, and is directed against the various irreplaceable assets provided by nature and the nineteenth century and, in Sydney, the eighteenth century.

Despite the comparative flatness of the continent, the absence of high ranges and the lack of dramatic scenic contrasts, the object of the pioneering cult is to reduce everything possible to the same level. If sometimes this object is beyond the scope of bulldozers, at least cemeteries can be placed on the highest promontories and factories can fill the winding valleys.

Despite the lack of water, and the national fear of drought, and the general agreement that dryness could be the worst impediment in Australia's boundless future, the object of the pioneering cult is to remove all sight and sound of water from everyday life. The city waterfront is the place only for wharves and warehouses. Factories have always gravitated to the river valleys where they had wonderfully convenient natural drains for the disposal of dyestuffs, sewerage and industrial refuse. The lowness and the thicker undergrowth beside rivers and creeks also recommended their valleys as official or unofficial dumping grounds for suburban refuse.

Despite the natural tendency of the country to overheat, despite the blistering outback legend and the constant search for relief even in the milder areas during the hottest weeks of summer, the object of the pioneering cult is to banish all shade from everyday life. Every lot is cleared for yards in all directions before it is considered safe for building.

Despite the nation's lack of attractive, dramatic historic background, and the temporary look of most of man's feeble efforts to subjugate the natural elements, despite the political advantages of national symbols at a time when the northern Asian waters are growing uncomfortably warm, the object of the pioneering cult is to push aside old buildings, whatever their historic or architectural interest, without a moment's misgivings—without the knowledge that there is any cause for a moment's misgivings, if the space is required for a car park or an unloading dock.

The object of the pioneer cult, in short, is to clear all decks for action, to reduce everything to the same comprehensible level so that something new can be put on it. The pioneer has never a moment's doubt that what he puts up will be better than what he tears down. In fact all he achieves is a more intense reduction of character in the background culture, allowing him even more freedom for the application of momentarily satisfying features.

Any sensitive visitor should be warned. He will be perplexed by the apparently senseless destruction of some old structures. He will ask what madness is it that causes the real-estate agents to direct a complete devastation of land before it is offered for sale, not content even to leave the degree of destruction to the individual tastes of the homebuilders. One can perhaps understand the mass destruction in the case of cheap land in the outer suburbs on the fringe of the bush. The gum trees here are probably too plentiful to command any respect, and the job of clearing is considered as inevitable for a home-builder now as it was last century for a farmer. Once the Housing Commission in Perth was persuaded by a tree-lover group to spare some of the native bush in an outer-suburban subdivision. The Commission agreed to leave two gums in each front garden. But six months after the estate was opened every tree had been removed by the occupiers.

Modern Australians have no especially psychopathic fear of the gum or the wattle, but no two trees could have been designed to be less sympathetic to the qualities of tidiness and conformist indecision which are desired in the artificial background. The Australian bush was made in one of nature's more relaxed, even casual, moods. Everything is evergreen, yet this term is often ironic, at least in relation to the ubiquitous gum tree. Certainly the eucalypt is not deciduous, but it is sometimes blue, often olive-grey, and occasionally brown. Measured against a fresh green European ideal, the Australian bush presents a slovenly scene. The grass grows long, ochre and rank. Most eucalypts are undisciplined in the extreme, their branches straggling wildly with disconnected tufts of leaves. It is quite impossible to trim one into the shape of a rooster or a kangaroo. They do not drop their leaves suddenly and predictably, but all through the year in a slummocky way, and are likely at unexpected moments to add to the dry brown mess at their feet a dead branch or length of bark which one of them has discarded, having finished with it. The wattle and other native trees are almost as indolent in their habits, lounging at drunken angles on the shabby, crackly, threadbare ochre carpet. The vertical limp leaves and the hungry earth consume whatever water they receive so avidly that within minutes after a rainstorm everything looks as dry as before and the yellow dust is free to rise again. It is all most unpleasant, measured against the European ideal. It is faintly frightening: not that it menaces, but simply because it is so unfamiliar, so strangely primeval: as different again from the European or North American landscapes as a tropical jungle. It disturbs the white Australian, the expatriate European, remembering, it seems, even at generations removed, his own northern lands where even the wild woods are civilized, with neat, compact trees changing beautiful hues, yellow and red, as bright as any painter's colour-card, and a layer of moist leaves, green grass and daisies on the weedless ground like a lovely Axminster carpet.

But the Australian landscape can be corrected, at least in the more populous coastal fringe, where the European plants do so well that a deciduous tree grows several feet in a season and a mature-looking, pretty garden can be created from bare soil in two or three years. The prolificity of leaf and bough has been the trees' own undoing. Undoubtedly it has contributed to the irreverence of Australia's attitude to nature. Trees are often planted in the streets, on the 'nature strip', as the six-feet-wide lawn between footpath and traffic-way is called. Plane trees are popular, but after each season when they sprout hopefully the shoots are pollarded back again to the knuckles by diligent council employees and the trees become grotesque arthritic knots of wood. Next season when it sprouts again the tree turns into the desired shape: a tidy green ball supported by a neat stick like a tree in a story-book illustration decorating red-roofed dolls' houses.

Contrary to the virility of many exotic plants in Australian soil, the smaller indigenous flora is fragile and delicate. Australian wildflowers are brilliant in colour and intricate in design, but usually spindly, diminutive and defenceless against weeds once the ground is broken and the foreign growths are introduced. They have great difficulty in prospering even when they are wanted. As they are generally not wanted, they have vanished entirely from cultivated areas, despite the efforts of a few small associations like the Native Plants Preservation Society of Victoria.

Thus progress is measured by the number of acres transformed from the native state of sloppiness to the desirable state of clipped artificiality. One exception to this rule proves the absence of psychopathic discrimination against native plants. The West Australian flowering gum, luxuriant, dark green and compact, is often accepted into the exotic deciduous family. This shows that the white Australian has nothing against gum trees on racial grounds; it is simply unfortunate that so few of them are neat enough in their habits to be acceptable. The bush is so far removed from the European image that

one cannot contemplate attempting to come to terms with it in suburban society, to meet it at least half-way down the garden path. A
principal article of suburban faith is that these primitive landscape
elements must be eradicated from the home environment in the same
way as one would deal with a disgusting-looking tramp seen weaving
his way in through the front gate.

Once the pioneer's aesthetic direction is adopted, practically
nothing that is natural to Australia fits in. One by one everything that
is native has to go, even if one has to hold a hose all evening to keep
the English grass green and the daphne alive. Most suburban councillors who make wood carvings out of the plane trees on the nature
strips, and most subdividers who shave their bits of forest bare before
offering them for sale, are probably, at home, nice family men not
inclined to regard themselves as arboraphobes. But the councillor, as
politician, senses the desires of society and is keen to satisfy them with
the municipal axe and saw, and the subdivider wrecks his little piece
of Australia not, he will tell you, to satisfy his own taste, but on
accepted business principles. He knows from experience that most—
not all, of course, but most—buyers of outer-suburban allotments see
greater possibilities for their Semi-Contemporary homes and the kind
of clipped garden they admire on a barren paddock than on one covered with untidy trees that will crack the concrete drive (when they
can afford a drive) and will block the drains (when eventually the area
is sewered) and will drop bark and leaves on the lawns and the beds
of annuals (assuming there will be water enough to spare to keep a
garden alive).

A rule of thumb could be stated for the guidance of visitors, over-
simplifying the case but giving a key to the different characters of
Australian cities: the more beautiful the area, the more contemptuous
the citizens are of nature. Thus Sydney, with a philosophy of over-
abundance, tramples down the attractions of its harbour reaches and

its rococo coast. When one inlet is filled with brown bricks and asphalt there is always another, green and virgin, round the next cape. If this tree is hacked down another will soon sprout in the warm sun, and when the dust and rust of the city grows too sordid to bear there is always the white beach, which is not very satisfactory for building or car parking, to lie on for an hour or two of health.

Melbourne, on the contrary, used to show a tendency to preserve the few better things provided by tight-fisted nature. Most beach fore-shores were reserved for public use last century. The Yarra River runs through parks or by a boulevard for much of its meander through the flat suburbs. This principle, however, succumbs to any real pressure. In 1962 the first section of a much-needed freeway to the eastern sub-urbs was built along the river's north bank at Richmond. The planners of this new road never faced up to the real problem: how to move back a strip of factories which had encroached almost to the river's edge. Instead they allowed the road to take the line of least resistance and to sidestep into the water, knocking over the last gum trees on the bank. A small forest of concrete piles paddling in the shallows and a cantilevered roadway overhead have now removed the last trace of dignity from the poor Yarra in this part. Nevertheless, this little grey trickle can be seen by visitors, drivers or pedestrians rather more easily than the great blue stretches of Sydney Harbour can be seen from Sydney's streets. On the other hand, Sydney people perhaps are not such rabid arboraphobes as the citizens of Melbourne and the smaller cities. Even in some of the poorer suburbs a number of trees can be seen between the houses. But one has the impression from the untidi-ness of the gardens, compared with the neatness of the gardens of more denuded cities, that the trees are there simply because no one has weekend time to chop them: everyone is down at the beach. Sydney people love their beaches, their harbour and their Blue Mountains. They know that they have at hand some of the world's

most magnificent stretches of water and most dramatic twists of headland. But these things are left strictly for playtime. The long-established
practice of allowing private ownership of the waterfront near the city
has effectively cut off this precious possession from the workaday life
of the city and from the sight of the visitor. The stranger who has seen
it from the air feels almost continuous frustration at being so near yet
so far from the wonderful dark blue stretches of water. He imagines
the wide views which he can only glimpse through slits between the
brown cliffs of houses and flats ranged shoulder to shoulder round the
harbour banks. When he finds a charming inlet that has not been
commandeered by cottages, it is usually cluttered with boatsheds and
broken-down piers. He looks at a distant green headland, standing
with its tanned feet in the blue ocean, and sees it through a tangle of
overhead wires and crooked poles. He stands on the high points of the
surrounding country, like Mt Kiera above Wollongong, and sees the
suburbs' stealthy crawl like dry rot eating into the forest edge. He sees
more trees being bulldozed from the yellow clay of the housing developments, as if the estate-agents and builders are determined to make
all the coast match the now-barren, windswept sands of Botany Bay.

But this is not, of course, their aim; nor is there consistency in the
aim. The generalizations already made are subject to regional variations. The suburban area of Sydney, like that of every big city, is
subdivided by scenery and snobbery into different class regions. New
areas are still as sharply divided in this regard as they were last century, although the difference between highest and lowest is now much
less pronounced. Monied-class suburbs are created no longer. No new
Vaucluse or Toorak is under construction. The leaders in industry,
commerce and professions who formed them in times of low taxation
now move up to make room for others of their kind in smaller houses
or flats built on their tennis courts. New graduates to the uppermost
levels of success have to be content with severely limited space in an

area which confirms their successful arrival, or have to become (to use A. C. Spectorsky's word for New York's new rich) Exurbanites: they move beyond the suburbs to outposts of urban living in especially favoured semi-rural areas. It hardly needs emphasising that Exurbia in Australia follows America's lead down to the proportions of a martini, but that it is more scattered and less organized.

The recent growth of Sydney is mainly confined to three zones. Out west, the wooden villa, or Villawood Zone—to use the name of one of its central districts—sweeps from Liverpool north through Parramatta. It is a fairly typical Australian working-class development, repeating the dreary, ill-considered housing growth on the outskirts of every Australian town: the same cold comfort conservatism of villa design with the regular sprinkling of primary-tinted features. The Housing Commission of New South Wales, speculative builders and private owners compete with one another to reduce the bush to a desert of terra cotta roofs relieved only by electric wires and wooden poles.

The same approach extends south into the Tom Ugly Zone, to use the name of a landmark near its centre: Tom Ugly's Point, where the George River opens into Botany Bay. Here the familiar suburban techniques are more destructive because the houses are slightly more pretentious and the country which they strangle was obviously more beautiful before man arrived. The fibro frontier is pushed right to the water's edge.

The really depressing parts of Sydney, however, are in the North Shore Executive Zone. Here some of the most dramatically beautiful country available to suburban commuters anywhere in the world seems to draw out a delinquent streak in nearly everyone who builds. Out through French's Forest and along the spine above Pittwater one can find three or four of the most notable modern houses in Australia. They are nationally, and to an extent internationally, known by their

photographs. But the photographs do not show their neighbours. The
few thoughtful buildings of the area are all but lost in a wild scramble
of outrageous Featurism clearly planned for the express purpose of
extracting a gasp of envy from each passing sports car. By the placid
water's edge on the road to Church Point, in one of the most charm-
ingly tranquil home-building sites one could imagine, is a structure of
multitudinous angles and rainbows of colour which exemplifies the
assault on the North Shore. At this point the visitor begins to recall
with some affection the paralysed conservatism of the Villawood
Zone.

The pioneering spirit which transforms the natural environment
is equally satisfied with transformation wrought on the products of
the architecture and landscaping arts of earlier days. The decade
before the Second World War in Sydney, and the decade after in most
other capitals, saw the most violent destruction of historic colonial
buildings. In that period Sydney lost many of its best old buildings,
including Burdekin House in Macquarie Street: a three-storey stucco
mansion of 1841, with two bland upper floors and a veranda-shaded
ground floor. Burdekin House was quite the largest, best known and
most handsome colonial house in Australia, and it had sufficient
charming Regency ornamentation and craftsmanship to ensure the
broadest popularity. Nonetheless it came in the path of progress and
was demolished, although its fine columns were preserved. They were
cut shorter and re-erected in their somewhat stumpy new proportions
on the veranda of St Malo, a cottage at Hunter's Hill on the Parramatta
River, which came under the protection of the National Trust of
Australia. But still it was hounded: two decades later St Malo itself
stood in the way of a new highway and soon it too was marked down
for early demolition.

The total loss of buildings like Burdekin House was almost to be
preferred to the mutilation to which other sensitive buildings of

Australia's infancy have been subjected. Elizabeth Bay House, a fine building of 1832 by one of the most cultivated of the early architects, John Verge, is periodically threatened. At the time of writing it still stands. Its elegant oval hall, perhaps the most famous architectural detail in Australia, is now painted in a contemporary two-tone treatment of green and creamy yellow. Australia's oldest remaining building, Elizabeth Farm, Macarthur's homestead of 1793, the cradle of Australia's wool industry, is poorly painted, crowded by the suburban houses of Harris Park near Parramatta, and forgotten or unrecognized by most of its neighbours. There is no malevolence here; only a painful void where a national sense of history might be expected. But at least these two buildings still stand while many as significant and beautiful in their time are gone. Of all the hundreds of examples of early work illustrated by Morton Herman in his *Early Australian Architects* only twelve were in a recognizably intact state when he published the book in 1954. 'No architecture in the world has been so maltreated,' he remarked. The mutilation took two forms: deliberate remodelling, sacrifice to some newer fashion; and wantonly careless additions: sleepout, fibro-cement screens to verandas, iron-roofed skillion blobs of various sorts buttoned on to the sensitive, or at very least careful, formal structure of the days before the home magazines.

In the busy house-building years after the Second World War Melbourne packed hundreds of mediocre villas into the few private gardens which remained from the early days in the better inner suburbs. The mansions of the boom years came tumbling down. In the space of a few months in 1955 three of the biggest—Werndew and Leura in Toorak, and Norwood in Brighton—were removed with extraordinary diligence. Not only were the large structures wrecked, but almost every tree was removed from the remnants of the estates which these houses had managed to hold round themselves. In each case the site was presented by the real-estate agent to a moderately eager public as a raked-over desert cut into little rectangles and innocent of any trace of the thousands of pounds and years of craft-labour spent on the vanished monuments, all hint of dreams and continuity gone. Destruction of this sort continues, and will continue despite the formation of the National Trust organizations.

The Trusts grew up in separate States in the early nineteen-fifties, like mushrooms in the raked-over ground, for the ordinary Australian's antipathy to nature and history is matched by the fervour of minority movements. The continuing destruction presents a hazard to anyone writing about Australian architecture and wanting to cite living examples. Before the ink is dry a building which seems important, permanent and invulnerable may be trembling to the first blows of the wrecker's mallet.

Certainly, some of the big old mansions of the boom period managed to find useful occupations in the twentieth century and live on borrowed time. 'Labassa', in Manor Grove, Caulfield, Melbourne, one of the most crested and curvilinear of them all, is still standing (at the time of writing) as a rooming house with its urns and statuettes and marble insets almost intact. 'Fortuna' is also standing. This was the vast home which George Lansell built himself in Bendigo, Victoria, beside the gold mines that provided his fortune. Lansell built the house with three floors of reception rooms, music rooms, banquet halls and galleries. He put statuettes on the parapets of the flat sunroofs, statues in the hall, on the stair landings, and in the temple of love that was reflected in the artificial lake. He put stained glass in each window—'east, west, home's best' round a circular stair well window—and mosaics on the drawing-room walls. He brought a shipload of furniture and features back from his trip to the Continent. His bedroom suite, in solid wrought brass, was a prize-winning exhibit which he picked up at the Paris Exhibition. 'Fortuna' was probably the most

Featurist house ever built. Now it is stripped down to some pretence of utilitarianism as an Army Survey Headquarters, and the strong southerlies blow a fine grey dust from the neighbouring mullock heaps over its broken plaster mouldings.

One or two other early houses have been taken under official wings and appear to be safely protected and preserved more or less in their original state, giving some impression of living conditions in the successful strata of the first pioneer period. There is Kirribilli House at Kirribilli Point, Sydney, a high-roofed Gothic house with carved gable ends and a turreted porch. It belongs to the transitional period, too late for the early colonial simplicity and too early for the furbe-lows. It was built about 1855, threatened with demolition in 1919, saved by the Prime Minister of the time, W. M. Hughes, and eventually restored to a romantic version of its youth in 1957 by John Mansfield, architect, and Mrs Gregory Blaxland. It is now used as a residence for overseas guests of the Commonwealth and contains a sprinkling of Australiana and soft gold ornamentation. In Tasmania there is Entally House, a historic Georgian home of the Reibeys at Hadspen, acquired by the Tasmanian Government after the Second World War and converted into a national house, open for public inspection. In Melbourne there is Como House, above Como Park, Toorak, built about 1843. Como has fared better than any other colonial house in the country, for it has been preserved with its original furniture and furnishings practically intact. It was the first acquisition of Victoria's National Trust. The original section is a white box wrapped prettily in a fragile two-storey veranda. Indoors, the rooms remain practically as they were, arrested in the middle eighteen-sixties when Charles Henry Armytage furnished it all, partially with fine, sturdy pieces, made by an undertaker across the river in Richmond.

The notable thing about the fate of the less fortunate houses was not simply their demolition. In most cases they occupied big estates in inner suburbs grown extraordinarily rich and crowded; they had to go. But the way they went was significant. There was no attempt to preserve any part of them or any part of their parklike settings. The fences, shrubs, and the enormous trees of gardens established as long ago as a century went with each house. There was a clear intention to eradicate every sign that the land had ever been occupied. Bulldozers nuzzled out every stone, stump and blade of grass. Then the bared paddock was cut into the narrowest permissible lots and sold piece-meal. Very slowly over the months which followed the lots filled with medium-sized houses and midget blocks of flats, all of them as representative of the noncommittal Featurism of our day as the buildings they replaced were representative of an equally expansive, almost as Featurist, but slightly more committed, era. On a purely architectural-artistic level it could be argued that little or nothing was lost in these obliterations of the old by the new century. Only space, trees and continuity were destroyed. But it goes further than that. The really disturbing thing is that the new culture is certainly no improvement on the old. Nothing was gained or learned in those hundred years.

No one seriously argued that always it was necessary to remove the old house in order to subdivide the estate successfully nor that always, along with the house, every tree had to go. A reasonably alert office boy in an estate-agent's back room could juggle most subdivisional plans to spare some of the garden, if that had been in the least desired by anybody concerned. No one appeared to consider any such thing, yet a normal healthy human being ordinarily can be expected to choose to make his home in a garden rather than a wasteland. It becomes necessary to analyse the pioneer cult to explain better this annihilatory urge and other allied phenomena of the Australian ugliness. In addition to the simple confidence that anything new one does today must be for the better, there are three less attractive qualities. These may be called Puritanism, Diggerism and Selective Blindness.

The first of these is a quality of Australian life, varying only slightly from region to region, which grew up with suburbia and the preponderance of private homes and the emergence of an ideal, family-group image. The years between the gay eighties when private houses were few, and the grey nineties when the first waves of small villas swept out from the cities, was the period when the female community saw to it that the doors began closing on the rumbustious life of their wild colonial boys. As gaslight gave way to electric light the streets grew darker, for most of the new light was in the family parlour, and from this time on anyone who was not settling down with an anagram or a crossword puzzle by the fire had to start minding his manners. As the century and the suburbs grew, one by one the privileges of city life were forbidden to the growing hordes of city dwellers: early closing of bars and restaurants; banning of more books, films, magazines; more permits required to do more things, a general tightening of licence and a gradually growing habit of censorship, ever-increasing prudery on the surface while the male community grew more ribald and appallingly blasphemous under its breath. The puritan movement finally expanded beyond its object of protecting family life in the suburban developments, and came to mean the public denial of every natural requirement of the human animal. The visitor to Australia encounters this immediately on arrival at his airport or dock. He will notice strange, coy signs on twin doors. Usually they will be silhouettes in black plastic on white plastic panels, one depicting a Regency gentleman holding a lorgnette to his eye, and the other a crinolined lady. Sometimes one will be a cigarette trailing a curl of smoke, and the other a powder puff. There are popular variations on peculiarly Australian ciphers designed to avoid giving definitive names to the unspeakable rooms with the plumbing. Sometimes again the silhouettes will be a top-hat and a bonnet respectively, or some other equally proper and irrelevant sex symbols.

Sometimes the twin public lavatories of hotels, theatres and other places of lighter entertainment are given names, but whimsically oblique ones like Romeo and Juliet, or Dave and Mabel, or Adam and Eve, or even more peculiar twin titles, as in the confused case of the Springvale Hotel, Victoria: Dave and Eve. In the State Theatre, Melbourne, an 'atmospheric' design from the heyday of the cinema, the male convenience was originally labelled, in old Gothic type, 'Gentleman's College Room'. This must have seemed too much even for the motion picture business, for now the echoing white tiled space is labelled, 'Gentleman's Lounge'.

It may be argued that these amiable idiocies are the product of suburban style, not a contributory cause of it. Yet their surrealist absurdity represents a philistinian-puritan denial of reality which is one of the wellsprings of the annihilatory approach to natural and historic facts. But if the female-inspired puritanism on the surface is the enemy of sensible development, the undercover male opposition is even more firmly set against any sensitive growths. Huddled whenever possible in the last refuge, the exclusively male bar, a sizeable proportion of the older generation of Australian men reaffirms the Digger tradition of the world wars in a stream of four-letter words which mean on translation: to the Devil with all sensitivity and sympathy. In the younger male, the Digger tradition often lives on in a more sophisticated way which merely takes the form of condemning epicurians, experts, connoisseurs, gourmets—all evidence of cultivated taste. Bill McIntosh has stated their attitude well. Mr McIntosh's handsome face creased in a puzzled sulk became familiar to newspaper readers in half-page advertisements. 'Wine Connoisseurs,' he was quoted as saying, 'they annoy me.' ('...all I know is Sienna Cream is my favourite sweet sherry.')

The third contributory cause of the Australian ugliness is a deficiency shared by the sexes. It is a special sort of cultivated, selective blindness. Perhaps it began as an involuntary defensive mechanism against the few ugly, hasty things in colonial and gold-rush times; then it grew into a habit, and encouraged more ugliness. Large elements of the Australian scene are invisible to the great number of people afflicted with the complaint. This explains several phenomena, including the faith in paint. It is quite misleading to imagine that paint is used so fiercely and vividly to improve the appearance or draw attention to the thing coated. Its prime purpose is only to be a symbol of tidiness. In Bacchus Marsh, Victoria, there is a little public park beside the municipal sportsground which was generously endowed last century with cast iron urns on masonry pedestals. For some years, apparently, the gay youth of the twentieth century enjoyed the sport of breaking off the urns. Mostly they snapped at the narrow stem, leaving jagged bases of various dangerous shapes. Later civic pride revived and a painter went through the park with a tin of pillar-box red, coating not only the few remaining urns but all the pathetic little stumps as well. Again, the appalling cabins of railway workers at Chullora, west of Sydney, and the shameful migrants' huts at Holmesglen, east of Melbourne, and at Gepp's Cross, north of Adelaide, are painted a variety of different colours. No one could want to advertise these hovels. No one could believe they look any prettier, in their contrasting hard-pastel tints, than the red stumps at Bacchus Marsh. But in this busy age ordinary taste has become so dulled and calloused that anything which can startle a response on jaded retinas is deemed successful: it draws attention to the fact that paint has been used and progress is afoot.

Tram, telephone and electric poles, and the spiders' webs of overhead wires which are strung to them, are more in evidence in Australia than anywhere. They form a ubiquitous veil across the civic scene, but like the sides of one's nose they never register on the retina. They are kept out of focus; eyes see through and beyond them. Even the central city streets of the capital city of Tasmania are equipped with regularly spaced, split and crooked tree-trunk posts, garnished with loops and tangles of wires, insulators, lights, brackets, tram connections and transformers, leaning at any angle but vertical against smart shop fronts or poking through carefully designed and neatly finished stainless steel verandas. Plumbers work more in the open in Australia than anywhere else; in very few areas will the pipes freeze, and external plumbing is one British tradition which is universally respected. Moreover, the vent pipes of sewerage lines are required by building regulations in most towns to rise many feet above the highest neighbouring window, and they aspire Gothically above the roof-tops in competition with the intricate ladders of the television aerials.

But the pipes and the ladders and the wires are not seen. A house can be selected as a 'Dream Home' by a national magazine though its sides are an angular espalier of drain, water, and storm water pipes, complete with towering vents and convenient inspection openings. A building can be admired for its shiny new grey-green glass curtain wall while some monstrous thing is stuck to its aluminium edging looking like a mad electrician's scrap basket, and immediately round the corner from the smart facade on the plastered side wall red and orange letters fifteen feet high announce once more the name of a popular brand of petrol.

The un-designed wires and poles do not mar the attractiveness of the street because they are not seen, because a street is not seen as a street but as a series of feature buildings to be viewed separately through the veil. The electrical and phone connections and the advertisements do not spoil each building for the admiring eye, because a building is not seen as a building but as a collection of features to be appraised separately: first curtain wall, then entrance doors, then lobby, then lift doors, then lift cage: unrelated in vision from the whole structure, and from the street, and from the city, and from the countryside.

In the darkness of the cultivated blind-spots some of the most painful damage is done to Australia in all innocence, as when, with the simple intention of making things nice for visitors who come to admire, scenic lookouts and beauty-spots are provided with desperately picturesque accoutrements of rustic stone and wood, and two brightly coloured concrete boxes which may be found, on close examination, to be marked with top-hat and powder-puff respectively. Bright colours are not intended to make lavatories more conspicuous, because it is assumed that they are invisible, but only to make them look nicer for anyone who requires to use them. The blind-spot contribution to the Australian ugliness occurs most frequently when the intentions are most honourable. Thus Tasmania, which is prouder of its age than most other places, which has an active National Trust and a Government which gives occasional recognition to the need for preservation, suffers worst from this somnambulistic sub-section among destructive practices. Private enterprise in Tasmania is not completely oblivious to the commercial possibilities of antiquity. At New Norfolk in the Derwent Valley, twenty-five miles north of Hobart, one of the prettiest places in all Australia, there is an enterprise called the 'Old Colony Inn'. Unlike some other historic places which have been ravished by caravan parks, this establishment has been carefully contrived as a coffee house with a 'rest chalet' and cabin accommodation especially devised for honeymooners. The publicity dates the basic building evasively as 'one of the several gems of 1815 vintage' (New Norfolk was founded in 1808 by a party from Norfolk Island), but the date is of purely academic interest, for the original has been almost unrecognizably altered, choked with the tourist trappings of chintzy old-lavender charm indoors and outdoors. The inn is a typically Tasmanian display, unfamiliar on the mainland, of killing architecture with kindness.

Hobart would be a beautiful big town if it were not a pretty little capital city. The state of capitaldom gives too much importance to what man has done round the broken bays and thrusting headlands of the Derwent River's magnificent harbour below Mount Wellington. Nature's scale, set by this stately precipitous rock of four thousand feet, is magnanimous; but somehow everything in the town that rests at the mountain's wet foot is just under life size. From the roofs of most of the three- or four-storey buildings of the town centre it seems one could throw a stone down the funnels of the liners at the wharf. Narrow streets with midget footpaths climb and circle the rounded foothills. In the low lobby of the little Parliament House the Doric columns seem to have been thumped into the cellar for a third of their lengths to keep them in proportion.

The average house of the early days was a doll's house: two wide eyes and a central nose under a brimless hat. It stood close to the street behind a garden that had no room for trees. The combination of a consistently diminutive scale and a feeling of solemnity in the stone-work produces a sort of lead soldier importance that is quaint, charming and distinctive.

The first generation after Hobart's founding in 1804 passed in savagery and beauty. The vicious slaughter of the Aborigines and the brutality to the convicts were accompanied by a gentle discretion in everything built. The prison at Port Arthur, fifty miles to the south-east on the Tasman Peninsula, exemplifies the early period, its relics of hideous inhumanity clothed now in mellow stone, gentle ivy and soft avenues of trees. In the simple matter of using bricks and stone, windows and doors suitably and without pretentiousness, the founders of Hobart could hardly do wrong and all subsequent Tasmanians could hardly do right. The city today is a monument to the destructive progress of twentieth-century Australia. The brutality of the foundation era is a closed book. Understandably, many Tasmanians wish not to be reminded of it. Historic documents have been left deliberately in some instances to rot so that the records of names, crimes and the awful penalties will be erased. Less methodically but as diligently the surface beauty of the early days also has been removed from all the more prominent places. The little houses have been wrecked without a second's thought, or were brought up-to-date with applied 'half-timbering' in the early years of the twentieth century, and with pots of primary-hued paint in the later years. Until the end of the Second World War Arthur Circus on Runnymede Street at Battery Point, named after Governor Arthur, was one of the charming sights of Hobart: a little ellipse of roadway in the Bath tradition with houses once occupied by military officers surrounding the road at attention, facing a park in the central space. The houses were minute, making a sort of architectural fairy ring. But now the lawn is treeless, and many of the little houses have been 'personalized', as they say, with many shades of paint in harsh, bright colours. A tangle of poles and over-head wires criss-cross the ellipse and some traffic authorities threaten to cut a road through the middle to speed the passing sightseer.

At times like this the Tasmania of today appears to be an island determined to lose any identity it has or had apart from the mainland. This is the pattern of the times. The Featurism which began in the fashionable centres of Sydney, Surfers and St Kilda Road, now oozes out evenly, flatly to the furthest places where Australians live. The cool green mountains of Tasmania and the edges of the stony desert a thousand miles to the north are now bound together by the brittle bonds of fashion: Georgian for high incomes, numb conservatism for the low, and for the great central majority coloured plastics, paint and flat black steel welded into hard geometrical shapes. These self-consciously 'contemporary' things now make up most of the veneer which smothers any indigenous materials and any cultivated aesthetic whether the object is a smart church in Darwin by a southern archi-tect, or a ski hut by a New Australian in the Australian Alps, or an

espresso bar designed by its proprietor in Brisbane. These things are
not in themselves important, for their power to attract will pass in a
year or two, but the spirit behind them, the emptiness of spirit behind,
shows every sign of permanence.

These things are not Australian inventions. The contorted black
frames and the vivid colours and accentuated textural contrasts are
only rough offshoots of international modern decorative design. The
meaningless space-age shapes are found by the truckload in
America—on juke-box and diner, in the sordid strip developments—
but there they are the muddy fringe of a driving movement of modern
design directed vaguely towards the confident (smug, if you like)
American dream. The blazing discords of colour are common enough
in the East wherever an ill-trained Oriental designer, unfeeling and
ignorant of the basis of Western style, essays Western fashion. The
inept mixtures of unrelated shapes and colours are found often enough
in Europe when unsophisticated designers attempt to emulate the
juke-box's excitement but fail to follow the method in its madness. But
nowhere else in West or East is the combination of smugness, ignorance and unsophistication sufficient to make a violent carnival style
the ruling of the land. In Australia it is not only the commercial eye-
catcher. It is accepted by strong-willed businessmen as the pattern for
their offices, by the clergy for their churches. It is the summer dream
of fresh young lovers planning the shape of their togetherness.

If the smallest signs of a reversal of the normal Australian drift
and a release from the ugliness could be detected, emotional despair
would be out of place in describing the scene. But there is no indica-
tion of a general change. There are, though, little hints of improvement
in certain somewhat restricted areas of culture. A return to the innocence of a pre-industrial peasant aesthetic is not to be expected, nor
necessarily desired, but a step farther away from innocence, towards
a more sophisticated sense of style, would at least clean up some of the

surface and buffer the shock assault of each new fashion. And in the foremost field of fashion, in clothing, there have been changes during the boom years which indicate increased awareness and an embryonic sense of style overriding the whims of fashion. The ordinary Australian woman's dressing may be as Featurist as ever and her collections of accessories and ornaments may still give visiting couturiers the vapours. But on the other hand more women now can afford to patronize better Australian dress-makers. And they can afford the more expensive and elegant materials which demand no fancy tricks in the cutting, no special feature inserts of richer materials, no festoons of art jewellery; in everyone's eyes the materials themselves look enviable enough to make diverting features objectionably irrelevant.

The advance in men's clothing has been more noticeable, and more significant because the very suggestion of attention to his own appearance is a retreat from the Digger's earlier stand when he allied smart male dressing with unnatural practices. The fancy-stripe mid-blue shirt is now plain and white. The last bunch-shoulder, multi-stripe navy worsted suit, by which Australian tourists once could be identified anywhere overseas, has practically worn out. Before 1955 men's tailoring was done as a country cousin version of Savile Row. Now it is American in pattern, style and cut, from the Ivy League stripe to the center (sic) vent. The tight, triple-toned brown Fair Isle pattern pullover, which was once wool's greatest contribution to informal masculine wear, and was worn throughout winter beneath the multi-stripe navy suit, has been replaced by various looser, bulkier sweaters in plain colours, Even the convict cut hairstyle is losing popularity. Frequently now the hair is allowed to extend down the sides of the head close to the level of the top of the ear.

Again, faint stirrings of fresh air may be detected even in the suffocating atmosphere of the popular furniture market. The carnival spirit is always at its maddest here, yet the plastic-coated contemporary is in fact an improvement on the fashion it is replacing. For some twenty-five years domestic furniture had been built around a three-piece genoa velvet lounge suite with waterfall back and boxed arms, almost as wide as the seat, inset with little shelves and panels of scalloped, walnut-veneered wood. The new popular pieces of vynex, laminex, black iron and bright brass may be gross perversions of the international modern models, but they are lighter and cleaner, figuratively and literally, than the musty over-stuffed, varicoloured velvet and the dusty-pink chenille. At least they narrow very slightly the great gap between the carnival and rational design, carrying the popular furniture store a fraction closer to the better interior decorators' salons with their few spare, graceful pieces, from Denmark.

But in the time taken for the consolidation of every increase of sophistication in some restricted area there is a proportionately bigger increase in the population and its ready money, in the spread of the background ugliness. For every new presentable piece of furniture there is a piece of the old boxed velvet still being made and numerous ornamental pieces of metal and plastic being twisted into insane shapes. For every fine building there are still some hundreds of blatant features thrust forward unhappily by unloved veneer villas, and wanton little shops, and worried big factories. For every new member joining a tree-preservation society or a National Trust branch there is at least one more suburban pioneer sharpening his axe. For every new creative worker in the visual media there is at least one new Digger with an active, vocal antipathy to any show of creative originality, with a moralistic and often bitter resentment of anything of unfamiliar appearance.

The influences tending to extend and encourage Featurism into further follies are growing stronger. This is the nature of the prosperity. There is no attraction to the idea of upsetting the comfortable *status quo* by fundamental re-thinking on appearances, while loose

coins in every pocket jingle eagerly to be spent on novel, exciting surface effects. As new industrial products, from cars to kitchenware,
appear from time to time they follow an inevitable course of decline.
They begin with an idea and arrive on the market cleanly and sensibly
pursuing the idea. But as soon as the first flush of success passes they
feel obliged to revive the newness. Yet all they can add is a new feature
or two in the styling. So every year the radiator of the car grins wider,
the handle of the refrigerator grows a bigger chrome escutcheon, the
control panel of the stove gets more Martian, the sets of saucepans and
bowls gleam with more jewel anodising, the concrete grilles get more
complicatedly geometric, the colours more vivid, the tiles more
random, and the light-shades—which always have brought out the
worst in designers—get more frantically pointed, holed, ringed, striated, twisted and miserable. And all the time, in case anyone should
begin crying for peace, the feature writers of the feature pages of the
magazines and newspapers are coaxing and encouraging more, more,
just one more golden crowning-glory feature, one more centre of
attraction to set off one's feature wall, one more outstanding, dramatically different feature, another touch or two of splendour for
everyman. It is the nature of the prosperity to make people feel not
unsettled but unsatisfied, to accept with complacence the muddle and
mess of the artificial backdrop to living but to feel a barely satiable
urge to brighten it up. A genuine desire to have things looking gay
and partyish is responsible for most of the conscious mutilation of the
colonial architectural heritage. It is behind, for instance, the circus
that is central Adelaide. The commercial party spirit is the reason for
old masonry buildings having their stones picked out in different
colours or faced with bright steel panels, for a charming colonial house
in North Adelaide being painted sulphur yellow, for the shady, tim-
bered, untidy natural banks of the river that recently ambled
unmolested past the University being bulldozed and terraced with

trim rubble walls and neat plants. It is the reason for the rainbow riot of Rundle Street: dark blue, green, orange, pink in a dozen shades, and candy stripes.

Consider the Red Lion Hotel, a pleasant relic of Adelaide's lustier days with the characteristic two-storey veranda. Its front to Rundle Street has not changed essentially for three generations. Drinkers still sit at tables on the first-floor balcony over the heads of the pedestrians on the footpath, and staghorn and ivy still hang above the heads of the drinkers. All that has changed is the atmosphere. The frail Victorian pomposity has left the cast iron and arches. Now they are part of a commercial party. The iron work is a smart charcoal and the wall behind is painted chartreuse, light grey, white and scarlet. The tables and chairs are a dozen different milky primaries and the four swinging bowls of floral Victorian ornament are now painted clear red, blue, yellow and green respectively.

The party spirit sometimes urges on tired little old buildings most inconsiderately, as on the two corners of narrow Union Lane and Rundle Street. On one side the old Belle Building has been pepped up with a ladder of persimmon-hued horizontal steel sunshades over the entire Rundle Street facade. This was painless enough, but on the other side an old brick warehouse, with its hoist still projecting willingly over the lane, has had teal green tiles pulled over its Rundle Street face like a party cap gone awry late in the evening. In King William Street, directly opposite the thoroughly over-ornamented but composed old Victorian Baroque ANZ Bank, it is possible for a student of Featurism to count nine different greens, ranging from lime to bottle, in the space of six narrow building facades. In Adelaide, rather more than in other capitals, the bright new party spirit is inclined to enter also the new office buildings. There is something festive about the three non-accessible balconies projecting at random from high on the face of the proud new Advertiser building, something of a party joke in the satiny, master-bedroom pink of the CML building, something reminiscent of a party drink in the bright little spots of cherry in the two-tone green glass walls of the Savings Bank of South Australia on the corner of Hindley and Bank Streets.

The span of the rake's progress of Australian taste can perhaps be seen most simply in a single little building: The Lady Franklin Museum near Hobart. Here is one story of its birth, as told by the late Hardy Wilson, long the doyen of Australian architectural theorists:

'There was another artist whose name I have never discovered. I believe he was a visitor with an eye for the beautiful and a joyous disregard for usefulness. He designed Lady Franklin's Museum, which stands on a knoll in a Tasmanian valley, encircled by classic hills. The story of the building, as I imagine it, runs somewhat as follows:

'One day, Lady Franklin, the wife of the Governor of that time, and this architect were riding through the valley when the beauty of the knoll and its surroundings attracted their attention.

'"What a wonderful site on which to place a Grecian temple," cried the architect.

'"It is very beautiful," replied Lady Franklin, "but how could a temple in this valley serve the folk hereabouts, who are as close to nature as their apple trees?"

'"Oh! as for that, your Excellency," he said, "there is no difficulty at all. Let us make it a museum."

'"But for what?" she exclaimed in surprise.

'"For apples," said the architect, "a museum where apples which grow so well in this happy isle, shall be displayed in shining rows of every sort and flavour."

'And so the temple was built and is known as Lady Franklin's Museum. And to this day it is used for storing apples.'

This passage is taken from *Old Colonial Architecture in New South*

Wales and Tasmania, 1924, the monumental work of Hardy Wilson, who on his own proud confession was more interested in pictorial beauty than in historical research. His drawing of the museum, dated 1915, reflects the gilded romance of his story of the two riders in the valley. The little building is shown lifted on to a mountain top amid cypresses and classical fragments beneath a magnificent Baroque sky. There are no figures about to give scale, and the shed looks at least twice its actual size. The architectural proportions are rendered accurately and the details with loving precision. Otherwise everything in Hardy Wilson's drawing and description was wild misrepresentation. He even had the wrong name. It was originally the Tasmanian Museum—this was noted on a lithograph built in under the foundation stone on 16 March 1842. A year later it was known as 'The Franklin Museum', and later it became 'The Lady Franklin Museum'. The point of interest about its conception was not that it was a pretty little snobbish conceit of an implausible dilettante and a grand colonial lady. The truth was more remarkable for its time in Tasmania. The building was a functional expression of the improving democratic ideals of good Sir John Franklin and his sympathetic wife.

Franklin, Governor of Tasmania from 1837 to 1843 and originator or supporter of many educational and cultural enterprises, was especially keen on promoting the study of natural history. Tasmania abounded in strange, unrecorded flora and fauna and the study of them should not have been above the educational level of the colonists. Franklin was disappointed but not daunted by his failure to impress the Secretary of State for the Colonies with this idea. He was not permitted to spend public money on the formation of a museum, but he and Lady Franklin built one. 'The story of the museum at Lenah Valley, Hobart, exemplifies the common task of husband and wife,' writes Kathleen Fitzpatrick in *Sir John Franklin in Tasmania*. 'Lady Franklin never considered herself more than an amateur of science—"I am hardly even a dabbler in science" she wrote once in her diary. But Sir John considered a natural history museum important for the colony, and Lady Franklin's museum is a visible expression of her devotion to her husband's interests.'

Lady Franklin selected the site, arranged for the design and the construction, and probably paid part of, if not all, the costs involved. At the same time it is apparent that she had plans to combine the natural history content with her own interests in art, which were not shared by Sir John. On 21 February 1841, she wrote to her sister, Mary Simpkinson, in England, asking: 'Do you think you could procure for me a pretty little design for a "Glyptothek"? I mean nothing more than two or three rooms of small size, though good proportions, to hold a small number of pictures and a dozen casts of the Elgin and Vatican marbles.' Sometime the same year she bought ten acres of land low on the slopes of Mount Wellington in an area then called Kangaroo Valley and now named Lenah (Aboriginal for kangaroo) Valley. Here on a little knoll between two gullies, the museum, one stone room, was built in twenty-two months. Long before it was finished the Franklins were in political difficulties. In July 1843 Sir John was recalled in undeserved humiliation, as Professor Fitzpatrick explains. By 26 October when the building was formally opened, not quite complete but furnished with a small library and some specimens of natural history, the Franklins were out of Government House and living in New Norfolk. Next month, before leaving for England, they signed a deed transferring the museum and its contents and ten acres of land to five members of the Tasmanian Society in trust for any future college or university.

The building they left beneath the towering blue backdrop of Mount Wellington, in a clearing between eucalypts, wattles and tufts of sweetbriar, was a superbly executed reproduction of a very small Greek temple in the Doric Order and prostyle tetrastyle form—that

is, three blind walls with a portico of four columns in the front only.
The proportions were perfectly in style and the simple mouldings
were as finely and lovingly carved as any classicist could wish. Almost
certainly the workmen were convicts—they were put to work on most
Tasmanian buildings of the time. In this case there must have been
masons of long experience among them.

As to the architect, all that we know certainly is that he was not
the gallant rider of Hardy Wilson's imagination. He might have been
Mr W. Porden Kay, a nephew of Sir John's first wife, working in his
little Colonial Architect's office in Hobart. And if this were so, it is
possible that Mr Kay and Lady Franklin decided to base the design on
the classic portico of the Old Sessions House at Spilsbury in
Lincolnshire, a building which both remembered. The Spilsbury
portico, however, is merely an appliqué design. In the museum the
portico is extended in depth to form the whole building. It is a classical building, not just a classical front. On the other hand, the
architect could have been James Blackburn of the Public Works
Department, an architect who knew the Franklins. And it is conceiv-
able that he was Sir F. Chantrey, in London, for Lady Franklin asked
her sister to sound him out when she first conceived the idea.

Three years after the Franklins left Tasmania in 1846, Christ
College was founded and the museum was duly handed over to it.
The College authorities had control of the building for the next eighty
years, and during the whole of this time they apparently were entirely
uninterested and unsympathetic with the idea. The building itself was
only an embarrassment. The rents from the rest of the estate which
the Franklins left were not sufficient, or not used, for its maintenance.
It was used as a store-shed for produce. Apparently apples were occu-
pying it when Hardy Wilson called in 1915. Gradually the little
building began to decay. Water from the edges of the roof streaked
the walls and ate into the soft stone at the base of the columns.

Occasional public protests at its treatment went unheeded. Cottages from the nearest suburb wandered up the hill and stood around awkwardly in the presence of decayed architectural gentility. In 1936, under an Act passed ten years earlier, Hobart City Corporation took responsibility for the building and in 1949 the Art Society of Tasmania reopened it as a gallery.

Now the neglect ended and the destruction took a new turn. The decay at the bases of the columns was patched with grey cement, practical galvanized iron gutters were added to the classical capping on the sides of the roof and downpipes zigzagged over the mouldings on their way to the ground. A public lavatory, painted green and yellow, was added near the back.

The Tasmania which the Franklins knew, and helped a little to reform, was a brutal young penal colony which had lately killed most of its blacks as objectionable fauna, still kept convict servants almost as slaves and administered bloody lashings for such crimes as insolent looks. The gradual ascent through the next hundred years into a considerably more humane and decent society coincided with the steady decline, at the same speed, of ruling standards of taste and sensibility. Presumably their paths crossed somewhere about 1900.

5

THE NON-FEATURISTS

Every Australian is not, of course, a Featurist or an Arboraphobe or a destructor in any guise. As the attentive reader will have noted, to every distressing action already mentioned there is at least a suggestion of reaction. In some of the widest generalizations in the previous chapters the small influences to improvement have not perhaps been given due attention. Little, earnest, weekender organizations of sensitive individuals, and talented professionals to guide them, have been present in almost every generation and in most towns. They have been regarded with tolerant disrespect by the mass as they tried to discover good ways to live in Australia. Their spirit was exemplified in many respects in a single building: a house in Toorak, Victoria, designed by Harold Desbrowe Annear for Senator R. D. Elliott about the middle of the First World War. It was called Broceliandi, a white roughcast cube, entirely unornamented with horizontal gashes of windows ingeniously devised to slip in and out of the hollow walls. The structure was on a module of three feet: the living-room carefully proportioned: 36 feet, by 18 feet, by 9 feet high. The big allotment was a controlled wilderness of gum trees not greatly appreciated by the neighbours in this conservative retreat. It was a good building trying to be sensibly Australian, and it was one of the world's early pioneers of rational architecture. The gum trees went in the nineteen-thirties; the building itself went while I was writing the last chapter.

All the destruction of recent times, unconscious and conscious, is not for want of critics or experts free with their advice. Anyone who has never visited Australia but who has studied the Australian press would be excused for thinking that Australians are passionate tree-lovers. At least since the last war every large-scale attack on trees in city or suburb has prompted some sort of outcry, and in many communities there are tree-lovers' associations, like the young, strong Tree Society of Western Australia, and societies for the protection of native flora, not to mention fauna, children, Aborigines, animals. The propaganda of these groups has changed the attitude of the axeman. 'I'm a tree-lover (swipe) myself,' he pants to the press columnist, 'but this one was too big. Its leaves were blocking the roof gutters and its roots were blocking the drains.'

In this practical sense tree-loving flourishes like town-planning. Every Australian city and big town has a plan, mostly sponsored in the idealistic flush soon after the Second World War and prepared laboriously, with gradually sagging spirits, during the next decade. The problems of the capital cities were too much for idealism. The plans which emerged from the various bureaucratic design departments promised to alleviate the worst tangles of traffic and industrial growth, but they were no help against ugliness. They did not pretend even to scratch the surface of the problems of the violent visual confusion of the streets of competitive architecture or the slightly psychopathic pioneering attitude to the landscape. The corrective plans had no artistic aspirations. They made no attempt to restore unity and dignity or to curb the self-advertising instincts of so many ill-trained or untrained designers. The other type of town-planning, the art, the sort of design which aims for a delightful total environment, is very rare; but it is not unknown.

From the very beginning there were cultivated men who tried to lead the way to better towns. Governor Phillip attempted to give pattern to Sydney only six months after his settlement had begun. He set aside wide streets and a public square and governmental centre. Colonel Light, in Adelaide, had the advanced idea of a park belt, one of the first 'green belts' in the world. He set out the familiar rectangular lots for the bulk of the city, but he allowed for public squares in the middle of the town and he dropped his straight-edge some distance from either bank of the River Torrens, leaving a wedge of river garden to divide the northern suburbs from the city's heart.

Artists and architects in Melbourne were criticising Hoddle's parallelogram plan for Melbourne even before the population outgrew it in the gold rush. In 1850 the *Australasian* magazine was editorially demanding the appointment of a leading London planner to advise the Board of Works for Melbourne. The city, 'perhaps destined to become the New York of the future United States of the South,' was described as it could be if the straight-edge principle were discarded and if Hoddle's plan was changed to suit the site, with 'a public forum surrounded by the town hall and post-office, a central fountain, public buildings in elevated positions united by broad streets...boulevards with rows of trees and broad footways encircling the town and separating the suburbs.'

Canberra, as has been mentioned, set out with good intentions and may yet succeed. The twentieth century also made some other, more modest, attempts to build model communities. Yallourn, a brown-coal town in Gippsland, eastern Victoria, was built in the early nineteen-twenties by the State Electricity Commission under the chairmanship of Sir John Monash. It was conceived as a model town, a symbol of the entry of the state into the new world of power and industry, a showpiece of the Commission. It was given generous children's playgrounds, sports fields, golf links, swimming pools, a toy town centre and an architectural policy reflecting the nicest taste of the time in cosy, slightly dolls' house cottages, with high-pitched roofs and suggestions of half-timbering.

Millions of words of discussion and proposal about city sprawling and satellite towns were written during the Second World War and in the readjustment period. None carried more weight than those published in 1950 by the South Australian Housing Trust, which was always the most powerful and vigorous of the various State housing authorities. This report led to the founding in 1955 of Elizabeth, the first self-contained satellite town to an Australian capital. It was seventeen miles from Adelaide and was planned, under Henry P. Smith, the Trust's chief town-planner, on an area of 5500 acres. Nine residential neighbourhood units surround the town centre, each with its own shopping centres, post-office, schools, churches and so on. A quarter of the whole area was reserved for parks. Each household was given half a dozen seedling trees for its future garden.

In the flush of industrial expansion about 1950 several new towns, like Eildon in Victoria, were built in remote parts to house the workers of new enterprises. In Eildon's case the work was a weir and when this was finished the town was sold to private buyers. Most of these towns were planned with a heavy practical bias. The principal buildings were designed by capable architects, but the quality of the whole was only slightly more enticing than that of an army camp. The one town which achieved the homogeneity which is the elementary aim of the art of town-planning was Mary Kathleen, a village of 1300 people in lonely outback Queensland, forty-five miles west of Cloncurry. Mary Kathleen was built in 1956–7 by an international octopus, the Rio Tinto Mining Company, at a cost of something under two million pounds, for the employees at Mary Kathleen Uranium Ltd, a mining and treatment works producing a fortune in uranium. The site selected was more than a hundred acres of comparatively luxuriant land for these dry parts: a wooded river valley three miles from the mine workings. The town-planners selected were unusually sensitive designers for this sort of work: Ernest Milston and Donald Fulton of Melbourne. Unlike other model towns, Mary Kathleen was almost a total design, nearly everything in it being made specially for it. The houses were not standard prefabricated cottages, but were planned specially for the gruelling climate. They were based on a pre-cut modular unit and made in a single string of rooms as cross-ventilated as a railway carriage. One side had a continuous veranda on to which the louvred glass walls of the rooms opened. All the houses were oriented on the north-south axis to catch the prevailing breeze and they were raised on long stumps two feet above the grassed flat which the river watered annually when it swelled in the wet season. The rest of the little town followed model specifications. The houses were placed in four neighbourhood groups round the town centre. The boundaries of each group were determined by the natural divisions formed by trees or rock outcrops. The roads followed the ground's natural contours. The town centre was formed as a ring around a wooded square. The school was reached by a system of footpaths connecting the backs of the houses and separated from the traffic roads. The buildings were trim, rectangular, economical to the point of austerity, but graced throughout by a touch of elegance in detail, characteristic of these architects' work.

In Australia there are these few pleasantly designed towns; there are also artists and nature-lovers and sympathetic souls—probably as many per head of population as in any country. If it were not for them, if the whole of man-made Australia were hideous, there might be more hope for a revolution. But even amid the worst squalor are moments of maturity and great visual delight. Separated by acres of the mean mediocrity of housing developments and miles of cynical ugliness in the commercial streets, there are the few buildings which have been produced by a sympathetic partnership of a sensitive owner and an imaginative designer. These works are the antithesis of Featurism and advertising architecture, and without their little flights of the spirit this era would be unredeemed, but the rare dedicated patrons and architects hardly can be looked upon as the potential saviours of the whole Australian scene. For one thing, although more trained architects per capita probably exist now than ever before, there are still so few that they cannot be expected to be responsible for more than an occasional oasis in the desert. If art is the cure of the ugliness, as many critics suggest, the twentieth century needs many more artists in every country, but here is a fundamental problem. How can the number ever be increased greatly? More schools of architecture with more sympathetic tuition might draw out more latent talents, but the best schools are limited by the capacities of the human material fed to them. They can train and encourage, but they cannot teach the spark of artistic invention which transforms building techniques. The inter-national architectural giants of the century were self-taught in the matter of their art, as are all creators. They were immensely stimu-lated, perhaps, by some personal contact with a master, but if they had formal training they succeeded in spite of it. Schools cannot be blamed if many practitioners of architecture are conscientious copyists without originality in their make-up. And even if every architect in practice had a brilliant creative flair and an indomitable will, still the greater part of building, being done without architects, by builders, publicity designers, engineers and others, would be unaffected. The architec-tural profession and its friends have always believed, and probably in the majority still believe, that this is the root of the trouble, that there is nothing wrong with the design of the world that a few more good architects could not correct. A vague article of progressive belief has been that, as time goes on, more and more buildings will be put into the hands of better and better architects until eventually, one assumes, a thousand Wrens and Wrights will be available to care for all new buildings in all towns. But in fact it is not possible to imagine educa- tion ever being stepped up to the high pitch required to produce enough architects to care individually for all the houses of Australia, not to mention the multitude of buildings required to shelter decently the more prolific human races of Asia, or the rest of the world.

It may be possible to imagine that some future Utopia could produce a race so cultivated and rich in creative talent that all its buildings could be designed at leisure by fine artists, but there is no practical lesson for the twentieth century in this dream. For we can envisage this world of art only in terms of art as practised now. Thus we can picture it only as the over-exciting if tasteful sort of chaos which develops every time a group of the most sensitive of the cen- tury's creators of form are brought together for an exposition. The world's creative leaders could not be expected to agree on the shape of a single building for Utopia if they were given a free hand by some benign world government. A paddock full of the modern world's twelve best architects' work would be more like a new World Fair than the fair new world which this century might have been.

The world-wide artistic problem of Featurism grows from the lack of any consistent aesthetic appreciation or digested artistic code permeating the building classes. The jumpy twentieth century has instead a nervous, wavering eye. It knows much about architecture but not what it likes. The international leaders have long been con- cerned by this and they propose various methods for re-instituting some sort of unifying code. Le Corbusier has *Le Modulor*, a system of proportioning based on the Golden Section, which he advocates for every draftsman and artist, hoping that its discipline would unite their separate activities in something like the way ruled lines in exercise books unify the writing in a classroom. Walter Gropius proposes team work, collaboration, groups pooling their artistic resources, to the distraction of the *prima donna* designer and the general elevation of the common taste of all involved in construction. Mies van der Rohe rests on the principle of intellectually controlled technology, for 'architecture is more reason than emotion,' he remarks. All of these solutions to the visual confusion of today deliberately curb to some extent the free spirit of the architect and imply firmly that the salvation of the ugly world can never be left to the great originators. However important and delightful their work may be in isolation, the more creative individualist architect's work is frequently as full of fight against its neighbours as a new service station. There are not enough artists to cover the world's architecture; but if there were it might be too many.

In the second half of the twentieth century the world has followed Gropius, Mies and Le Corbusier, if not exactly in the way they intended, to allow modern technology to produce unselfconsciously its own building type. This, of course, is the glass box, the international urban vernacular building of this century, counterpart of the carpenters' and masons' languages which are still the vernacular in parts of the country. City office blocks in Australia, as everywhere else, adopted the glass box soon after 1950, following the example of the United Nations Secretariat in New York. The first free-standing, fully fledged glass boxes in Australia were the Imperial Chemical Industries building by Bates, Smart and McCutcheon, and Unilever building by Stephenson and Turner, which transformed Sydney Harbour about 1956, and the most impressive before 1960 was ICI House in Melbourne, also by Bates, Smart and McCutcheon, on Eastern Hill. ICI House also turned out to be the tallest building in

Melbourne, having successfully beaten its way through a nineteenth-century height-limit regulation of 132 feet. It is more than twice as high as this, twenty storeys, and elevated on land already some hundred feet above the retail valley. Thus it is decidedly a feature of the city skyline; but it is not a Featurist building. In form it has a clear, simple concept of a tall, thin, blind tower of services hugging the side of a much broader and slightly shorter slab of glazed offices. It is a finely polished example of the international glass filing-cabinet type of office block and as good a representative of this type as one could find. It is in fact as good a representative of the crystallized mid-century style as can be found anywhere in the world. Others soon followed it, polishing the glass and metal a little more carefully every time. Next door to ICI a little three-storey cube, Feltex House, built in 1959 by Guildford Bell, has an even simpler window grid, and has eliminated even the subdued colouring of ICI House. Shell House on Bourke Street and William Street corner, 1960, was designed by the giant American firm of Skidmore, Owings and Merrill (and supervised by Buchan, Laird and Buchan), and is again more direct and sober, with great dark sheets of glass held in dull aluminium frames. Meanwhile in Sydney other glass towers were even higher, if not so polished, and eventually there was not a country town which did not have a glass box or two serving as a bank or an insurance company office, or perhaps a factory, a school, or even a church.

Thus technology upset the even tenor of architectural development by beginning to fulfil a promise it made a century earlier in London's Great Exhibition of 1851. It became capable, with its standard steel sections and its prefabricated curtains of aluminium and glass, of delivering mass-produced, factory-made shelter. This is a modern wonder which promises the only satisfactory means yet invented of covering one day the world's exploding population. It promises a way to end Featurism. It also promises, if industrial development continues in a straight line, the eventual elimination of the artist-architect.

ICI House demonstrated that even in a frantically Featurist society a non-Featurist building can be a popular success. In the first week after its opening, visitors were welcomed, and twenty thousand of them paid nearly two thousand pounds to charity for the privilege of looking over the building. It continues to be popular, but despite its non-Featurist design, not because of it. Other equally simple glass boxes without ICI's claim to sky-scraping were criticized frequently by laymen, from the Governor-General (Sir William Slim in 1958) down. People want Featurism. It fills a need. Its success is a symptom of maladjustment in modern society, which has failed so notably, and not of course only in Australia, to adjust itself to changed conditions on two levels: firstly to the machine, to the replacement of an artist-craftsman by a production line of workers and wiring circuits; secondly, to the disappearance of the patron. After the political and economic struggles were won by the forces of democratic equal-opportunity, there remained the problem of the adjustment of the equalized democrat to the new toys and opportunities, to the realization that the shape of the world around him was no longer safely in the hands of his social superiors. The old patrons of the arts, with the time, means and inclination to cultivate good taste, were seldom now in a position to promote architecture; they wrote books about it which other patrons read. The new promoters of building were corporations, governments, private businesses, and the new class of mammoth speculative builders, the 'Developers', all of which will never make an architectural move until, directly or indirectly, they have asked the equalized democrat for his artistic opinion. A share in the responsi-bilities of the patron was divided out to everyone with his share in the responsibilities of government and trade. But of course it was not accepted. The citizen still exercises practically no control or interest in the shape of his daily surroundings until the sudden need for a new home goads him into a brief predatory quest for the most acceptable good taste. A sort of cottage-and-castle division lingers in equalized society, the ordinary man and woman clinging to the cosiest traditions in their own home while content to leave the nature of all the rest of their environment to others.

The only ultimate cure for visual squalor is the redirection of public interest and responsibility to the entire field of the artificial background of life, and a first step to this end is a better understanding of architecture's aims and means. However, most attempts to promote this step which have been taken in books and articles of architectural propaganda take the form of a short course in the history and compositional devices of building; and so much of this is confusing and irrelevant. The aim cannot be to make a world of amateur architects. Furthermore, although artistic values may not change, new rules are needed now. For one thing, the effects of industry remove the architecture of this half of the twentieth century from anything but academic connection with the great buildings of the past. The scale of expansion in all younger countries, the enormous spread of cities, the speed of travel everywhere, have increased the scale of visual comprehension in public places. What was once a fetching intricacy of ornament is likely now to be merely finicking, and what was once a bald box is likely now to be a satisfactorily bold element in the vast mosaic. But an elementary article of Featurist lore is that no technological or other new conditions should be allowed special concessions. Anything new must attract the bustling modern worker in exactly the same way as craftsmen-carved masonry used to attract the leisured classes.

The plainness of the new curtain-wall boxes was never accepted as a relief from the visual confusion of the city. 'Imagine a whole street of them!' complained the Featurist. Industrial processes, having no wish to offend, responded to the complaint and dressed themselves ingratiatingly. The glass and metal panels of the curtain walls were inclined, very soon after beginning, to look back to decoration of the repetitive type to which a stamping press or a moulding machine so readily lends itself. Technical problems aside, the age of efficient industrialization of the building industry is held at bay by the aesthetic barrier. Awaiting the long postponed conquest by technology, the world today is witnessing a transitional stage. During this time the industrial product is trying to carry on in the tradition of individual building, making each structure appear as personal to the occupants and as individual for the circumstances as possible. The central part of Queen Street, Melbourne, displays more separate new glazed walls than almost any other street in the world—and more variety: two dozen different ways of combining glass, metal strips and coloured panels, all doing precisely the same job. This variety can be provided only at the expense of the economics inherent in the industrial mass-production process.

Mass-produced shelter—whether it is a single box, or a balloon, or is made of adjustable components—has by nature a universal neutrality, a negation of individual character. At the most it may be a chameleon in the colours which it adopts. Its form is fixed by the requirements of the central factory and the general demands of the average human animal, not by the demands of any specific site or occupant. If the prospect of a world of frankly industrialized shelter is depressing to some minds, the prospect of these shelters being less frank and attempting a pretence of sympathy is worse. The idea of anything but neutral character being mass-produced and endlessly repeated has a farcical note; one is reminded of a *New Yorker* cartoon of a tract development of houses, each with a reproduction of Frank Lloyd Wright's 'Falling Water' with its own diminutive waterfall.

On the other hand, if the industrialized building is left to its own nature, to be negative, anonymous and impersonal, it will never offend an educated eye; it will never disturb. While remaining neutral, it may be beautifully neutral. If it is wisely and sensitively directed, if the advice of the great teacher of universal principles in the machine age, Walter Gropius, is heeded, if the terrible temptations of the stamping press and the injection moulding machine and the industrial printery are conquered, then the impersonal aesthetic of the machine may provide a background to life which will restore the dignity that was lost about the time Australia was founded.

If the housing industry were to embrace modern factory methods with even half the enthusiasm of the car industry, in no time it would be producing standardized components or space-enclosures of some kind which could be assembled in various ways to suit the needs of each buyer. Gradually the family itself would become the designer of its own pattern of standardized units, as suggested by Walter Gropius as early as 1909, changing them about if necessary as the pattern of the family life developed. To be sure the spaces themselves and the outside of the house might be as impersonal as a new washing machine.

Whether we like the idea or not it would be blindly unrealistic not to recognize in the ICI and Unilever offices on Sydney Harbour a hint of the machine-made character which will ultimately overtake all construction. Their glass and metal walls were forerunners of a future now forecast with bated breath by research men, of a coming age when the space-enclosure fabric of any building—office, church, home, or school—is some sort of plastic sandwich coursing internally with all kinds of creature comforts, and these sandwich skins, propped perhaps on central service masts, are made so they can be linked together in a matter of hours to make a structure to suit any requirements, and unlinked as casually to change the shape when the needs change. It is a future which will have many jobs for technologists, but no studio to offer the special sort of artist who has been known hitherto as the architect. He might instead be occupied as one member of some large town-planning organization and his old art of space manipulation would be confined to the siting of various standard components. It would be a future in which the world at long last would be free of Featurism.

It would not be, however, a future free of features. The research man's forecast of an industrialized landscape wiped of all individual expression is profoundly disturbing to some people; it is also as unlikely as the familiar film set of a city on Venus. Someone will always insist on featuring something: if not a free citizen wanting to feature some symbol of his own success or aspirations, then governments featuring the symbols of their power. Shelter, food and features seem to be fundamental human needs; this is understood. The construction of features only becomes an ism when the object featured has no intrinsic importance or claim to be featured; for instance, the popular 'feature wall' of interior decoration: featured for the sake of creating a feature to occupy momentarily the dull, hedonistic eye.

If the negative, impersonal industrialized landscape is considered only as a background on which genuine features may be arranged to taste, it becomes a more acceptable idea even in our present state of visual delinquency. It is the black velvet on which the gems are sprinkled. It enhances the feature gems. They would stand in relief, magnificently featured, like Christopher Wren's churches among the phlegmatic brick houses of Georgian London, or Francis Greenway's in Colonial Sydney. But however attractive may be the vision of this future of two clearly defined architectures, it could not evolve easily or naturally from the present twilight world of commercial design, with its established and accepted false effects and empty imitations. The realization of non-Featurism would demand fulfilment of two conditions with which the present age is not in a mood to comply. One is the purging of advertising-architecture and ornament and all pretensions to expressive art from the industrialized buildings of the background. The other is the stepping up of the architectural quality of the foreground: the feature buildings worthy of special design and construction. Bathed in such limelight architecture would be obliged to wade out from the present pleasant luke-warm shallows into greater depths of artistic perception.

A recognition of the split between creative architecture and honest machine-building, and the elimination of in-betweens, has many side effects. The prospect is not attractive to a workaday designer who likes to do his best with any industrialized products that are available while injecting them with a tasteful portion of his own modest personality. He will fight hard to retain the pleasant status of a semi-artist. The prospect will not be welcomed universally when it comes close to home. It may be argued, even by people who are aware of the inexorable approach of industrialized structure, that a neutrality in architectural character is not an essential concomitant. It may be said that the hodgepodge of the vast suburban plain, stretching between the artist and the machine, is not simply the work of advertisers. It can be argued that the average untrained suburban house designer, though he may be motivated entirely by sales-appeal, gives the community what it wants in his heartless repetition of saccharine house trimmings: even a coarse and crippled colonial Georgian effect or the hybrid empirical style of the veneer villa is socially valuable if it gives the community a sense of familiarity and security. So the developer argues.

The machine is fairly accommodating. It may be turned without economic disaster to produce Georgian or Modernistic or any other style, and for many years yet it will spend a lot of its time, undoubtedly, in the reproduction of handicraft designs. And many who live behind the shallow facades will continue to delude themselves into believing that their mass-produced copy of a caricature is lending them some sort of individual personality. The irony is that prefabrication of the physical matter of the house is not progressing as quickly as was expected largely because people objected to the idea of being regimented; yet the same people accept a much more chilling prefabricated thinking which grips the very spirit of the private home. It is not simply that the mass-produced designs of many site-built houses are as impersonal as the products of any machine; the paralysis goes deeper than the thousandfold reproduction of the conventional veneer cottage.

Even when a building is a lone product on a ten-acre paddock, free to be or to express anything, the strong modern tendency is for it to be cast in a standard mould, like a character in a soap opera. Its conception or motivating idea usually bears no burden of original thought, no artistic passion, no inspiration stemming from the heart of the particular human problem of shelter. The quality which may recommend some new building to our passing interest usually is contained in but a single feature of its front. At the best, architectural

quality is often no more than one of a few generally accepted 'treatments'. For the convenience of the workaday designer a little
unofficial stock of standard architectural characters gradually has
built up. Each standard is a more or less conscious plagiarism of one
of the few spirited leaders of architecture. Select the flavour that suits
you best; here is Instant Architecture. Your home? Simply add water
to Frank Lloyd Wright. Your office? Simply add water to Mies van
der Rohe.

House-building postpones the economies of mass-production for
fear of losing individuality and personality around the family hearth-
stone, and the trade perseveres with ancient craft methods barely
modified by the atomic age. But if these laborious site-construction
methods are to be directed by a pattern of design-thinking which is
mass-produced, their greatest asset is wasted. Workaday architecture
is in—not a rut, but a number of parallel ruts, each producing no
more than a thin shadow of the qualities by which architecture could
be transforming building materials. In all the thousands of acres of
new housing developments across Australia one can count on ten
fingers the different basic types: Brick-Area-Conservative, Georgian-
Nostalgic, Holiday-Contemporary, Young-Executive-Contemporary,
New-Old-Colonial and so on, each symbolic of a certain economic-
social-cultural level to which the area and the occupants aspire.
Underneath a few 'personalising' features, hundreds of thousands of
individually produced villas almost give the impression that they want
to appear mass-produced, just as potentially mass-produced buildings
of metal and glass want to look individually produced.

Nearly half a century ago a certain group of European rebel
architects, Mart Stam, Hannes Meyer and others, revolting against the
various forms of Edwardian artiness, declared architecture's abdica-
tion from the fine arts and attempted an entirely rationalized process
of design, wishing to skip from function direct to technique without

an intervening stage of artistic conception. They were always frustrated because somewhere during the nimblest skip the form of the functional arrangement had to be determined by a mind, and something of the emotional quality of that mind rubbed off on the building. The rebellious school gradually accepted as inevitable this discoloration of the science of building and crept back, somewhat shamefaced, to the fringe of the fine art fold. But while the scientific morality of this early splinter movement faded and was forgotten, the search of economy through standardization and mass-production kept reducing the architect's area of free creation. In commercial buildings now the area for artistry is so restricted that, almost without realising it, we have come close suddenly to the once desired but unattainable state of inartistry. At last buildings can be erected without trace of an architect's individuality or evidence of any flicker of emotion.

The great architectural significance of modern technology is that it marks the beginning of the end of the gentleman's profession of architecture which has served the world with varying success for two centuries. Gradually the science of space-enclosure is drawing away from the creative art of building. It has been a long struggle for modern architecture since the day when a little leaderless international band of explorers turned into the twentieth century and discovered the ethics of design for function and total simplicity. Not all of them read into these ethics the elimination of the artist; on the contrary many recognized them from the beginning as liberating him to create free architecture uncontaminated for the first time since builders began toying with painting and carving. The world's response to the discovery of total simplicity lacked enthusiasm. The naked forms fought against prejudice through the first half of the century. Although the new architecture thought of itself as being in the forefront of the fight for democratic culture it did not share in the victory of the First World War and was denied a place in the League of

Nations building at Geneva. But it gained ground steadily between the wars, and then, after the Second World War, it was recognized publicly and internationally in the United Nations building. But even now the glass boxes are usually accepted for the wrong reasons: not as the welcome forerunners of a negative, impersonal background to everyday living in which building technology at last is permitted to come into its own, but as ivory towers, exciting things expected to occupy the same place in our consciousness as the old-fashioned art of creative building.

For as long as the novelty lasts the plain boxes will indeed give a touch of visual pleasure, like fresh air after too long in a fuggy room. But since there is little intrinsic interest in a plain curtain which is merely clean, the excitement derived must be even more transient than that which diverted the world from Gothic to Classic and back again in and out the years of last century. This new fashion, like all the old ones, has no solid cultural foundation. Before long the plain glass walls will be asked to convey something more than wobbly reflections, and the clever stylist will be only too delighted to respond to this challenge. The simplicity is only skin deep; already it begins to pall. The tendency to ginger it up is likely to increase during the next few years. The design of the Chevron-Hilton Hotel in Sydney includes at least six different wall treatments in its two attached but contrasted blocks. The curved slab of the BP sky-scraper in St Kilda Road, Melbourne, has its bold white spandril strips between windows teased by a shallow key pattern, like a dress-makers' braiding. Before long the architectural equivalents of a car's tail fins may spring above parapet lines and urban architecture will retire back to the position in the cultural scene which it occupied when the century began. The trouble is that the boxes still have pretensions. They even introduce sometimes a cautious, unoffending mural to try to prove they have a soul. If they were honest with themselves the boxes would admit that emotional expression was the last consideration at the time of their conception.

The Australian ugliness does need an injection of emotion and poetry, but even if Australia could learn to turn out Frank Lloyd Wrights like she now turns out tennis players and champion swimmers, still there would not be enough architects to give individual attention to all the buildings required. Wright himself offered as a solution to the world's architectural problems nothing more than the proposition that all designers of worldly goods eventually should cultivate the strength and type of imagination which he himself practised for sixty years. But since few enough of his own disciples at Taliesin were able to reach his creative level, this engaging prospect cannot be anticipated with any confidence. 'A building without poetry has no right to exist,' Wright told his Taliesin Fellowship on his second last birthday, in the Spring of 1957: 'it should never be built.' But an evening or two earlier when he was asked if he believed that there would ever be enough artists to design all the buildings the world required, he shook his head slowly and answered, 'No.'

A world where everyone lives, works and plays in structures of high poetry created by brilliant self-portraitists is as unlikely as a world where everyone lives in pure bubbles of technology, and in some respects both prospects are almost as forbidding as the present disjointed mess produced by men who avoid commitments to either side.

The solution, then, is to recognize that there is an appropriate time and place for both the technology of space-enclosure and the architecture of expression, and to work to eliminate the neuter type: neither scientific nor artistic. There is no fundamental conflict between the two logical extremes, between, say, Sydney's Opera House and her Unilever House, for they are not comparable. The poetic expression and the glass box are no more commensurable than the horse and the motorcar. And in the years ahead, as the science of space-enclosure grows more involved, exact and impersonal, the two will inevitably grow further apart—except that science and art, like the opposite ends of a straight line, might meet in an inverted infinite future. On some distant day the scientific builder might arrive at a point he recognizes as perfection, and might realize that his old colleague of the early twentieth century, the artist-architect, might have arrived at the same point from the other side if he had lived long enough. Scientist and artist could meet in a time of perfection, one guilelessly sheltering men whose lives and minds have discovered order and the other intuitively portraying those lives and minds. But we may be fairly certain that the buildings of such an era would bear no more resemblance to any buildings we know now than a perfectly ordered era would bear to our competitive, Featurist society.

And there is the basic objection to Featurism: a moral objection. No matter how successful it may be in pleasing the passing eye, no matter if it pleases to the extent of being judged beautiful, the entirely superficial, frivolous appeal of a Featurist object can never assist human awareness, wisdom and understanding. It is for this reason alone as degrading to human nature as it is to art.

To the average family, unimpressed by architectural theory but eager to get the best house possible, the acceptance of a clear division between creative and machined shelter should provide not less but more satisfaction from the experience of building. Those who derive pleasure from architecture and have the means to indulge their taste would, as always, consult the artist-architect of their choice. He, as always, would create in form and space a sort of personal portrait of the occupants and himself. Those who have no wish or patience to patronize the art of architecture would turn to the machined shelter, would find in it much more space-for-money, and might find even more opportunity for personal expression in arranging and appointing it than they can find now in the conventional housing market.

Indeed, the sooner that the break between the space-enclosing technologist and the creative building-artist is recognized, the better for all concerned. Then the pretence of artistry might be dropped by the great mass of buildings which now only pretend by habit, because it seems the thing to do. Then architecture would not present an even gradation from the sublime to the ridiculous; instead the streets of a cultivated community would present only two types of face: good particular and good universal. When architecture accepts the division a clear line will be drawn below the creative artist and those without his passion will be no more inclined to imitate him than they would ape a conductor's arm movements. Then the art of architecture will be left to those with capacity in the creative medium of shelter while the science and technology of space-enclosure will develop faster free of sentimental strings.

But the problem of Featurism is not, we know, confined to the mother art. It involves all her visual offspring, through engineering, to industrial design and craft work of every kind. The Sydney Harbour Bridge, with its entirely redundant pylons built as features to camouflage the honest steel, may be the crowning achievement of Australian Featurism, but the pylons differ only in scale, not in principle, from most things on three million Australian mantelpieces.

Perhaps two pictures in every hundred which hang in Australian homes and waiting-rooms and the foyers of business offices are not there for Featurist reasons, are there because they mean something as paintings to the person who hung them. The other ninety-eight, whether original oils or reproduced water-colour, whether traditional or modern, impressionist or abstract, serious or decorative, good or bad, are hung because someone first decided that something was needed there on the blank wall: something to destroy the frightening honesty of the blank wall: a Feature.

The way out of the Featurist jungle in the broadest field of architecture—the elimination of the in-between building, neither wholly rational nor poetic—may be a gigantic process requiring the re-education of the public eye. But the principle is applied more simply to individual buildings and articles. Indeed non-Featurism is already practised every day, not only by professional designers but by any talented houseproud woman who appreciates that the wholeness of the total effect of her house is a hundred times more valuable than any feature, and who realizes that, if there is anything more destructive to art than a feature, it is two features.

The non-Featurist housewife with her homogeneous living-room is, however, more intent on creating a delightful home environment than the bargain-hunter who can never resist the draw of the oddments-counter in a furniture store. The tragic irony of Featurism is that it is practised in the name of beauty, on the assumption that all things made by man for use in the workaday world are necessarily ugly when naked, until they are given the extra enlivening life of a few extrinsic eye-catchers. The Featurist is not prepared to consider the simple proposition that no object which is true to its own nature needs cosmetics.

Throughout the whole artificial backdrop to everyday life, as in architecture, there are two sources of genuine form: hand or heart: process or poetry. The man-made object may follow the mute logic of materials and techniques, or its entire nature may be shaped in an attempt to express some idea beyond the utilitarian. These are the black and white, the negative and positive approaches to genuine design, and each in its appropriate time and place could make a shape for Utopia. But the Featurist will not admit this. He is afraid of the naked, guileless truth of the plain utilitarian product of craft or technology. And he is not prepared to cultivate an appreciation of expressive form. The only visual excitement he knows is recognition of a familiar shape or a symbolic surface treatment of fashion. The Featurist way of design, indecisive and indeterminate, is a grey mixture, not directly from the hand or the heart: never a plain anonymous structure and yet never a message, nothing to say but a cry for attention, never a plain wall, never a strong painting, only a decorative mural.

The attraction of a Featurist object is sudden, sharp and shallow. It counts on claiming love at first sight, guessing that love never grows gradually towards anything which relies wholly on cosmetics. The really successful Featurist object instantaneously seduces its observer, who then begins gradually to cool, until complete disenchantment is reached usually about twelve months before the time-payments are completed. Because it is non-intellectual, non-emotional and entirely optical, a Featurist effect cannot be accumulative, inviting deeper study.

On the other hand, either of the genuine sources of design can provide forms of lasting value. Through the centuries warm feeling has produced boldly expressive art in numerous guises, and cold logic has produced boldly functional objects galore: from primitive tools to Quaker implements to fry-pans and aeroplanes. The hand has made some things satisfying and the heart has made others involving.

If Australia, or any other prosperous country in the modern world, had any desire to rid itself of the ugly evidence of Featurism, it would turn to both the genuine sources of design. Then the workaday backdrop would gradually be shaped by physical laws and the features would gradually be shaped by ideas. Not all the ideas would appeal to all men, of course, but somehow each feature would be meaningful to the person who featured it and nothing would be governed only by the meaningless, heartless habits of fashion.

The ideas are the essence of this hypothetical Utopia. Without them the prospect of an unrelieved, impeccable, impersonal background can enthuse few people. The key to release from Featurism is a promise of more, not less, visual interest. The Featurist can be offered the prospect of richer optical treats in the various objects which will always demand or deserve to be in the foreground: the houses of parliament, houses for kings and kingpins, churches, galleries, gift-shops—and within each of these the principal chambers, salons, altars, thrones and sales counters. If each of these things is to justify its assumption of prominence without calling in outside symbols, it needs a formal idea: something that will reconcile all the conflicting material and human requirements and create order at its touch, something that will make one whole thing out of all the necessary parts.

Plato made what must be the first recorded attack on Featurism when he explained the need in every work of art for unity: the cohesion and interrelation of all elements, as in nature. This theory has stood as an axiom in practically all artistic criticism. If there is no unity there is no work of art; two or three unrelated works of art there may be, but not one. Featurism, of course, works on the contrary principle that one cannot have too many good things, even conflicting things, provided the eyes are kept entertained.

In every attempt to design a Platonic non-Featurist object there are three stages: the programme of physical requirements and limitations, the formal concept, and the technique. The middle stage is the time for ideas. This is when form is set and character develops as a synthesis extracted from the programme. The idea comes to light as the designer seeks a unifying theme, a motive; or it fails ever to appear. The idea arrives, if at all, suddenly, complete, in the guise of a discipline; a motive, like character in a person, which makes for a certain consistency, reliability and predictability in all behaviour.

In buildings, which are the most complex and pervasive objects in our lives, character naturally may be more elaborate and subtle than in a chair or a tea-cup, but the principle is the same. In the moment of decision the architect cannot conceive every element as a painter might conceive the guiding form of his canvas. At this stage he may not even decide the form of certain major parts; rather he conceives a formal limitation for the project. Ask any creative architect how long it took him to design his favourite building and he will reply: five minutes, give or take a minute. Maxwell Fry tells how he and the others of the Le Corbusier team designed an Indian city in one conversation. Yamasaki tells how he designed an office block one Saturday morning when he happened to race back to the office for a moment and glanced again at his problem-littered drawing-board. Wright told how he designed an art gallery for Baghdad gazing out the window of his plane on the flight home. Most architects like to tell about the moment of perception on their favourite works: these are the high moments of their lives. The briefer the moment, the simpler and stronger the idea—and the more unified the subsequent building or city is likely to be.

The three stages of design do not, of course, always appear sharply separated in a finished product, but an analysis of any design and the extraction of the central, motivating idea is always helpful to understanding. The Featurist is inclined to judge appearances on the results of the first and last stages of design and to ignore the essential middle stage. For instance, if he happens to enjoy brightness and warmth at all times he is likely to approve a building which invites streams of sunshine through wide windows. On the other hand, if glare induces headaches he is unlikely to approve any building that looks very glassy, even if he never has to enter it. But the degree of natural illumination is a question which properly belongs in the first stage of design, the programming, when all the desirable qualities for the building are discussed before the designer puts pencil to paper. Again, the popularity of a building generally depends on qualities of the surface treatment, which properly belong in the third stage of design, the technique, and have little or nothing to do with the shapes or overall architectural form. A cosy sort of Featurist may be disturbed by hard, glazed finishes of tiles and metals, while the many who are Flash Gordons at heart are impatient with what seems to be the sentimental attraction of woody, warm, rugged textures. Personal taste, even in something as superficial as colour, often diverts attention from the essential form and makes the difference between approval and antagonism in the attitude to a building.

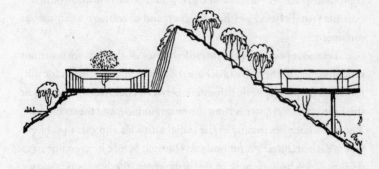

For the exercise, consider the work of two of Sydney's best known architects: Sydney Ancher and Harry Seidler. These men have much in common. For about ten years after the Second World War, before they were joined by members of a new generation, each concentrated on house design and without much help from others separately kept modern architecture alive in Sydney's suburbs. One or the other won most of the awards given during this period for distinguished work. Each of them had at some time to defend his architecture in court. Each has followed his own chosen line of development with rare concentration and lack of deviation. Each works within the central discipline of modern architecture. Yet within these limits their work could hardly be less similar. If the central discipline may be assumed to be a perfect balance between, on the left, the human emotional requirements in building and, on the right, the rational intellectual theory of building, Ancher draws the line a little to the left and Seidler likes to draw it to the right. If both were to set out to build themselves a house on the same slope of Sydney Harbour, one could anticipate, on previous showings, that Ancher would dig his house into the slope and Seidler would project his forward from the slope on some sort of cantilever. The materials also might be different: easy-going carpentry on the left, formal concrete on the right: but whatever was chosen there would be no distortion of materials for visual effect by either designer, and of course no extraneous ornament.

Yet most people, surveying the houses of the two men cannot remain neutral. They love one, hate the other. And the reason for this, for the great atmospheric difference between characteristic houses of these two architects, stems from the programming and the techniques. The difference lies mainly in the initial attitudes and extra problems which each architect gratuitously sets himself before he even begins to design. More important than the differences, the houses of the two architects have one element in common; each is based on a strong design idea which permeates and brings coherence throughout the building of each house, in short, is intensely non-Featurist: a whole thing; and two such whole houses can sit beside each other more amicably than any two Featurist houses which are already ragbags of oddments. For this reason an Ancher house and a Seidler house, for all their atmospheric differences, would never be bad neighbours to each other. No matter if the former is disciplined by an idea of external form and the latter by an idea of space and structure. No matter if each idea is not absolutely original, underivative and apt. The important thing here is the fact that the houses always have some idea and are thus united in the higher order of ideas, while Featurist villas without ideas or integrity are always at war within themselves and with their neighbours. While the Featurist jungle is torn by all manner of strident cries for attention, all things made with an idea and an integrity can sit happily together, however different they look, and can be simultaneously appreciated by us without vacillation of principles. The way to escape from the Featurist mess throughout the whole world of design is not to attempt the impossible task of standardising people's preferences in the atmospheric quality of the environment, by seeking a common denominator in popular tastes in living habits or materials or techniques, or by trying to find an acceptable style to which everyone is prepared to conform. The way out of the mess is not by way of taste, but by way of cultivating the quality of ideas in design. Any object lacking a strong central motivating idea must be lacking intrinsic interest and coherence, and untrained eyes will look immediately for features to add the visual entertainment. Even trained eyes may hanker after some central feature on which to rest a while. Hence the over-prominent entrance feature on three out of four buildings. But in the presence of a virile, meaningful, characterful motive, even the least experienced eye will be conscious that a strong order prevails, and will realize that its discipline would overrule irrelevant additional features, that they are not necessary and indeed might be objectionable. This realization is the only thing that will break the grip of Featurism on those people who practise it now with the best intentions of creating beauty.

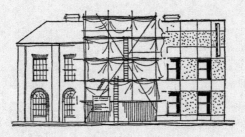

6

THE INNOCENT ERA

In some ways it is not hard to explain why Featurism caught hold in Australia with even fiercer grip than in most other countries. For one thing, the foundations of popular Featurism were begun in England during the expansion of the Industrial Revolution early in the nineteenth century, just at the time Australia was engaged in battering back the bush frontier and creating quick impressions of civilized conditions in the townships. Again, it is easy to see how the monotony, the infinite sameness of the eucalyptus bush, the awe-inspiring plainness of it all, encourages the thought of setting up features. It is easy to understand how Featurism flourished through the golden boom days when the successful gold-diggers collected European treasures to dress the crude colonial bodies of their structures, and the unsuccessful felt obliged to make a hollow pretence of success where it counted most: say, around the front door, or on the mantelshelf. It is understandable that the attitude persists now in a period of accelerating development, when Australia's British roots, always thrown a little off-kilter by a Mediterranean climate, are entangled with American trimmings.

If somehow in the resultant mixture Australia often loses the reserve and critical capacity of the British, the flair of the Mediterranean and the sophistication of the American, she also loses a few degrees of the excess pressure of older countries. One of the nicest qualities of Australia is her impatience with discipline for discipline's sake, and with politics, polish, theory, or work for their own sakes. The fact that Featurism is untenable in theory, and is disastrously undisciplined by intellect or ethics worries her not at all. That it is lazy man's design is no concern to her. Featurism gives the required effect by the simplest means to people anxious to get on with the practical things of living. Featurism satisfies those who care least about appearances as well as many aesthetes who care most about beauty, and Australia has, by the law of reaction, a considerable number of the latter to counter the majority in the former class. All she lacks is any sizeable body of people, between the two extremes, prepared to contemplate natural and manufactured objects as they are without comforting masks or contrived eye-catchers. Australia is content with Featurism because it can make anything prettier without anyone building up a head of steam over principles. Featurism gives the desired effect without anyone having to work Saturdays to get the whole thing right. This is reasonable; anything more would be sheer fussiness.

Firm decision, strong motivation, self-reliance, an unequivocal statement: these are the essential ingredients for positive non-Featurism in any field of human expression. They add up to the rare invaluable quality that is at the heart of fine work in any field; the creation of whole designs, whether they be pieces of music or refrigerator-cabinets or the frozen packages inside. This quality is produced by a certain kind of talented man or woman given due encouragement, stimulation, time and money. Some countries, like the USA, recognize the kind of talent required immediately that it shows itself, and they feed it well. Australia does not. Perhaps the pioneer, the digger and the puritan will always resent this kind of talent, or perhaps the reason is simply that Australia at this time is moving too fast to notice if she tramples on tender buds of expression and initiative in the arts. In any event, constructive talent of the kind essential to the initiation of ideas in all fields is given lower rewards, proportionately to the country's richness, than almost anywhere else. While every man who prints a magazine and every boy on the corner who sells it receives fair payment for his labours, the man whose writing appears in the magazine is often lucky if he clears the cost of his paper and postage. Australian newspapers with respectable circulations—half a million or so—are in the habit of paying the national oracle on any subject five or six guineas for a special article. The highest-paid Australian actors or actresses receive, while a season lasts, less than a competent carpenter is paid continuously. A municipal council in 1955 advertised for a refuse collector and an assistant architect simultaneously, naming a higher salary for the former. Perhaps a dozen painters and as many writers in the whole of Australia make their living solely by practising their art. Visitors from abroad are frequently flabbergasted by being offered a fee for a television appearance of roughly the same sum as their hotel bill for one night, or by being offered nothing at all for a lecture to a richly clad audience. This is the pattern. Nearly everyone who has a part in the presentation of any form of cultural activity: the cameraman, the sound engineer, mechanic, printer, distributor, manager, agent, is protected by unions or professional organizations or trade practices which ensure him a fair share of one of the world's highest living standards; but one member of the team frequently is paid very little or not at all. He is the one who supplied the creative idea which made possible the whole project. It is not simply a matter of resentment or meanness; the men of culture have shown themselves not to need money. Through many artless years they have indicated frequently that they are quite satisfied, indeed eager, if they are merely given an opportunity to express themselves. And so it has been assumed that a man who is egocentric enough to want to display his talent owes it to the community to display it freely and can be called upon to write, paint, lecture, and make sculpture or films in his spare time. Many talented and potentially creative Australians accept this laudable, charitable role in society. They do not starve. They make a good living at something else and practise their art as a hobby. Others leave the country. A list of successful Australians in creative fields in London and New York suggests that there is something about the Australian sun and the meaty diet that produces a high proportion of talented people: Sidney Nolan, Arthur Boyd, Loudon Sainthill, Albert Tucker among the painters; Eileen Joyce, Arthur Benjamin, Charles Mackerras among the musicians; Peter Finch, Robert Helpmann, Cyril Ritchard among the dozens in theatre. Australia still produces for export only a prodigious number of singers. Covent Garden has been called satirically an Australian Expatriates Club. Its director, farewelling the contralto Lauris Elms when she left to return home to Australia in 1959, said: 'Come and rejoin your fellow Australians here when you can't stand it any longer.' It has been argued that the principal reason for the absence of original Australian television is the shortage of adequate writers; yet Iain McCormick won an English television Producers' Guild award a few years ago for the year's best script. He is one of a number of Australian writers, including Alan Moorehead and the late Chester Wilmot, who were not public-spirited enough to stay and pursue their writing at night while engaging in a normal, healthy job by day.

The tradition of minimum payment for creative work is generally accepted not only by those who should be paying more but by those who should be creating more. However little an Australian ideas man is paid, his employer can buy syndicated American ideas for less—or better still can pick them out of imported magazines for nothing at all, plagiarism being the most expertly practised art in Australia. Under these circumstances most employed artists are not inclined to adopt a bold, demanding attitude. Instead they learn gradually to put into their work no more than the encouragement they receive in return.

This one aspect of under-payment for creative thinking is probably where Australian development differs most from the pattern in America, which many of her developers admire so much, where the man of ideas is a sort of prince of the community. The making of ideas in art, of firm decisions in design, the cultivation of self-reliance and unequivocal statements, are specialized activities taking experience, concentration, and time, as well as certain native talent. But this is not the sort of work that is as apparent as the work of choosing and devising attractive features to disguise the absence of an idea. Therefore Australia habitually economizes on the formative phase of any production. Hence the scarcity of motives in the Australian backdrop. Hence Featurism.

And yet Australia was not always like this. There was a time when Australians appreciated seeing their own reflection in the eyes of their own artists, actors, cartoonists, comedians. And there were times without salesmen, without urgency or anxiety or special policies and products to be put across, without market surveys or home-magazines or any other sources of compulsion on the maker to divert the way which things fell naturally in response to requirements. At these times there was no Featurism; just sensible construction.

Sydney's and Hobart's records for good building were hardly broken by a single vulgar display during some forty-five years before the other capital cities were founded. The universal structural system was a robust masonry wall punctured regularly but sparingly by upright double-hung sash windows and capped by a plain hipped roof. The style was purest in warehouses, stables and other utilitarian shelters. The old row of warehouses in Salamanca Place behind the Hobart waterfront still stands as evidence of a half-century when entire blocks in the two oldest cities were built simply to work. Buildings that were not entirely utilitarian, like inns, usually added one discreet feature: a semicircular fanlight over the entrance door. A tiny cottage at the corner of Hunter Street and O'Connell Street in Parramatta, New South Wales, is practically perfect as an example of the lightly ornamented, but beautifully balanced, whole designs of the period. In New South Wales the veranda was usually an integral part of the plan and structure and was given a flat plaster ceiling like the rooms inside. Usually, as in this cottage, slender wooden columns supported the veranda edge. In this case the lightly moulded columns, the six-panel door on the corner, its semicircular fanlight, the low veranda, the shuttered windows, are all in excellent proportions—which means they are excellently balanced in the Georgian tradition so that no part dominates to the disruption of the whole.

Not far to the north along O'Connell Street, across the river on the corner of Ross Street, there is a bigger house, Roseneath, of the same style and period. Roseneath suffers slightly from modern paint and electrical connections, but it is still perhaps the best remaining example of the single-storey pre-Featurist colonial house. Its evenly spaced veranda columns are slightly stouter, which robs the house of some of the fragile charm of the little corner cottage, but its wider door with semi-elliptical fan and sidelights, its twelve-pane windows and its low, flagged veranda protecting the three visible sides, provide a model of co-ordination and integrity.

The back blocks of Tasmania are practically undisturbed for a searcher after the old dignity that is lost behind the age of Featurism. The houses, the stone walls, the cylindrical oast houses, the stables,

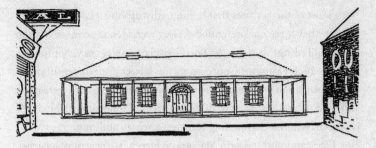

lofts, storehouses, pigeon towers, nearly all obey the most simple and rugged masonry lore, and each is shaped by ancient empirical rules to follow its own function. Even the pretentions were modest in the eighteen-twenties. A water-mill dressed like a gazebo on a rise by the river at Woolmers, in Longford, Tasmania, is octagonal in plan and has a Gothic arch on each side, but all is done so plainly and ingenuously that the little folly remains in harmony with the functional farm buildings. Wanstead, a lonely house on the Tasmanian midland plains, built in 1827, is a classic example of the two-storey homestead vernacular. Its foresquare plan and hipped roof are unrelieved except by the evenly spaced windows. A plain veranda applied to the ground floor is so lightly supported that the slim columns seem to be holding it down rather than up.

Such buildings formed the familiar background of life in their day. Few of them were consciously designed and none knew fashionable architects. They were the equivalent of the glass-walled contemporary suburban style of this day. But they were not, of course, the only kind of buildings. A decade before the rot set in during the eighteen-forties, one of the most polished architects ever to live in Australia, John Verge, was at work on his elegant houses round Sydney. Against the plain masonry background of common building, the houses of Verge and the more talented of his colleagues were the features of their day. However, they differed in an important respect from most of the features that began to disturb the scene a decade or so later: they were not pretentious. They were designed mostly in the fashionable English style, the late Georgian or Regency, not for the reason which exhumes Georgian in the late twentieth century, but simply because it was the manner in which their designers were born and bred. Moreover, each of these feature buildings was within itself balanced, without dominating features, a whole building.

One can stand today in Macquarie Street, Sydney, on the corner of King Street, and see the two kinds of building which made the first Australian urban scene. On the south side of King Street is St James's Church, the first fine feature building in Australia, the piece of jewellery. Opposite, across Macquarie Street, are the Mint and, further north, Parliament House. These are two remaining parts of one building: the old Rum Hospital of 1812, one of the last representatives of the anonymous veranda-shaded background, the black velvet. Neither the gem nor the black velvet is in quite as good shape now as when it was built. The Rum Hospital lacks its central body and St James's has had several additions since the first service in 1824. But none of these alterations destroys the complementary effect of the two designs. Each wing of the Rum Hospital is a whole thing because it is innocent of features. St James's is a whole thing because its features are controlled by the masterly hand of Francis Greenway, probably the most talented and certainly the most famous architect in Australia's history.

To use the term innocent in any connection with the Rum Hospital may be questionable. As Morton Herman has recounted in *The Early Australian Architects*, this ingenuous-looking building with its two storeys of colonnaded verandas was the subject of extreme discomfort for good Governor Macquarie, and is linked historically, through Greenway, with St James's. The Government paid for the hospital not in money but by giving its three builders a virtual monopoly of the rum trade. The building cost some £40,000 but the monopoly was withheld from the builders. Macquarie was censured from England. In 1816 when Greenway was appointed Civil Architect and Assistant Engineer, his first commission was to survey and report on the structure of the hospital. 'He tackled the job with the enthusiasm of a man determined to prove his superior abilities,' Herman writes. 'It would be tedious to list all the defects he recorded with savage delight...Of the fronts of the buildings he said: "There is no classical proportion in the column, not being regularly diminished. Its shaft is set wrong upon its base; the cap is set wrong upon the column, and is of no description ancient or modern..." '

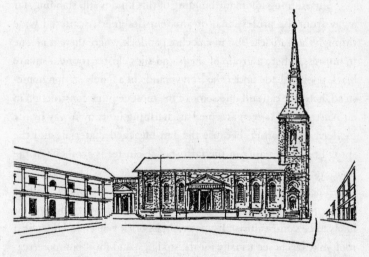

This was an architectural stylist's, if not a literary stylist's, description of a non-scholarly building whose designer did not consider himself important enough to see that his name was recorded somewhere for posterity's information. Under all the circumstances it is not surprising that the frustrated, vain, impatient Greenway entertained himself by castigating all evidence of incompetence that he

could find. But in fact the hospital's innocent shattering of all the correct English rules of how a column's cap and base should go was a
featherweight counteraction to the extraordinary strength of a design
which was really too good to know better. Whether the unknown
designer was an untrained tradesman or an inexperienced gentleman,
and despite all the monkey-business in connection with the contract,
the integrity of the Rum Hospital's design cannot be questioned. Its
two storeys of evenly spaced windows, its round columns spaced their
own length apart, and its plain hipped roof, together make up an
example of unaffected, direct employment of simple building materials which could still serve as a model today.

Unassuming idiomatic building of this kind is still standing, far
away from the professional or amateur designers, scattered wide
through the outback. Out in an ochre paddock where there is no one
to impress, where a group of sheds and silos cluster round a square
black pool of shade under the iron veranda of a lonely station homestead, here one can still find some of the most genuine construction in
all Australia. It is even accepted as charming in its own way by the
modern city worker, because the sun-bleached materials and the
sprawling informality of the farm-house cluster is symbolic of the
basic strength and romance of the nation.

The ordinary modern suburban house of the speculative builder
who is not too harassed by his competitors or his advertising agent is
likely to be non-Featurist. Its materials, its brick veneer and high tiled
roof, may be chosen usually for the stodgiest and most pompous reasons, but when the whole easy-going statement of the conventional
Australian villa box with its projecting lounge-room is made in the
lazy Aussie drawl of a brickie and his carpenter mate it has its own
rough dignity. Without doubt the plainer examples will be held in
some reverence as genuine products of their day by future generations
of serious architectural students. Australia's vernacular villas fall short

of their own best intentions only in the uncouth treatment of finishing and decorating. When a district of them is given a touch of control, co-ordination and stylistic direction, as in the Department of Works' housing in parts of Canberra in the middle 1950s, the social triumph of the nation's housing policy is justified artistically. In Narrabundah, by Captain Cook Crescent, the Australian dream comes close to breaking through the surface into reality. Unfortunately, however, the number of unfussed non-Featurist cottage-villas is diminishing as the small speculative builder-designers begin to succumb to organization-builders modelled on the American image: their houses often complete with American Colonial details.

Areas where the old non-Featurist development is general enough to make an environment have been eroded continuously, but fortunately some can still be found. It happened that certain pioneer districts lost their popularity after only a few decades of settlement and thereafter remained for all practical purposes suspended in the middle of the nineteenth century. In this way many outback town-ships have been comparatively frozen.

Perhaps the most accessible area still displaying the remains of the old vernacular is in Victoria. The drive between Melbourne Airport at Essendon and the city is as Featurist and forbidding as the drive to any other big city from its airport. But, conversely, the con-tinuation of this drive in the other direction, from Essendon away from Melbourne along the narrow Bulla Road, in the footsteps of the first pioneers, is rewarding. These are the yellow plains which attracted so many of the earliest settlers in Victoria and so few of her subsequent citizens. The road twists crazily at intervals to cross sudden gorges, through arid, pretty, heartbreaking country dotted with little centenarian buildings. The place has hardly been changed, except by rot, since the middle of last century. A wooden hotel by the roadside decays like a sheep's carcass in the field behind it—a few of the original wooden shingles still clinging to what ribs remain of the roof skeleton. Most of the wall and fence construction was done in the basalt of the area, the hard, heavy rock known as bluestone. This is slightly variegated, ranging from a deep brown to grey, but the predominant colour is a dark slate hue, with a touch of blue. It is extremely durable but its hardness makes it difficult to work, and the early builders were usually content to leave it with an axed rock face.

The typical cottage of the area is a diminutive bluestone box with a hipped galvanized iron roof and a veranda all round. This, unlike the Sydney model, has a separate roof tucked tightly up to the underside of the gutter of the main roof. Two of the earliest Victorian settlers squatted on the hard ground here in 1836. They were William Jackson and George Evans, members of John Pascoe Fawkner's party of adventurers who came that year in the schooner *Enterprise* from Launceston. William Jackson's brother was Samuel, the architect. He missed the first trip in the *Enterprise* but caught it on its second voyage and followed his brother out to the northern plains. The two of them built the first substantial shelter in the district: two rooms, one the living-room in white-washed pisé with a wide split-log roof, the other a skillion bedroom in wattle and daub. This house lasted only twenty-four years. Samuel Jackson had a native talent, probably very little training in England, and an unembarrassed primitive approach to the historic styles. He soon moved down to the centre of things at the river settlement which was to become Melbourne, and as one of the first two architects (Robert Russell was the other) he participated in the early building boom. Nearly all his buildings of this relatively unassuming early era were suddenly outgrown when gold was found, and most of his Melbourne work was removed or remodelled almost before the mortar was set. The only memorial he left in Melbourne which has not been badly treated by time is his panoramic drawing of 1841 showing the frontier town he was helping to build. It is said that he crouched inside a beer barrel erected on a wall of his own half-erected Scots' church in Collins Street and drew what he saw through the slits in the barrel's side as he removed and replaced one stave after the other while turning slowly round. The finished sketch is twenty feet long and about two feet high. It is in the National Historical Museum in Melbourne, and is a vivid illustration of the non-Featurist opening years: muddy, horsey streets inhabited by a few pelt-clad Aborigines and fashionably dressed townspeople, and a community of little eaveless-box houses and shops, one or two more substantial masonry buildings, and beyond them all the ring of straggly gum trees retreating slowly before this strange invasion.

George Evans built more solidly than his neighbour William Jackson. He used the abundant basalt and his house is still standing firm, the oldest if not the prettiest of several bluestone buildings in the Sunbury area with the authentic early earthy charm. It is just out of Sunbury on the north side, away from Melbourne. Signboards term it 'Victoria's Oldest Homestead'. A stony road runs two-and-a-half miles to Emu Creek, a rocky seasonal watercourse, on the far side of which the old house sits among its barns, a picket fence and a bright cottage garden. There is an ornamental monument erected on the centenary: 17 August 1936. Unlike nearly all buildings which have survived a century or more in Australia, George Evans' house is very well kept by owners conscious of its historical importance.

Nevertheless it is possible to imagine what it was once like beneath the cream and green paint. It consists of two blocks, built at different times, set in a right-angled L. The walls are colour-washed basalt, and the roof, now galvanized iron but probably shingle or sheet-iron originally, is pulled down in a sad, droopy brim over the flagged verandas. The L turns its back to the afternoon sun like an Aboriginal settling for the night, and the rooms are strung in single file along the wings, approached through solid wooden doors from the verandas. The windows are stock colonial twelve-pane double-hung sashes. The house is called, with terrible nostalgia in this yellow-ochre country: Holly Green.

Sunbury itself is a dark green patch in a valley of the bleached hills. It is atypical of Australian country towns, with its comparatively narrow roads and lack of an indisputably main street. Sunbury is a spoilt village. In a country where there are no unspoilt old villages this term can be complimentary, for Sunbury is only spoilt, not ruined, and it is still possible to see what it was in the pre-metal age, in Victoria's quite early youth before gold and cast iron. The basalt buildings are only partially overwhelmed by advertisements. The shady trees still meet above the dusty yellow footpaths. Several shops look undisturbed after a century. One on the corner of Evans Road and Brook Road exemplifies an early nineteenth-century style which has disappeared from Melbourne: a two-storeyed shop with an almost inaccessibly narrow balcony on the upper floor cantilevered on pro-jecting timber joists over the footpath.

Most of the architectural history of the world could be adequately covered by an account of roofs, and most of the distinctive qualities of Australian building have been concentrated in the shapes and mate-rials of roofs, designed in the country to give shade and to collect water and in the suburbs to give an air of permanence and to hold gargoyles. Corrugated galvanized iron and, more recently, corrugated asbestos-cement, are the staple materials of the north and the outback. From the air, the cities grow progressively freer of colour as one travels inland. The grey-white corrugated sheets give a non-Featurist coherence to man's feeble assault on the outback, and practically unify many country towns. From the air, even a town as big as Alice Springs is a whole town. The iron roof is accepted in the country, and can be sentimentally regarded by an armchair bushman of the city. But when one transplants the sheltering corrugated iron parasol from a country house to a suburban cottage in Melbourne or Sydney it is judged hideous, as estate-agents attest. Then if it is moved again to a beach area it is judged highly contemporary and pleasing again, for Featurist aesthetics are sensitively relative to social position. Nevertheless, that elusive thing, the Australian national style of architecture, is most likely to be found, if it can be found at all, in the droop of a roof.

A wayward example is at Geraldton, WA, over the Wicherina Reservoir. It is all roof, the biggest in the country, measuring no less than 17 acres. It is made of fragile corrugated asbestos-cement on a hefty wooden frame, and was built simply to reduce evaporation by protecting the water supply for Geraldton from the direct sun's rays. Here, then, are all the ingredients of local colour: water so precious it must be housed, the local eucalyptus wood—jarrah—given the gruelling task of supporting wide spans while standing deep in water, and a favourite adopted material, asbestos-cement, all put together with bush carpentry and a bold idea. From the ground it seems nothing. The frame is flat, a few feet above the water surface, and the asbestos-cement sheets are loosely butted together without the usual laps, for their only function is to provide shade and certainly not to divert rain water. From the air the whole roof can be appreciated as a model of Functionalism. It is straight on two sides where it abuts roads, but for the rest has a wandering perimeter following the natural contour of the water below. Indeed by moonlight it looks so wet that the pelicans of the area are continually breaking the sheets and killing themselves by landing at high speed, feet thrust forward in expectation of water. It is said that the reduced evaporation saves the drought-afflicted town annually about twenty million gallons of water, or £2,500. Nevertheless, the big roof probably would never have been thought of, or built, except for the Depression, when it was conceived to make work.

Some of the main clues to the realities of Australian building are likely to be found in unrespectable buildings of this sort, rather than in the charming examples of Colonial monumental architecture which are still to be seen in preserved relics under the protection of organizations like the State National Trusts. And although modern Australia naturally is proud of her rising sky-scrapers and spreading factories, the visitor will not find anything particularly indigenous in the steel frames, aluminium curtains, and glass walls of the busy commercial and industrial buildings. He may eventually decide that Australia's main contribution to civilization during the twentieth century is in the experimental development of the unexciting region that is neither lonely nor busy: the suburb, where most Australians live, in private houses which many have built and many own, and where even those under-privileged by nature and by society may own a private domain with a certain degree of civilized comfort. It is in the suburb, the real Australia, the home of Featurism, that one must look first for any improvement in the Australian ugliness.

In the decade after the Second World War much of the national economy and most of the resources of the building industry were devoted to the provision of separate houses and the few small schools and shops which are scattered among them. The growth continues at slightly reduced rate. These single-house suburbs are a creation of this century: they are the late-nineteenth-century English suburbs cut down to one storey, stepped up several degrees in architectural temperature and made available not only to the middle class but to every class and category in society. For half a century Australia has taken for granted that every man deserves his own house and should be able to shape it in some special personal way.

Modern Australia is not entirely suburb; there is still the outback and the night-club, the woolshed dance and the art-film society; but it is mainly this half-way area, a crosshatched smudge on the map round each capital city and larger town, in which may be found all the essential drabness and dignity of Australia. Much earlier than those of

America, the Australian suburbs demonstrated the attainable heaven of the common man's century, the little private detached castle, physically as comfortable as the latest mass-produced techniques could make it and as individual as your own necktie. The suburb is Australia's greatest achievement (not 'proudest' achievement; there is little or no collective pride in the suburb, only a huge collection of individual prides). More people, per head of population, over a longer time, have enjoyed here the dear millstone of a detached house, separated from the next by at least eight feet, a private den for the family not visited by squire or servant. Statistics show that Australia—along with New Zealand, as usual in these things—has the highest number of privately owned separate houses per head, with the highest number of separate bedrooms, the greatest volume of running water in the most bathrooms, the tallest ventilating stacks to the most conscientious sewerage systems—all in all, indisputably the world's highest minimum standards of health and safety ordained by building codes. Ventilation, for example, is particularly well provided for. Most State or municipal building codes require every house to have permanent holes through the external walls of all rooms, and in some places even the spider-ridden darkness beneath the bath must be ventilated. However, all the statistics and regulations which prove the country's unchallengeable claims to one of the highest levels of suburban development do not mean that a new Australian house is bigger or better equipped than, for instance, a new American house. It is not. The statistical superiority merely shows that Australia started much earlier along the same road.

Australia never had much tolerance with the idea of very rich or very poor people, and, except on the harbour banks near Sydney, has not built many big apartment blocks. Residential architecture began with adaptations of English country houses, strongly coloured by Colonial experience in India, spotted on the hills round Sydney

Harbour. On the sixty-feet-wide lots into which the town of Sydney was divided by Governor Phillip, little bald box cottages kept their own company, well apart from the neighbours and well clear of the border of bushland surrounding the settlement. From the beginning one of the dominant influences which helped to shape communities from primeval Africa to feudal Europe was missing: there was never a necessity to congregate for mutual protection. However, when Sydney and the other centres began to grow to towns of reasonable size the houses naturally began to draw closer together, not for safety but simply for convenience, to reduce walking distance.

The second half of the nineteenth century was the heyday of the terrace house; one, two, and sometimes three storeys high, the single-fronted, narrow houses pressed together with identical brothers in long lines close to the footpaths round the industrial areas. The terrace era ended with improved transport. As the suburban railway systems spread crooked fingers out from the city hubs into the surrounding farmlands, the concept of Australia's space as inexhaustible was reawakened in townspeople. Now the toiler of the industrial revolution saw for the first time an escape from the scaly environment of the factory. Here the worker who knew his worth, and none knew this better than the late-nineteenth-century Australian, could find a good reason for slaving at the bench. Out in the hills he could have a home which he could call his own without stretching the economic facts too far.

Thus in the late eighteen-eighties, as the cities fattened, the foundations of the suburban ideal were laid. These of course involved much more than a house for every family. They introduced a suburban lore that became known, some seventy years later, as the Australian way of life. By the time it was known by that name, recognized and extolled, by the time, in short, that it became self-conscious, Australia's popular culture was becoming inextricably tangled with the American and the lore was losing distinctive flavour, but in the meantime a number of characteristic qualities had become ingrained. There are still in Australian suburbia many indigenous ingredients mixed up with the stone-veneer garden barbecues, the flourishes of wrought iron and other features of the fashionable home which seem like a distorting-mirror image of the advertisement pages of the *Saturday Evening Post*. The essence of Australian suburban life is unreality: frank and proud artificiality. To this extent it is English. In some countries, like Sweden, the suburb may be supracountry. In America it may allow itself to be coyly rustic. But in Australia it is the city's bastion against the bush. In certain areas—parts of Wahroonga and Castle Crag in Sydney, Beaumaris and Blackburn in Melbourne, St Lucia in Brisbane—gum trees prosper among the houses and a countrified air is not discouraged. But for the most part modern Australian living is represented best by the shorn look already noted. The countryside in which the suburb grows is shorn of trees. The plot in which the house builds is shorn of shrubs. The house itself is shorn of the verandas which the colonists knew, shorn of porches, shelter and shade. It sits in sterile, shaven neatness on its trimmed lawn between weeded, raked, brilliant beds of annuals, between the grey paling fences which separate each private domain from its neighbours. Very little is planted in the first place which is expected to be or is capable of growing high; and nature never can escape the tidy gardener's sheers. The pioneering spirit still means change from nature, right or wrong, and the Australian suburban objective is still to carve clearings in the native bush and to transplant on to naked soil a postage stamp replica of the ruling idea in international high-life.

Sometimes the early architects tried hard to reach a compromise with the Australian climate and the indigenous materials, but the exotic model usually dominated. The ruling styles came in turn from England, Italy, Holland via England, Spain via California via New

York. The flow of fashion may be traced from adaptations of the laws of unoffending Georgian taste in the first half of the nineteenth century, through exotic romanticism in the second half, through promiscuous plagiarism in the first half of the twentieth century, to general Americanism in the second half. But while the pattern of imposed fashion has thus fluctuated over the years, the basic policy of tidy artificiality has remained unchanged since the moment when Governor Phillip's sailors of the First Fleet leapt ashore and made the first clearing by the beach. The white man is still a foreigner in Australia, still looking at the fragile greys and ochres of the landscape through European eyes. And in common with his contemporaries anywhere else he is also still a stranger to the industrial age. 'We can't bear its ugliness when it's not turned on,' the Featurist aesthete says of the one naked, unaffected, unprettified thing in his living-room: the television screen. He puts beautiful Oriental cane doors to fold over the glass tube when visitors come. A sense of reality would appear to be the last thing desired. This may be consistent with the avoidance of realities in other aspects of Australian life, with the prim censorship and with ostrichisms like the blue laws which rule the Australian night. But is it what the Australian really wants?

No one can answer this question because the Australian, in common with most people in the world, has never seen so much as a glimpse of the alternative. Featurism is continuously sold to him by the unofficial international propaganda machine for conspicuous consumption: not merely by the overt advertisers, but by the mutually boosting mass-communication decorators: the *Houses and Gardens Lovely* magazines from far and near, the syndicated home-maker tips in the women's pages of the daily press, the decoration service of the paint and wallpaper and appliance companies; everyone selling the thought: you can never afford a good home but you can always afford another nice feature.

Nowhere in Australia is there a significant sign of an escape from the shallowness of this approach. On the contrary the drift seems to be downwards again. The crusader spirit which followed the Second World War produced eventually a high point in co-ordinated progressive endeavour early in the nineteen-fifties, when it was possible for the master plans for the bigger cities to be adopted by popular consent and for Elizabeth, Australia's only experiment with a new town in the European sense, to begin building north of Adelaide.

Elizabeth, as already noted, started with some idealism. If it had not the most imaginative site—the flattest of treeless plains when there were pleasant slopes nearby—it had at least the full treatment of satellite town-planning theory. But look at Elizabeth now after some eight years of construction, with about sixteen thousand people living in the scientifically spaced separate houses, with its civic centre and shopping malls. Here is a horizontal slice of pure contemporary Australia, all the best and worst of it, and most of the unique qualities of it. English migrants make up much of Elizabeth's population. There could not be a better place for them to assess the typical Australian way of life while they are making up their minds whether or not to identify themselves with the new country. Apart from a few three-storey flat blocks under construction near the centre, almost the whole of the town is single-storied. Among the bungalows, as the English occupants call them, an attic design appears at rare, regular intervals. Otherwise the town presents a rippled sea of low pointed roofs with a surface some twelve feet above the plain and extending a mile or two in every direction, unbroken but for pipes, wires, and television antennae. In designing the houses the State was benevolent. The South Australian Housing Trust did its best to conceal its formidable powers. Confronted with a rare and wonderful opportunity to create a unified environment, an Australian suburb with visual direction, the Trust instead calculated with all the science at its command a balanced reflection of the average established Australian taste. Anxious not to expose itself to the criticism that it was regimenting people into soulless barracks, it produced a variety of designs, ranging from a low glassy Contemporary to the attic style already mentioned, with its touch of the Tudor. The proportion of each style in the mixture was apparently calculated to be relative to the proportion of acceptance of the style in the community at large. One result is that the charge of creating a monotonous, controlled design has not appeared among the criticisms of the Trust. So successful has the Trust been in this regard that it is difficult to tell where its design ends on the Adelaide side of the town. And it is difficult to pick out the free lots in the neighbourhoods where normal private design and construction are permitted.

Elizabeth, so Australian, is the visual antithesis of new towns in Europe which have been based on similar international town-planning theory. It is also the antithesis, socially as well as visually, of European urban housing as found in the Hansa district of West Berlin. On the fringe of the iron curtain, at the same time as Elizabeth was being planned, a number of world-famous architects were invited there to contribute one design each to a park to be spotted with multi-storey flats. The appearance of the complex when opened in 1957 was co-ordinated, controlled and exciting—very conspicuously so, for the propaganda effect of consciously progressive housing on eyes behind the curtain was even more important to West Berlin than progressive housing. Here families lived in the smallest possible huddle of rooms as high as fifteen stories above the lawns but almost within feeling of the pulse of a city's life. In Elizabeth each family has a quarter or more of an acre to itself, a lawn for its own games, and some seventeen miles to go to the nearest rumble of urban stimulation. Compared with the Hansa development on any intellectual or aesthetic or artistic or stylistic basis Elizabeth is a complete and derisive failure. Yet on a social basis it promises a prospect for family life second to none in its economic range anywhere in the world: as healthy as any, more private than many, and more capable than most of sustaining non-conformist life.

When so good at heart, why is Elizabeth so depressing to the eyes? This is the crux of the problem of the Australian ugliness. So look at the town more carefully. Each house taken separately is adequate in design. More sophisticated stylists might have coaxed public taste a little further to the left than the Trust's kid gloves drew it. But, taken separately, the architecture of each house is not important. Elizabeth could have been given the same team of international star architects as was gathered for Berlin; there could have been masterpieces in the collection of houses and yet if everything else were the same Elizabeth would still be a depressing sight. One reason is the absence of trees. The only growths above roof-sea level are the few trees in public planting reserves by the roads. Somehow very few of the young trees which the Trust provided for gardens seem to have escaped above shears height. Only about one household in a hundred is encouraging any sturdy growth, and only one in a thousand seems so eccentric as to be growing gum trees. On the other hand, look over any low front fence and you are likely to find neatly clipped lawn and tended flowerbeds and a red cement urn holding a cactus, or a stork with scarlet legs, or a yellow cement bunny, or a gnome with a coat greener than anything else in Elizabeth. So it is evident that these houses are loved, which is all the justification they need for having been built on their separate lots on their hot, flat plain seventeen miles from town. It is also evident that the language of love is at fault. But more than that, the attitude to trees on the one hand and to gnomes on the other goes deeper than unsophistication in matters of design. The trouble is a deep unawareness, and a wish to remain unaware, of the experience of living here, now. The visual failure of Elizabeth is not the fault of the benevolent State authority or its technicians or professional advisers. It is the choice of the majority, many old Australians and English migrants finding common ground among the cement bunnies.

The contrived variety of house styles to suit all tastes in Elizabeth is not a concession to the people so much as a humiliating insult to them and to the materials of which the houses are built. The attic houses, the conventional suburban villas, the semi-contemporaries and the contemporaries are not different primarily for the sake of difference in character to suit people of different living patterns. This would be most reasonable. But these houses have essentially similar plans and are made different mainly to suit different tastes in decorative external styling, or dreamhousing. The designers must have known which of the styles was the best they could do. All the others were sops to the conservatism or fashion-consciousness of hypothetical future occupiers.

The answers to the problem of building houses for good living for average Australian families are not unknown or obscure. Something close to the ideal can be found empirically by any unselfconscious builder. The text-book logic of Elizabeth's subdivisional plan is a good beginning. With a small injection of Colonel Light's kind of daring and conviction it would be excellent. The ordinary evolved suburban house plan is satisfactory. With a little of the freedom won by the pioneers of modern domestic architecture, from Annear to Ancher, it could continue to evolve sympathetically in response to new, less formal, living habits. As for the structural form, the principal problems were solved years ago. If bricks and timber are being used, the methods and shapes of the old colonials were usually exemplary. With a little injection of the ethics and disciplines of twentieth-century design they would be impeccable for today. If new materials or techniques are being used, the machine can be allowed to dictate its own methods. In following the machine and the engineer into unfamiliar shapes, there need be no fear of losing the way so long as the new techniques are concerned with improving the quality of the enclosure for the occupants. There are no real difficulties in the planning and shaping of good houses for Australians, no real reason why every house built is not good. The difficulties are made only by the urges of fashion and prejudices and the misdirected desire to beautify. These are qualities in the community which cannot be very effectively countered by any amount of artistic integrity or technical skill wielded by individuals. They are qualities not confined to Australians. The Englishmen at Elizabeth, like most New Australians in any suburb, are quick to adopt old Australian tastes and tricks. But the uneducated, unguided urge to beautify is a quality in the community which is probably given more expression in Australia than anywhere else. Nowhere else do the ordinary man and woman with untrained, unopened eyes have quite the same opportunity to parade his and her taste in public. Any private decorative indiscretions in the new Berlin apartments are hidden within a fine co-ordinated package made perhaps by Walter Gropius. Everyone is fashion-conscious to some extent, but the Australian, because his home is under his own design control, is fashion-prone.

The cure to a large part of the Australian ugliness is through the Australian eye. Nothing done in this region will clear the slums or put the wires underground or stop the need for outdoor advertising, but it could remove or restrict the most discomforting source of the ugliness: the attempts to beautify.

Visual re-education could be quite formal and idealistic, beginning with youth. School curricula could include, not necessarily more art history, but the subjects of Awareness and Design Integrity. The scholastic approach, however, seems improbable. The shape which visual re-education will be more likely to take in the next few years is informal and commercial, as has proved fairly successful in America. Firms connected with the promotion of all but the cheapest and most essential consumer goods will begin conducting unofficial propaganda for better design as a means of finding new fields for expansion. At a certain point in the course of prosperity the manufacturing establishment realizes its customers are passing through the Featurist barrier and are ripe for attack on a second level of appreciation. At this stage the gear is changed in all advertising and promotional matter to meet an 'upgrading' of popular taste. A living example of the power of a commercial stimulus to taste is the town of Tanunda, in the wine district not far north of Elizabeth. Civic spirit here is stimulated by the brandy that bears the town's name, and one result is the most unmolested and pleasant street-tree-planting to be found in any comparable town in Australia.

There is little immediate promise of any sort of broad visual re-education. The schools are still not concerned enough and the manufacturers are still not quite rich enough. And since any kind of educational guidance takes at least a decade to be effective, the prospect for the next ten years is not encouraging. The nineteen-sixties, often announced as Australia's most promisingly rich decade, sometimes threaten to be also richer than ever in the pepped-up party spirit, in mutilation of anything non-carnival in atmosphere, in wild Featurism—foreboding perhaps by 1984 a nightmare of a kind George Orwell never considered. Not a drab spiritual nightmare of regimentation but a mad visual nightmare of indiscipline. But happily this prospect is not inevitable.

A major part of the whole consumer-product manufacturing and advertising world has at present a vested interest in Featurism. No one as yet has a commercial interest in whole design. But as mass-production of advanced technical processes turns to prefabricating larger and larger components of the house, as more mechanical appliances become less status-symbolic and more a routine minimum demand, the commercial need for encouragement of the idea of wholeness, for an Anti-Featurist movement, will arise. A big section of the communications machine will grind into reverse to present the alternative picture, and twenty-six weeks later society's immutable concepts of beauty will be turned inside out. To gain some idea of the effect, it may be helpful to consider a hypothetical suburb. Imagine a hillside about five miles beyond the rim of the sprawl of any Australian city. At the present time it is occupied only by a cottage, a low wooden place with white walls and a green galvanized iron roof extended to a veranda on all sides, surrounded by shrubbery, and sitting at the top corner of an apple orchard. The orchard takes about one-quarter of the hillside. The remaining three-quarters are wooded. An occasional wattle shows among the gum trees and the undergrowth is flecked here and there with the orange or violet spots of wildflower.

First consider what is most likely to happen to this hill when the familiar suburban sprawl catches up with it. Look at it two or three years after the subdivider's bulldozers lurch in. A grid of streets is laid across it. All the trees, native and fruit, are down, except in the garden of one house near the top. This house is wooden, with a low corrugated iron roof, and the owners have a name for being eccentric; it is said they haven't a television set. Elsewhere the trees have been replaced by rows of electric and telephone poles and the wildflowers by tidy beds of English annuals. The houses which line the streets, standing respectfully back twenty-five feet, are all different—or are they? The colours are different: fuchsia pink, ocean green, Miami tan, Californian yellow, and other contemporary shades—in pastel tints on the walls and full strength on the solid panels below the windows; tiled roofs are striped, speckled and spotted; front porches are fancy with the latest fashion shapes in wrought iron and concrete. But look closer: surely all these people must have identical families and identical living habits, for the plan is clearly the same in every case, and each big picture window stares across the street into the practically identical eye of the picture window opposite. Of course neither sees the other for each window is permanently sealed by a venetian blind: it gets pretty warm behind all that glass. The one cool-looking house in the area is the old farmhouse, now used as a service station; one can still see it behind the smart new brick front with the neon signs.

Down where the central road meets the passing highway a little explosion of colours and alphabets marks the shopping centre. This is rather special. For three years before it was built a big signboard announced 'Glamorous American-Style Drive-In Shopping Center'. It is a row of shops set back from the street quite far enough to park a row of Volkswagens in front on the yellow gravel. The building is made of fibro-cement but one would hardly guess this because each sheet is painted a different contemporary colour, and there are enough advertisements pinned on the front to make the building stand up without any wall whatever. All the shop windows slope forward alarmingly and altogether one couldn't wish to see a more exciting building. The best of the houses is equally enticing. It is on the corner of the highway opposite the shops, a split-level design with a stone porch made of hard polyvinyl plastic and fibre-glass weather-boards finished in two tones of Las Vegas Sand. It is a little too contemporary for most of the rest of the citizens of this new suburb of Applegrove, but still they regard it with envious respect. It has a kidney-shaped plastic swimming pool set in the concrete stone slabs of the front garden.

This is the likely development, following current practice. What is the alternative? Picture the hillside now developed in a different way, by a community slightly more mature, calmer, realistic and keen to enjoy the best things of life even in the suburbs. Firstly, in such an enlightened community, the very fact that the hillside is developed at

all indicates that it has some natural or acquired features which recommend it for residential use. A town-planning authority with real
authority and the money necessary to back its decisions must have
zoned this area for private housing. Secondly, a certain sympathy with
the shape of the land and its natural growth runs through the by-laws
of the municipality and the plans of the subdivider. The streets are not
in a rectilinear grid. The main roads sweep round the hillside following the contours. The trees were not entirely bulldozed by the
developer; only those in the way of the roads went at first. The others
were left on the allotments for each owner to decide whether or not
he wanted them. The wires are out of sight at the backs of the blocks,
or underground. Two or three acres at the crest of the hill are set aside
for community use and a few communal amenities such as a swimming pool of swimmable proportions are set in lawns in a central
clearing. Many of the area's residents have shares in the little company
which built and maintains this park. These and other co-operative
enterprises provide a potentially pleasant background for the residents
of the area. But the third and most important aspect of this new community is displayed in the way each citizen has treated the little slice
of Australia under his control.

The houses now are all the same—or are they? They seem to be
built of similar materials and they sit amicably together among the
trees because none tries to dominate. No front porch or sky-scraper
chimney cries for special attention. The visitor can seek out the front
door he wants, but all front doors don't seek him out. There are no
special excitements. But on closer inspection it can be sensed that the
occupants do not all have entirely the same number of children and
precisely the same habits, for their different requirement and tastes in
living seem to be reflected in the essential form of each house. One lies
in a long thin line along the contour of the hill, the next one curls itself
round a courtyard, another steps down the slope crabwise. Yet the

whole hill is homogeneous. The shopping centre is clearly an independent unit, but it is part of the pattern.

The homogeneity is partly because of a mutual respect for the
natural contours and growth of the hill, partly because of a mutual
desire to subdue anarchical display in order to create a whole community, and partly because most manufactured building products in
this hypothetical near future are less frivolous than they are today,
having accepted their responsibilities to the world's homeless millions.
Industry saw its opportunity in the growing public reaction against
Featurism and the growing desire for more unity and dignity in the
home environment. It turned its resources to producing big sectional
parts for buildings. It submitted to regimentation to the extent of recognising and adopting standard sizes. This was the big break-through
for reason. Suddenly everything fitted together: all manufacturers'
wall panels, floor and roof sections, baths, air-conditioning packages,
stoves, sinks, were interrelated and interlocking. Each buyer was able
to make his choice of structural units and the new unobtrusive appliances and to arrange these jig-saw fashion during evenings of
togetherness, into a plan suited to his family living pattern of the
moment. Next year he might change the arrangement, buying a few
more wall panels or an extra bathroom package.

The first part of this picture: the planned community with an
easy acceptance of nature, mutual respect and a common artistic aim,
is no dream. It is seen today in non-Featurist areas in many parts of
the world: some suburban areas of Scandinavia, very occasionally in
the USA, and, even more tentatively, in parts of Australian suburbs
which are known to be slightly rustic and unconventional.

The second part of the picture: the sectionalized houses mass-
produced at a fraction of today's costs while providing infinitely more
amenities, is also on the brink of realization. It is postponed all over
the world pending a hint to industry that the public is ready to live in

logical, realistic, honest-to-goodness shelter.

When people are ready to return to the qualities of the innocent era, while restating them in twentieth-century terms, both parts of the picture will come to life in ordinary suburbs. Then we will know that a psychoneurotic visual block which afflicted the world early in the Industrial Revolution has been cleared, and the world has broken the grip of Featurism at last.

PART THREE

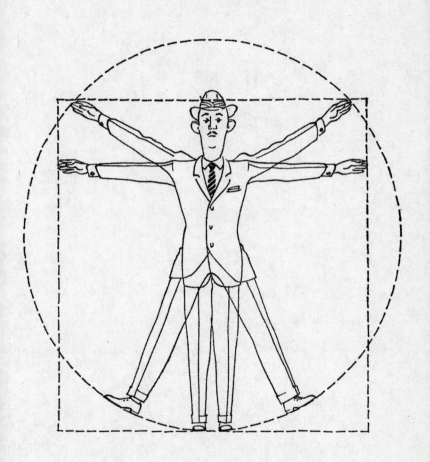

7

THE PURSUIT OF PLEASINGNESS

In earlier chapters it has been suggested that the basis of the Australian ugliness is an unwillingness to be committed on the level of ideas. In all the arts of living, in the shaping of all her artefacts, as in politics, Australia shuffles about vigorously in the middle—as she estimates the middle—of the road, picking up disconnected ideas wherever she finds them. If Australia wanted to build up her mental development to match her muscles she would have to begin by valuing her own ideas more highly, encouraging more of them and gradually building up a climate of confidence and self-reliance. For sake of the argument this undefined term 'ideas' has been used earlier to describe a sort of elixir required to transform the crowded, confused, prettified mess of the man-made environment.

Since ideas are the key to all design, and architecture is the key to all the other visual-functional arts, it is not sufficient to leave the nature of the architectural elixir in a muddy state, to substitute for explanation a theocratic term like 'beauty'. It is necessary to examine more closely the action of ideas and aesthetic theory in architecture, the major field of design which shapes Australia. If and when the grip of Featurism is broken by technology, this triumph for rationalism in the industrialization of building would have to be followed up quickly, to avoid something worse, by the clearest possible expressions of architectural ideas in the buildings which somehow achieved a position in the non-standardized foreground.

Unfortunately, at this time in international architecture ideas are not developing very vigorously. It is a time of action. Ideas, manifestos and the intense, hot eyes of reformers cooled when modern architecture achieved worldly success. About the only article of faith that the modern Modern architect can state with any fervour is that the plain white cemented box of the old Functionalism was not enough; it was materialistic, narrow, dull, even undemocratic, because it reduced man to a sack of flesh and bones and denied him psychological demands, let alone spiritual aspirations. This criticism of the early, simple, butter-box type of modern building is valid if one is judging architecture by conventional values of beauty. But many of the early modernists were fighting for something they felt was more important than beauty. What really mattered to them was 'the ten-fingered grasp of things', as the American Louis Sullivan described it. Their arch-enemy was the aesthete.

Looks were important to the early Moderns, of course, but not what we call good looks. They wanted the look of a functioning thing, the look of a naked, guileless thing. They wanted in seeing to be intellectually convinced of the necessity of every part. They knew of nothing smaller than an architect who thought he could improve on the necessary minimum. On this concept of physical necessity they built up a moral code for building, demanding 'honesty' in expression of functions, 'truth' in construction and 'integrity' in the whole—the first secular architectural theory in history.

Perhaps one should enlarge on this metaphor, for here is the crux of the whole situation in architecture today. The classical aesthetic, for instance, was pagan, with its exacting gods of orders, proportion and ornament which would sanction almost any delinquency if they were appeased. Present-day architecture on the other hand is moving towards theism, without concern for a moral code but sustained by a blinding faith in the unerring rightness and self-justification of one god: Beauty. But the very idea of any sort of deification was anathema to the early moderns, who were brothers of the religious Rationalists. They may have been agnostically unable to describe the actual shapes into which their architecture would eventually turn, but they would have snorted at the thought of introducing a mystical riddle—in this case the word 'beauty'—to cover the unknown.

There was nothing new in the old Moderns' demand that every building showed integrity, wholeness and devotion to its own idea; every architectural or aesthetic code requires as much. There was nothing new in 'truth'. Some of the maddest excesses of the Gothic Revival were done in the name of Honest Architecture. Even the application of science to design was as old as Pythagoras. The past was littered with scientifically reasoned mathematical systems intended to guide the designer. There was, in short, nothing of world-shattering novelty in the old Moderns' theories of design practice. What was revolutionary was their concept of principle, of the aim and the end of design. For the first time a definable, concrete, material goal was substituted for the indefinable, semi-mystical qualities hitherto referred to, with varying degrees of unctuosity, as beauty.

Functionalism promised much more than cold, articulated efficiency. It held a beacon up on top of the hill at the end of the road. For if architecture were ultimately to serve every physical need of man with scientific exactness while understanding and obeying precisely the physical laws of matter, then it would succeed in identifying itself with creation; or, if you like, architecture would merge into the cosmic pattern—not directly but through man. When that day came, fashion, taste and style would slough off, and pure architecture would stand alone, the supreme art of man. Along these lines the materialist philosophy promised ultimate exaltation, which raised it from the level of the time-and-motion studies and made it a religion, like atheism.

Every architect in every new design had the opportunity to push a little closer to the ultimate in physical perfection. The aim of the old Modern was clear and unconfused. And because of this the discipline along the way was accepted without question. It was seen to be full of meanings and compulsions. But as time went on and a lot of practice within the discipline turned out to be concentration on the more mundane aspects of creature comfort, and much of it was something less than inspired, architecture gradually lost sight of the beacon at the end. Then the discipline became merely a nuisance—especially restricting and irritatingly austere in a rich, expansive era. Gradually the code was broken. The glass box—basic unit of Functionalism—sought ways of making itself, not more suited to housing the human frame but more interesting, more pleasing to the hedonistic eye. The box began adding the features: fascinating textural effects, gift-wrappings, art work at the entrance, and water, water everywhere. Shell structures took on extraordinary forms as architects sought to make them, not more related to human activities, but more evocative or more fun, like abstract sculpture or mud pies. Thus the new Modern grew up, seeking to win back the attention of the wavering eye, seeking to enchant, to uplift, to excite, to create the Kingdom of Heaven here, now, suddenly, by intuition.

But this is not good enough for the vital art of architecture. Beauty is not good enough; it is too full of mysteries. In the rare instances when this indefinable quality can be tied down, it turns out to be a private understanding between an observer and an object. When beauty is the sole motivation in design, it has a tendency to die at the moment of birth. Nearly all the worst excesses of Victorianism, Revivalism and Contemporary Featurism have been perpetrated while the designers were courting beauty ardently and fairly sincerely. Most of the Australian veneer has been applied in the name of beauty, and most of it gave to its designer and owner a brief moment of pleasure, like any bad habit. This sort of uncommitted visual beauty is one of the greatest dangers. Some different aim is needed to restore a sense of sane direction to the man-made environment. What, then, is a better description than beauty for the quality that moves us in great architecture?

The most cursory examination of the history of building indicates that the first essential in design is the clarity of a ruling idea in the form. Architecture needs some unequivocal statement strong and convincing enough to sway a whole building. It needs, for example, the plain box and unbroken rhythms of a classical temple, or the concise symmetry of a Palladian villa, or the ascendant sweep of a medieval cathedral. On the other hand it may be satisfied simply by the staccato repetition of a factory's units, or the decisive all-embracing form of a music bowl, an opera house or a culture centre. Probably the earliest and still the most common method of achieving clarity is to plan the building within a single containing shape, like packing a suitcase. The most elementary type of architectural suitcase is the kind that grows vertically from a geometrical plan: a plain rectangle, a triangle, an exact square. The circle has been considered 'the most sublime form' for the plan of a building of worship from Stonehenge to the Roman Pantheon to Palladio's Church at Maser to Saarinen's chapel at Massachusetts Institute of Technology, to half a dozen new suburban churches in Australia. Every regular geometrical figure must have lent itself at some time to the overall plan of a building. In his Fifth Book on Architecture, 1547, Serlio recommended the ellipse, octagon, hexagon and the pentagon among the ideal plan shapes for churches. The last suggestion eventually was taken up by the US armed services for their headquarters in Washington. In addition many composite but simple geometrical plans have been used through the ages: the Greek Cross, the equilateral Y of the UNESCO Building in Paris, the square ring of the US Embassy in Athens, the circle cut from the square plan of Roy Grounds' house in Melbourne. Plans in the Soane Museum by Thorpe, the sixteenth-century English architect, include a triangular house enclosing a hexagonal courtyard and a house planned in his own initials: I.T.

There are symbolic plan shapes: the cross of the cathedral, the fish-shape of the Church of St Faith in Burwood, Victoria, the sham-rock of an Irish exhibition pavilion, the five-pointed star of the Moscow theatre. In all these cases the walls rise more or less conven-tionally from the geometrical concept of the ground plan. But the horizontal geometry is not necessarily expressed in three dimensions and the final mass of the building may not reflect the quality of the plan. A more subtle architectural overall is the three-dimensional geometric form, not confined to a plan shape: for example a pyr-amid—point up as in Cairo or point down as in Caracas, or an all-embracing dome as in Canberra, or a spiral as in New York.

In all cases the effectiveness of the suitcase selected depends pri-marily on the scale and the complexity of the functions to be sheltered. In a comparatively small, single-cell structure: a temple or a chapel or an open living-room, the form is perceptible inside as well as outside and the desired effect of oneness, of an all-inclusive formal idea, is achieved in the simplest and purest way. But as the building grows and is subdivided, it reaches a point where it escapes comprehension unless the human eye is assisted mechanically. The idea behind the vast Pentagon Building in Washington cannot be sensed by a pedes-trian. One may gain some impression of it speeding by in a car, and if the human eye is elevated by an aeroplane the building shrinks to a child's toy and the pentagonal ring reads clearly again for the first time since it left the drawing-board.

Glass assists the architect who tries to keep the overall form visible within a building which function demands must be subdivided. By using glass-topped partitions and low 'space dividers' he hopes to minimize interruptions to the form of the main enclosure. But there comes a point, even with the help of the most fashionable substitutes for walls, when the size of the whole or the number of subdividers grows beyond comprehension and the eye loses the impression of singleness. Another familiar type of motive which does not suffer this unfortunate disadvantage is the cellular scheme. Some unit of structural space, based on either a geometric plan shape or an overall form, is adopted as the largest common denominator of the spaces required in the building complex. No matter where or how this unit is used, no matter how informal or unruly is the arrangement dictated by function, the steady repetition ensures an all-embracing unity. Thus a medieval town or a motel may achieve its homogeneity. But sometimes the unit is not recognizable in its multiplied form and the eye loses track again.

The idea, then, may sometimes be no more than an abstraction, a draftsman's diagram which never could be perceived after translation into the various volumes of an actual, usable building.

The degree of impressiveness of the idea ranges from lost abstractions up to the comparatively rare succinct visual image so simple and sharply focused that it is photographed on the brain after one short exposure. Between these extremes architecture has various subtle means of imprinting itself on the perambulating eye. Although a great architectural complex often is not comprehensible from a single viewpoint, an image builds up in the course of time as the observer passes round and through: thus the tenuous connection sometimes made with Einstein's space-time concept. Again, the form may be based on a motive of some intricate regularity or internal geometry producing not visual simplicity but an ordered and clearly directed complexity. Sometimes the form may have no apparent basis in geometry—as in the voluptuous Baroque facade, or Sydney Opera House—and yet still be manifestly controlled by an idea comprehensible to the observer.

Even the simplest container rarely is sufficient in itself without various adjuncts, and openings to admit light, air and people. The additions to or subtractions from the basic form may make new points of emphasis and change the direction; indeed the main ingredient of many designs is subtraction, the effect of hollows, voids, and spaces on elementary forms.

With complicated modern functions the search for a motivating idea grows more difficult. What is required now is a simple interpretation which crystallizes or typifies the complex functions. Without this any form which naively follows function will undoubtedly appear to wander aimlessly, and a combination of forms may be so involved and uncertain that all the artifices of composition, all the desperate beckoning to a centre of interest, cannot endow the whole with a single meaning. The great idea is no more and no less than a suitable discipline to mould gently but firmly all the inert matter of the physical requirements, pointing to a reconciliation of all conflicts in a united presentation of a clear statement.

As the psychologists' theory of gestalt indicates, the unanalytical eye is the busy Featurist-designer's greatest ally. The conscious mind tends to extract a memorably compact, articulate image even from incoherent form combinations. It gravitates gratefully to any feature. The casual observer, like the tourist with a camera viewfinders' eyes, is inclined to ignore any elements not directly relevant to the gestalt, or dominating image, the feature eye-trap set by the architect. The test of the comprehensiveness and value of an idea is not simply the persistence of an image, but the extent to which that image recalls and represents the building or composite of buildings.

Advanced techniques now make it possible to extend the range of ideas in economical forms of structure into the subtler shapes of solid geometry: parabolic arches, the twisted planes known as hyperbolic paraboloids, and complex curves as in the giant funnel of Melbourne's Sidney Myer Music Bowl by Yuncken, Freeman, architects.

With each exciting new mathematical form in pre-stressed concrete or tension cables the world gains a confusing but optimistic impression of change, invention and progress. Undoubtedly many more unfamiliar forms lie ahead of the century, but no shape in itself has ever added to the strength or depth of architectural communication. Experiments with structural shapes and expressive shapes fascinate many of the most prominent and imaginative architects and a new shape is often fortunate in its first showing. But novelty's fascination may be delusive. An unexpected shape sometimes gives an effect so startling that the observer is deceived into crediting it with more power than it really possesses over the whole building. The test is whether the shape, new, second-hand, or antique, is in fact the ruling motive of the entire building or whether it has been applied like a feature: a scoop of flavouring to a tasteless pudding. Technological developments assist architectural expression only as they extend the potential range of motives. The great idea seldom is found in a floundering sprint ahead of the engineers by an architect in search of spectacle; it grows from a wide background knowledge of general technical potential and from the specific information which has been gathered on the problem in hand.

If the architect cannot produce a strong formal idea at the beginning the building must plod on to become either an incoherent assortment of practical solutions or coherent in a contrived, noncommittal, stereotyped routine, begging to be enlivened by features. But it takes a really rabid Featurist to demand features on a structure as self-reliant as Melbourne's Music Bowl.

The making of any artistic statement strong and clear is of course not enough if the statement happens to be irrelevant. And when, for instance, an architect has not properly assimilated the programme, or when he is by nature impatient with the details of programmes, it sometimes occurs that he prematurely pounces on a motive which bears little relation to the physical requirements. The crystallization of a theme is usually a point of no return in the process of design, the strong idea bringing with it a compulsion which few architects have the strength to resist. During the developmental stage they may discover that the theme does not suit all the conditions; consequently something must suffer. According to temperament, some architects twist the theme to suit the programme. Others amend the programme to fit the theme; as happened in an extreme way in Wright's spiral Guggenheim museum in New York: a triumphantly non-Featurist building with a motive so strong it appeared to overwhelm even its author. In this case it seems that Wright was never adequately briefed on the gallery requirements. The motive struck him with what must have been sledgehammer force while he was isolated in his desert workshop. There it possessed him. At no time did it permit him to bend to the practical requirements of those who had to run the museum. When he learned their problems later he had to dismiss the problems ('If the pictures don't fit, cut them in half'). The spiral now ruled everything. One may find other examples of incompatibility between requirements and motive in some self-consciously monumental buildings in Australia. Their obvious functional failure is observed intently by the Featurist, not without a hint of sadistic pleasure. They confirm the Featurist's distrust of firm statements and his adherence to a non-committal basis for all design. They almost give him a touch of intellectual justification to add to the powerful economic argument in favour of Featurism.

But the great idea in architecture is not simply a matter of geometry. When the architect confers an idea on the building project, he experiences a rare phase of his work when he is as free of the worst nagging practical considerations as a sculptor contemplating a block of stone or a painter confronting a clean canvas. If he is moved, if he has the desirable flash of inspiration, something within himself ignites it. This may be the desire for a certain atmospheric quality in the space to be enclosed, or a certain structural bias, or an attitude to the environment of the proposed building. Irrational influences will enter; the moment of conception will be shaded by the architect's own background and mood, by sympathy for a charming site or stimulation by the personality of his client, by religious dedication or good humour or any other private emotional response to the situation set by the programme, the site, the surroundings, the social implications, the entire building problem. And the great idea is also influenced by one's understanding of the nature of architecture.

Through the ages, at least before the arrival of modern technology, circumstances have changed people and their shelters, causing great differences from nation to nation and from region to region in the colour of skin, in language, taste, haircuts, table manners, dress, church services and so on. But underneath all the material and physical differences, underneath social, psychological and taste differences, underneath the cultural veneer of civilization, human nature is always human nature and architectural nature is architectural nature. The ancient question of this nature, the continuing essence of art in the mother art, is the crux of any philosophical discussion of the shape of the man-made world. Now it has to be examined again; for the best counter to Featurism is real architecture, and the only hope for real architecture lies in much wider understanding of its potential. What can architecture do for an occupant that a non-committal building with a nice couple of features can't do? What, in short, is the secret of architecture?

In the course of picking over the world's history for features that would add a moment's titillation to pedestrian structures, Australia built up a smattering of knowledge about architectural styles and a scorn for architectural theory. In the pattern of an active people, happier when doing than when theorising, the Australians most interested in architecture, including even the keener students of architecture, have always inclined towards a concentration on fine detail, craftsmanship and elements of good taste, rather than a puzzling over the reasons for the different basic shapes and forms of building. Nevertheless it was hard to avoid noticing that the revolutionary movement that went under the general heading of Modern Architecture was not in fact a single style but a number of different styles, some of which could be given names: for instance, the 'Organic' and the 'International Style'. There is in fact a forest of fashions, mannerisms and misunderstanding within the modern movement, and this is profoundly unsettling to many architects, whose work means nothing if not the attempt to create order. At this time the schools are full of questions. Should a building express its function or its structure? Can it be free to express an emotion? How can one reconcile humanism with mechanization, and which way is architecture to go now that the opposing traditional styles are all vanquished and it has nothing to fight but its own confusion? There is now no agreed basis for argument firmer than taste, and few people are so unwise or unsophisticated as to believe they can always rely on that.

In some periods when most cultivated people shared the ideals of the artists, the ground was ready prepared for the critic. When he made pronouncements his audience understood and appreciated the scale on which he was judging. In any of the golden eras of building the critic, the architect, the patron and the educated public agreed on a code of design. There was room for critical discussion only on interpretation and execution of the code. Today in some other arts a code applies; not in painting or sculpture—the disagreements between schools and individuals and the lack of accepted values often produce chaotic contradictions in the criticism of these arts—but a code applies to some extent in music and literature and to a great extent in the livelier arts. If a drama critic writes that such-and-such a play is unreal, unimaginative and the acting is unconvincing, every newspaper reader gains a fairly precise impression of the evening that lies ahead of him at that theatre. But if the same adjectives are applied to a building—and of course they can be applied without change of meaning—no one is much wiser. The sensitive layman, wanting to know more, seeking experiences parallel with those he has enjoyed in the understanding of other arts, seizes on the word imagination.

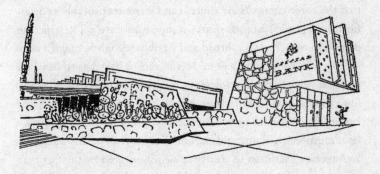

But immediately he is lost again; between the desert Taliesin of Frank Lloyd Wright and one of the flashier new private bank branches in any progressive Australian town lies practically the total range of architectural sensitivity, creativeness and sincerity; yet there are cultivated and sensitive laymen who can hardly distinguish between the two.

In all periods without a code of artistic behaviour the more thoughtful critics have felt obliged to provide one, hoping to formulate rules which would have universal application and be binding on all, irrespective of emotional incidents and individual tastes. In the Augustan age of Rome Vitruvius first performed this task for architecture. He specified the three essentials: '…strength, utility and beauty'. 'Strength,' he wrote, 'arises from…making a proper choice of materials without parsimony. Utility arises from a judicious distribution of the parts, so that the purposes be duly answered, and that each have its proper situation. Beauty is produced by the pleasing appearance and good taste of the whole, and by the dimensions of all the parts being duly proportioned to each other.' Sir Henry Wotton, paraphrasing these remarks in 1624, defined the elements of architecture as 'commodity, firmness and delight'. Sir Henry's definition is still the staple of architectural theory, despite Sir Geoffrey Scott's objection that the three elements are diverse and incommensurable and can furnish no general estimate or true comparison of style. The tripartite definition nevertheless is broad and flexible enough to make a convincing and convenient axiom. It is in fact so broad as to be of no practical value in guiding anyone through the shoals surrounding the few clear landmarks of modern building. For more exact guidance various critics and the more articulate architects have tried to formulate additional axioms and definitions; indeed the insecurity of architecture's position in society is well illustrated by the fact that everyone in the last hundred and fifty years who has essayed a book on architectural theory has felt obliged at some stage to invent a new definition of the art.

Complacent fanciers of architecture scorn all these earnest efforts. While admitting the desirability in certain circumstances of a code of criticism, they oppose all attempts to tie art down to any sort of formal agreement. 'Does it *look* right?' they ask. 'That is the only test.' They quote Oscar Wilde: 'There are two ways of disliking art; one is to dislike it; the other is to like it rationally.' Any rule binding any art, they claim, will choke all life and subtlety out of it. If a man has not the native taste to appreciate a fine building, no amount of argument will convince him; if he has, don't hound him. Let him enjoy it in his own way.

Here is the difficulty which arises in some form in every study of any art: should we attempt to define it, to tie down what 'right' is when we say something looks right—right to whom, when, where?— or must we leave it free? Or can we do both, define it just sufficiently for comprehension and appreciation on the widest plane but not sufficiently to dampen enjoyment of it on any plane? No doubt every critic of every art and age has tried for this compromise, and today the architectural critic is still trying. He is seeing a total order, a coherent pattern in man's flimsy structures on the face of the globe. His order is not the architect's order of beautiful plastic form. He sees that the most sensitive intellects which twentieth-century architecture has produced might create only a more refined sort of chaos if their buildings sat down together to reform the world. His is not the planner's order of a blueprint for expansion of city or nation which may untangle the traffic and pipe-lines and even on occasion provide a glorious perspective to the war memorial. It is not a practical, nor an aesthetic, nor even a visual order. He is intent on the order of ideas, on the ultimate order of man's motive for building.

The search leads many critics where few can follow them. Last century John Ruskin found his order in a divine purity of decorative style, and he passionately felt the need to communicate his discovery to others. Before he could write a book on his dearly loved *Stones of Venice* he felt obliged to write a preceding volume laying *The Foundations* of his appreciation. He wished to determine 'some law of right which we may apply to the architecture of all the world and of all time; and by help of which…we may easily pronounce whether a building is good or noble, as, by applying a plumb-line, whether it be perpendicular.' He thus led himself to state 'three great branches of architectural virtue': that any building should act well, speak well and look well. By acting well he meant in effect the first two parts of Sir Henry Wotton's tripartite definition: commodity and firmness. He insisted that a building should answer its purpose 'in the simplest way, with no over-expenditure of means'. His third virtue, to 'look well', was Sir Henry's 'delight', and his second, to 'speak well', meant that a building should express its purpose in its character. But he was not quite sure how this should best be accomplished so he was content to leave the question of architectural expression 'for incidental notice only' while he subjected the other virtues to laws.

With every respect for the Venetian magic we do not see St Mark's Square today through Ruskin's eyes. Even in his own day he was criticized for insisting on using the words 'beauty' and 'ornamentation' interchangeably, and his rhapsody on Venice as a series of ornamented boxes finds little response with us, who are more impressed by the spaces, perspectives, and relationships between the buildings and their two paved squares and the vertical exclamation marks and the great open vista to the sea. Ruskin's metaphysics succeeded only in doing what many earlier architectural theorists had done: in building an order upon the moist foundations of his special private delights, preconceptions and prejudices in building.

We may be as precise as Ruskin was about the things we admire in Venice, and no doubt a future generation, reading the various appreciations of St Mark's Square still being written in the twentieth century, will respect our reasons for admiring it, as we can respect Ruskin's. But when we try to devise an order, immutable rules of architectural behaviour, on the strength of our own visual reactions, we are being pompous and ridiculous. The beauty of the square may well be attributed by a future generation to qualities unperceived by us, and not consciously intended by its creators. If we are seeking universal canons we should be wary about stressing our preoccupation with space. We may turn out to be as misled as Ruskin was in his concentration on the intricacies of opaque form. He who could not be daunted even by the prospect of the next century went so far as to censure ICI House and the whole curtain-wall era. Ruminating on the great glass spectacle of the Crystal Palace in 1851 he saw a future which he could not approve, for it fitted no pattern of the past. 'It is thought by many,' he wrote, 'that we shall forthwith have a great part of our architecture in glass and iron, and that new forms of beauty will result from the studied employment of these materials.' He saw no cause for optimism. The glass, he believed, would lead firstly to the degradation of colour and secondly to the end of the majesty of form. 'You can never,' Ruskin insisted, 'have any noble architecture in transparent or lustrous glass or enamel. Form is only expressible in its perfection on opaque bodies, without lustre. This law is imperative, universal, irrevocable.' But it was not of course any such thing, and the 'new forms of beauty' are recognized by us in some, if not all, of the shimmering, reflecting transparencies of modern commercial building.

There is no constancy in the appreciation of architectural forms. The conception of beauty, the things that delight, may change radically within a few years even in the towers of architectural learning. A thousand styles of mass and surface treatment have had their day somewhere, sometime, when they were judged sublime. The task of extracting from them specific universal laws of architecture is like seeking universal manners of good taste in social intercourse. Yet architecture has always been clearly distinguishable from routine buildings; there must be a single golden key which turns in any age and transforms unfeeling stone or steel: the key to the critic's order.

The search for this key has led many to amplifications of the Platonic and Vitruvian theories, and others to poetic analogies. 'Architecture is frozen music,' Schelling mused, to the delight of a romantic generation. The twentieth century is not satisfied so easily. In its search for something more precise and businesslike the themes of integral order and organic unity reappear frequently. 'Only those buildings can be accepted as architecture which are transfigured by a gesture of unification and have acquired the tension character-istic of an organism,' wrote Victor Hammer in 1952 (*A Theory of Architecture*), drawing heavily on Sullivan and Wright. The key is seen by many to be contained in the idea that architecture is a vital and sympathetic expression of society. 'Architecture sums up the civilization it enshrines,' wrote Lewis Mumford in 1924 (*Sticks and Stones*). 'Architecture is the art of making the content and the forms of a civilization coincide,' wrote William Lescaze in 1942 (*On Being an Architect*).

The four spiritual fathers of twentieth-century architecture, who have or had little else of theory or practice conspicuously in common, subscribe in their writings to most of the above generalizations and come close to agreement on definitions of their art. 'Good architecture should be a projection of life itself,' said Walter Gropius in May 1937 (*The Architectural Record*). 'Architecture is that great living creative spirit which from generation to generation, from age to age, proceeds, persists, creates, according to the nature of man and his circumstances as they change,' wrote Frank Lloyd Wright in 1939 (*An Organic Architecture*), later giving capital initials to the Great Spirit. Le Corbusier also speaks of 'the pure creation of the spirit' and in 1937 he defined architecture as 'the harmonious and proportional disposition of materials used for the sake of erecting living works' (*When the Cathedrals Were White*). Mies van der Rohe, contrary to appearances, agrees with the others in writing on almost all counts. Regarding the

Great Spirit of architecture and its pure creation from the human spirit, he said in 1950: 'Architecture is the real battleground of the spirit.' Later, speaking of architecture as a projection of organic nature, he explained that his aim in building is to 'emphasize the organic principle of order', and touching on the question of artistic unity in the design he told of the ideal of 'achieving the successful relationship of the parts to each other and to the whole.' On architecture as the expression of society he said in 1923: 'Architecture is the will of an epoch translated into space; living, changing, new.'

Thus it seems that the different camps of modern architecture can still meet under the one roof, provided the eaves are broad enough. Despite many conflicting ideas, technical habits and personalities, unanimity of aim still shines through. But immediately the definitions are made more precise, dissenters start to drift away. Even Louis Sullivan's attractive and widely accepted idea that architecture is a further stage of organic form ('Nature who made the mason made the house') is not acceptable to Joseph Hudnut. In a series of lectures in 1952 titled *The Three Lamps of Modern Architecture* he tried to snuff out some of the new, more pretentious lamps while defending architecture as a vital and eloquent medium for an artist. He dismissed the thought of an architect being able to extend organic nature, or express progress, or democracy, or anything but himself. Our buildings, he said, involuntarily express something of our era, our technologies and our democracy, simply because they exist in our time, but architects cannot take any credit for this and should not continue to believe that it excuses them from the performance of their duties as creative artists.

Sullivan's most famous maxim, 'form follows function', the banner under which most modern architects rallied for half a century, is now questioned in theory and often discarded in practice. Under the prevailing influence of advanced engineering and geometry, form follows fabrication. Every specific rule built up by some camp is demolished by another, yet as long as architecture remains without accepted codes or canons it cannot remove the barrier between it and the busy man in the street. Creative architecture will tend to remain the province of a coterie of individualists, *prima donnas* and dedicated if somewhat befogged reformers; and ordinary building will remain in the hands of commercial Featurists.

But is a code really necessary? Can it be true that the key to classification of the architectural ideal is simply to be found, without intellectual help, along the primrose path to beauty? Then what is beauty? No matter how liberal we may attempt to be in defining universal laws of visual enjoyment, we can be sure someone will disagree. For one thing, we will be limited by the narrowness of our experiences to this date. With the most perfect understanding of the aesthetic education of Western man, with the broadest outlook on the whole world story of building, still we must be limited by our ignorance of the future's eye. If a canon of architecture proposed now is to be worth anything it must convince that it is capable of embracing all the buildings which civilized men have loved: a stone temple, a glassy cultural centre, a medieval cathedral, a hyperbolic shape in concrete, and anything which the future may produce including new forms for new social orders, soft walls, wind curtains, and other mechanical, electronic, or chemical devices which may extend our range of vision and understanding. Any narrower view of beauty is doomed to be soon as obsolete as Ruskin's measured prejudices.

Undaunted by Ruskin's failure to describe his sublime architectural vision in terms of permanent meaning, other writers tried to illuminate the darkness as the seven lamps grew dim. In his study of Renaissance building, Sir Geoffrey Scott in 1924 counter-attacked Ruskin on behalf of the quattrocento, dismissed his pontifical artistic laws and explained the phenomenon of architectural beauty in purely

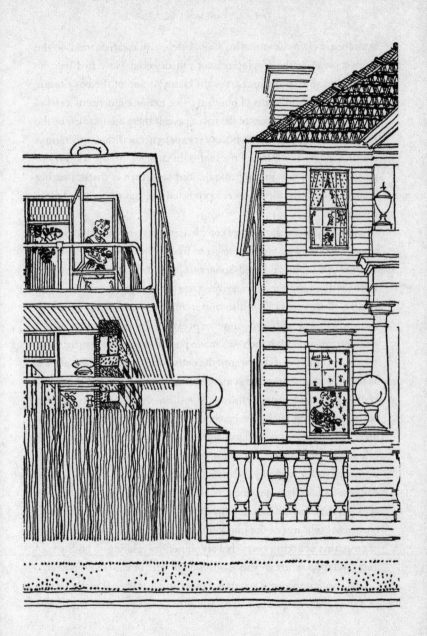

humanistic terms as empathy, *Einfühlung*, visual satisfaction on the highest plane. In the development of a theory established by Lipps, he described the architectural art as the transcription of the body's state into the forms and terms of building. The major elements of a structure give certain promises to the roving eye; if these are fulfilled by the remainder of the elements, beauty is experienced; if the expectations are unanswered or falsified the end is dissatisfaction, the contrary of beauty. Again, any grossly unbalanced structure is discomforting because it disturbs the observer's projected feelings of his own bodily balance.

These generalizations are convincing, but they are all but demolished by an untenable example given by Sir Geoffrey. Top-heaviness discomforts us, he said, and 'sooner or later, if the top-heaviness…is sufficiently pronounced, every spectator will judge that the building is ugly.' But even as he wrote this architects were toying with top-heaviness as a valuable new expression in their language, a qualification of bulk which was made possible by frame construction, and by the middle of the twentieth century top-heaviness was almost as familiar in the streets as symmetry was in the middle of the eighteenth century. Urban buildings stood on sheets of glass, houses balanced on thin sticks, everywhere heavy loads projected in cantilever, defying gravity; and beauty grew with familiarity. Finally Oscar Niemeyer designed a museum for Caracas which is a pyramid upturned and caught by its apex as it was about to tumble down a dangerous hill. Top-heaviness could not be more pronounced, and eyes practised in balancing feats quickly judged it one of the most beautiful buildings of the mid-century. In short, the specious theory of empathy, of architectural beauty somehow relating to bodily balance, collapses when we move outside the aura of classical repose.

A more impressive statement of a similar theory is made by one of today's *avant-garde*, a structural innovator whose buildings command the greatest respect for any of his philosophical comments: the Italian, Pier Luigi Nervi. For long he has been attracted by the idea that some sort of measurable relationship exists between technical and aesthetic quality, and he says: 'I have examined the greatest possible number of meaningful structures of the past and present and have come to the conclusion that for all great structures, without exception, the indispensable premise for architectonic beauty is correct technique. This is probably due to the fact that the intuition and sensitivity to statics which in a more or less confused form may be found in all people are satisfied by those structures which immediately reveal the play of forces and resistance which define its equilibrium.'

On an up-to-date plane and from an unimpeachably up-to-date commentator, here is Sir Geoffrey Scott's thesis restated. Nervi is saying that even untrained eyes know intuitively when the technique of structure is perfect, and he castigated buildings like Sydney Opera House for 'the most open anti-functionalism in statics and construction'. But is it possible that any eye, especially the layman's eye, really can sense statics in any detail? Can anyone tell by looking whether or not redundant material has been used to support an unfamiliar roof of reasonably sophisticated design, or whether a cantilever is correctly shaped? And how many eyes, however well trained, can tell from a finished shell concrete structure how thick the shell is and how clumsy or clever its technique? It seems more probable that the eye reacts best with experience. It gradually finds more confidence and tranquillity as it grows accustomed to what once appeared startlingly unfamiliar escapades in engineering.

Others in the twilight of eclecticism early this century contributed to the short shelf of books begun by Ruskin, books designed to open laymen's eyes so that they might share the delights with architects. The most explicit and complete of these was a labour of love by an American, Talbot Hamlin, first published in 1916 under the title

The Enjoyment of Architecture and covering all significant periods
of building to that date. Thirty years later he rewrote the book as
Architecture—an Art for All Men, and now included the modern
movement, which had grown from infancy to some sort of maturity
in the years between. This new architecture he saw, not as a revolutionary artistic movement throwing rules and restrictions to the
winds, but as another responsible variation in the continuum of
Western architectural expression. Thus he applied the same rules and
guides to the Roman Colosseum, a modern hotel, and Santa Sophia,
and virtually made bedfellows of Michelangelo, Le Corbusier,
Bramante, and any man with his name on a hoarding in Pitt Street.
He found the rules under the Greek columns, Gothic carving and
aluminium sheathing, in 'a substratum of what seems to be universal
law'. Architecture, as an art of form and colour, has its stable codes
and approved criteria, and, 'whatever may be their basis', he wrote,
'certain qualities seem to be possessed by any works of painting or
sculpture or architecture which the consensus of opinion of mankind
has judged beautiful.' He noted that unity was the essence, and examined 'the dominant qualities that are common to all beautiful and
unified buildings'.

Once these are understood, he promised, sound criticism of
architecture as pure form is simple and inevitable. He then defined at
length the principal accepted academic rules of composition applicable
to architecture: balance ('the parts...on either side of an imaginary
line...shall be of apparently equal weight'), rhythm ('units shall bear
some rhythmic relation to one another'), good proportion ('the several
parts...so relate as to give a pleasing impression'), good scale ('the
observer gains some conception of the actual size'), harmony ('not a
single element...to appear disturbingly distinct and alone and separate'), and the need for a climax ('some spot in a building more
interesting than the rest').

The shades of this code of composition may be discovered in most famous historic buildings and, as standard ammunition for instructors in architecture, the rules guarantee a certain satisfaction whenever conscientiously applied by an earnest student. The nature of this satisfaction, this approved state of building beauty, is indicated by Hamlin in remarks dropped during his analysis: 'restful and charming', 'the eye, as it wanders over a large building, grows tired if there is no single feature on which it can rest', '...a sense of repose results at once, and consequently the building appears beautiful.' All is to be restful, reposeful, serene and unoffending.

Other books on the shelf seek the same unruffled calm. 'Every really good architectural work is clothed, as it were, in an atmosphere of repose,' wrote John Belcher, a Past President of the Royal Institute of British Architects in *Essentials in Architecture* in 1907. He listed one or two other rules leading to the desired end: breadth ('a certain comprehensiveness of form and firmness of line') and grace ('a dignified seriousness of purpose'). A. S. G. Butler, in *The Substance of Architecture*, 1927, emphasized the importance to the sense of repose of a notable centre of interest, a fulcrum round which all the weights are balanced and to which all lines lead, so that 'gradually, as we study the arrangement, we find a focus—as it were the heart of the thing—to which our eye returns gratefully and rests there.' Butler, however, could see that this conception of architectural expression smacked a little too much of quiescence, not to say ennui, and he defined a 'deeper meaning of the word "repose", as that effect of vital stability in the appearance of a building which we enjoy in our appreciation of its harmonious unity: the sense of tranquillity which...beautiful architecture provokes with its just adaptation of those two elements...We lean on it and it rests us. Hence repose.' He explained that a ball-room, although properly enticing, should still be as much in repose (in its own somnambulistic way, one supposes) as a farmhouse in a sleepy valley.

Before the modern movement was generally accepted in Australia, a compromise was successfully negotiated by many prudent architects, leading to a brief Indian Summer of the Renaissance between the two world wars, with buildings stripped of Victorian romanticism, and ornamentally reserved, but dedicated to the Classical concept. Many of the most carefully designed buildings of this period, for instance, the war memorials in most capital cities, had potential power in their conceptions. The Canberra National War Memorial had a thunderous motive of a courtyard plan pinned to the ground by a heavy, domed tower. It was bare for its time, in that it had fewer and shallower mouldings than were usual. And its grouping

of windows and arcades, its massing of solids were bold and effective. It did not permit features of detail to be prominent enough to destroy the motivating concept. This destruction, however, was achieved by additional compromise elements: intermediate steps between the tower and the base, thin buttresses on the tower, various other softening transitional steps between parts, and numerous rests and cushions for the eye. Here architectural composition in the grand manner may be seen more isolated than is usual, thanks to the general simplicity of the masses. All the academic rules, of symmetry, good balance, climax, good proportion and so on as recommended, are followed meticulously, and with some originality and sensitivity; and the result exudes nothing if not the architectural repose of which the writers of the twilight were speaking. The vigorous motive is not permitted to rule the building; instead it must submit to the rules of eye-resting: the tower not too high (step it in near the top), the base not too long or too low (break it somewhere; soften it). Lead the eye gently, no surprises, no shocks; we aim to please; the customer is always right. It would not be fair to say that all the strength of the Canberra memorial is lost in the scholarly composition. It has the requested degree of dormant vitality. It is in fact a sleeping giant of familiar mien; one has surely met him many times before in different clothes in other countries.

The revolutionary twentieth century movement opened with a blaze of protest against the ancient dogmas; early buildings struggled to free themselves of rules of good proportion, scale, taste and eye-resting. But today one could fire an antique cannon down many a street of modern buildings and not strike a single rebel. Ornament, as understood by the ancients, is not altogether free again, and simplicity of massing, the accent on space, transparency, suspension and mechanization have changed the expression of buildings. But architecture has returned nonetheless to an essentially classical concept of its aesthetic function. It aims to please, to rest; to soothe—though now in clean, uncluttered lines instead of ornamental plaster, and with light, air and grey-tinted glass in place of massive shaded permanence. The rules of composition apply again, if in a freer way; one talks again of good proportion, scale, balance and attractiveness as things apart from a building's motive. The notion of a universal character returns, a translatable quality not relative to the eye of the observer and certainly not affected by his mental attitude or the psychology of the moment, an elevated, nebulous, mysterious quality which may rest on cathedral, house, or factory, not necessarily in the same shape every time but providing the same visual balm. On the lowest plane this concept is an instruction to every architect on every project to achieve sweetness and light, a winsome smile, a pretty setting for beautiful people surrounded by charming pictures in lovely golden frames. On the highest plane it is the ancient search for a universal perfection of form, a return to Vitruvius.

In his first book, the second chapter, Vitruvius defined good architectural arrangement as the disposition in their just and proper places of all the parts of the building, and the elegance or pleasing effect of the whole. 'Pleasing Effect' then became the slogan emblazoned on the banner wherever the classical tradition was carried. To realize this universal property of pleasingness the ancients sought a golden rule, the vital touch of nature's design, the key to a perception unlocking the innermost secrets of the design of the universe. Characteristically they began the search on the surface of the human body, believing that the secret of the design of its form would be the key to all creation.

Vitruvius started methodically at the navel, noting it to be the natural central point: 'If a man be placed flat on his back with his hands and feet extended, and a pair of compasses centred at his navel, the fingers and toes of his two hands and feet will touch the circumference of a circle described therefrom.' He also explained that a square may be discovered in the body, for a man's arm-stretch 'will be found to be the same' as his height.

This picture of the man in the circle has pleased many generations. Somehow it seems evidence of our importance in the scheme of things, suggesting at least a comforting niche for our mortal frames in the cosmic pattern, if not positive proof of our being made in God's image. In his study of the Renaissance, Rudolph Wittkower disagreed with Scott's theory of empathy, and with the humanist's simple aim to please the eye. On the contrary he pictured the age in earnest search of a mathematical and harmonic integration of architecture in the cosmos. The Vitruvian Man 'seemed to reveal a deep and fundamental truth about man and the world', he said, 'and its importance for Renaissance architects can hardly be over-estimated. The image haunted their imagination.'

The artists of the Renaissance delighted in illustrating the concept. Leonardo's famous diagram is the most thorough. His man has a body fixed in the centre of a superimposed circle and square. Man's limbs are shown in two positions, with legs spread easily and arms raised in a V to touch the circle, and with feet together and arms stretched wide to touch the square. Other artists pictured the Vitruvian figure differently. In 1511 Fra Giocondo, the first to publish a drawing, had Man's arms horizontal and his legs comparatively close together. Cessariano's edition of Vitruvius in 1521 spread Man's legs into an acrobatic split. Francesco Giorgi in 1525 had to bend his Man's arms to contain them within a circle which had suddenly contracted for some reason not suggested by Vitruvius until it almost touched his head. Notwithstanding the different postures, all these universal men were contained precisely within the perfect geometric form of a circle. This is not remarkable since artists can adjust posture and proportions at will. All the men in the pictures are proportioned differently, as indeed are men in life, and the artists could just as well have turned their pens to prove that man bore a striking resemblance to a triangle, or a tree—which may be a more convincing hypothesis.

But the circle attracts because it is the most obvious basis of cosmic geometry, and a circular container adds dignity to our physical form. It reminds us that, however vulnerable and ungainly our body may be in comparison with the forms of some of our four-footed co-inhabitants of the world, it alone when spreadeagled can fit inside the shape of the universe. Nevertheless, if we were cats we would fill the Vitruvian circle much more snugly and in our sleep.

Vitruvius scrutinized his fellow men more closely to find further evidence of harmonic pattern. He was delighted to discover that their frames carried a network of mathematical divisions: 'The human body is so designed by nature,' he wrote in Book III, 'that the face from the chin to the top of the forehead and the lowest roots of the hair, is a tenth part of the whole height; the open hand from the wrist to the tip of the middle finger is just the same, the head from the chin to the crown is an eighth, and with the neck and shoulder from the top of the breast to the lowest roots of the hair is a sixth...' and so on. Furthermore the face is a veritable graph: 'The distance from the bottom of the chin to the underside of the nostrils is one third of it, the nose from the underside of the nostrils to a line between the eyebrows is the same; from there to the lowest roots of the hair is also a third comprising the forehead...The other members too have their own symmetrical proportions.'

It is difficult to believe that such wishful thinking ever could have commanded a sizeable body of artistic thought. If the proportions stated for the body or the face were exact everyone would look alike. If they were intended to be only approximate, then they mean nothing as a rule for design, since it is the subtle little differences in proportion which express major differences of character in the human design. And if the ancients were not considering ordinary mortals but only an ideal, a perfect human, a god, then who among the artists are we to follow? Where is the perfectly proportioned human on which we can base our proportions of building? No doubt he is an athlete, tall, trim and bronzed, poised against the blue sky of ancient Greece, or perhaps a modern Olympic competitor. Western, of course; Caucasian and all that, and male. The Vitruvian figures were always male, sometimes aggressively so.

Illogical as it is, the belief that the elusive 'perfect' human body holds a secret of universal proportional beauty was carried high through the Renaissance and appears triumphant again today in the roguish figure with which Le Corbusier embellishes his measuring stick *Le Modulor*.

As already mentioned, Le Corbusier proposed *Le Modulor* after the Second World War as a method of standardizing and 'harmonizing' dimensions of all manufactured goods, while reducing the obstacle created by the irreconcilable metric and foot-and-inch systems, which are now splitting the world. It takes the form of a graduated scale, a useful tool for draftsmen, and is based not on the repetition of even units— inch upon inch—but on a logarithmic progression of lengths. Starting at a basic dimension of 2.26 metres, the intervals diminish in steps of even proportion towards zero, and in the other direction (beyond the length of the rule) enlarge in the same progression towards infinity.

The basic dimension of 2.26 metres was selected by Le Corbusier as being the height of a man standing with one arm raised. He proposed this as a standard dimension for the ceiling height of rooms, a measurement based on the human being rather than the arbitrary inch or metre. The man whose arm is raised is taken to be six feet tall. In earlier experiments with *Le Modulor*, Le Corbusier recounts that he and his collaborators had adopted a human height of 1.75 metres, but this was not proving satisfactory in some of the practical details of conversion to feet and inches. Then one draftsman suggested: 'Isn't that rather a French height? Have you ever noticed that in English detective novels, the good-looking men, such as the policemen, are always six feet tall?' So they amended the basic measurement to 1.8288 metres (6 feet) and this solved their problem.

Le Corbusier was not prepared to leave this measuring stick at the utilitarian level. Having selected rationally if not very scientifically a basic dimension keyed to human scale, he diverted to the mystic 'mathematics of the human body, gracious, elegant and firm'. In the body he expected to find, as the Ancients did, 'the source of that harmony which moves us: beauty'. On the measuring instrument he drew in his familiar easy scrawl the outline of a man—the English policeman, presumably—with one enormous hand raised above his head to the 2.26 metre line. He discovered that the figure could be divided vertically into sections of pleasing mutual relationship. He used the navel, not as a socket for the point of a pair of compasses, but to mark one of the 'decisive points' of the human body's occupation of

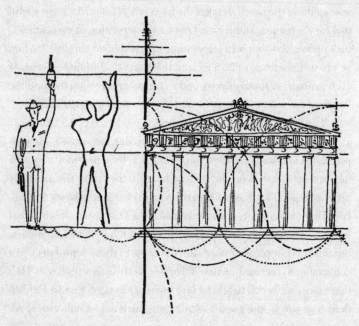

space. As he shows it, the policeman's navel is conveniently situated half-way between his toes and raised fingers. This central position of the navel, as noted by Vitruvius, may apply universally to athlete, policeman, giant, or pigmy, because all proposals of this sort avoid specifying whether the raised arm should be stretched or bent, and any differences may be adjusted at the elbow.

Le Corbusier then took three 'decisive' dimensions from the figure of his policeman, measuring from ground to the navel, to the top of the head and to the raised fingertips, and from these three he developed the entire system of *Le Modulor*. By combining two simple mathematical progressions, a range of dimensions was obtained from 2.26 metres (basic ceiling height) descending in decreasing steps to the smallest measurable size. It was intended that a tape so graduated should be at hand on every drafting board, eventually supplanting the foot or centimetre rules. It could eliminate arbitrariness in the subdivisions of building. The architect or draftsman, after being led by functional requirements to an approximate dimension for any detail— for instance the height of a sill—would consult the tape and select the nearest *Modulor* size. As all *Modulor* sizes are linked in a progression, the dimensions of the building would be linked or 'harmonized' to each other and to human scale.

While Le Corbusier was careful to explain that this measuring tape did not relieve the artist of any responsibility, while he reserved for the artist the right to make a 'personal interpretation' of the proportions which it suggests, still he claimed that *Le Modulor* would help a draftsman to select the most pleasing proportions not only for the parts of architecture, but indeed for sculpture or painting as well. He was naturally delighted when Albert Einstein wrote: 'It is a scale of proportions which makes the bad difficult and the good easy.' Durisol Inc., a company in New York, undertook in 1947 to market *Le Modulor* as 'a scale for harmonic measurement of space', and Le

Corbusier saw himself entering the country of numbers, '*passe la porte des miracles*'.

Anyone else is entitled to select other key features of the human frame—for example the joints: knees, pelvis and shoulders—and claim for them more decisive roles in the body's occupation of space than that enjoyed by the immobile navel. A different scale could thus be drawn up from the relative positions of these features, no less logically related to the body. Someone else may prefer to base a system on the proportions of the width of a policeman to his height. A dozen different systems of proportioning could be devised on the results of a brief run over a human body with a tape-measure. But of all the possible points of reference and combinations of dimensions, Le Corbusier was led by his practised artist's eye direct to the one set of proportions which accorded to the classical designer's golden rule; he selected a division approximating the mathematician's extreme and mean ratio, the traditional conception of perfection in proportion, the Golden Section.

If the rational movement in architecture cannot accept any mystical connection between the figure of a man and a divine system of proportion, it is nonetheless as impressed by mathematicians as any aesthetician of antiquity. In *Architectural Principles in the Age of Humanism* Professor Wittkower went some way towards presenting a disenchanted post-war generation of architectural students with a creed. Many saw a new direction for a Functionalism that had lost its way as they followed him through the historic progression of the idea that architecture, in the company of the musical scale, may reach through a system of mathematical ratios finally to the being of God himself. Wittkower traced the growth of number symbolism and mysticism from the Pythagorean conceptions (for example: 'Three is the first number because it has a beginning, middle and end. It is divine as the symbol of the Trinity') through Plato's suggestion that cosmic order may be obtained, and the harmony of the world expressed, in a pyramidal lambda of the figures 1, 2, 3, 4, 8, 9, 27 ('the ratios between these numbers contain not only all the musical consonances but also the inaudible music of the heavens and the structure of the human soul'). Renaissance architects, practical men, converted the heritage of harmonic theories into workaday techniques. They modified the strict classical modular system and developed new codes. Palladio in the mid sixteenth century gave a general rule to harmonic proportions for the height of rooms in relation to their width and length. 'A wall [was] seen as a unit which contains certain harmonic potentialities,' said Wittkower. 'The lowest sub-units, into which the whole unit can be broken up, are the consonant intervals of the musical scale, the cosmic validity of which was not doubted.'

Gradually the search for a key to the cosmic harmony was abandoned, but the belief in the existence of a universal beauty and a science of proportions lingered on into the middle of the eighteenth century. Then a new tide of rationalism engulfed it with the cold water of the ideas that architecture and music are not comparable since they communicate with the mind through different organs, and that architecture and mathematics operate on different levels: note how a building's apparent proportions change as the observer moves about. The effects of proportion depend on the association of ideas, not an abstract reason, and are relative to the beholder, his nature, his time and his place. Thus Burke, Kames, Knight and others argued in the eighteenth and nineteenth centuries, and in the twentieth a leader of the modern movement restated the most obvious objection to all golden rules: 'Beauty is relative because men are different,' said Piet Mondrian, a painter for whom an utmost delicacy of proportioning in lines, spaces and solids constituted the very means of expression. 'Attachment to a merely conventional conception of beauty hinders a true vision...'

For two centuries, then, bridging across generations of the picturesque, the romantic, the worldly, and deep into the revolution of the functional, the thought of universal harmony lay dormant. Men with all kinds of conflicting artistic approaches could agree at least on one principle: whatever the style, art was a task for artists and not for mathematicians; it was an understanding between an artist and an observer; it was in the eye that received a satisfying message.

But the closed door of the mathematician's study slowly regained its fascination for the architect. Everything he saw through the keyhole as the twentieth century developed suggested analogies with the problems of his own creative work. When the mathematician advanced in his studies of three-dimensional geometry the designer saw new prospects in plastic forms, and when the mathematician directed his attention to a fourth dimension the architect could scarcely contain himself. Hence the world-wide enchantment of the title which Sigfried Giedion attached to his famous account of the origins of the modern movement: *Space, Time and Architecture*.

Many architects today still respond to an old magic and look to their profession for somewhat more than creative satisfaction. The polite apathy which the ordinary cultivated layman extends to architecture is counter-balanced by a high intensity of feeling on a certain thin professional stratum from which architecture is viewed not simply as the ultimate art of man, for this much is self-evident, but also as a dazzling light now shaded by ignorance, a saviour of mankind's soul—not to mention his body. On the day when all building accords to the cosmic harmony, all men will live in order and peace of mind. The secret of the harmony escapes us temporarily, but who can deny that the Greeks were close to it on the Acropolis?

Thus the search for inspiration in numbers is revived, if on a somewhat less emotional plane, and linked now to the technological demand for an international module to reconcile the metric and foot-

and-inch systems and to facilitate the prefabrication and international exchange of parts. High-level meetings of professional men and technicians in Italy and England have discussed the physical details while aestheticians re-examine the complex arithmetic which the Greeks brought to perfection in the Parthenon. The geometry of the medieval mason is drawn out into the daylight. Even Chartres Cathedral's asymmetrical facade is found, by Professor Levy of Massachusetts Institute of Technology, probably to be following a mathematical 'melody' of dimensions based on an octagonal whorl in the Gothic section and a modular scale in the Romanesque part.

Le Corbusier was never alone in his experiments with *Le Modulor*. Once again he was leading his profession, this time in the revival of a concept and an argument which had been discredited for two centuries: the concept of an objective system of beauty which may be applied to all men's construction. But what made his invention profoundly significant as an architectural development in the middle of the twentieth century was that it returned, beyond the numbers, to the dawn of philosophy to try to find some sort of mysterious link for the system with the proportions of the body, some hint of divine inspiration. The sheer reaction of these suggestions coming from one of the spiritual leaders of twentieth-century architecture might have been expected to take the rational movement's breath away. Instead, thousands of Le Corbusier's disciples round the world began to play with *Le Modulor* and to claim to see some part of the miracle which the inventor himself all but experienced. Some criticism was made at the time of inherent difficulties in the practical application of the scale, but there was no sign of shock; only a movement which had retained its rational principles would have been shocked.

The 'Golden Mean', 'Golden Section', 'Golden Cut', or 'Divine Proportion', which were revived from near oblivion by *Le Modulor*, are artist's quasi-mathematical terms for one of the geometrical propositions which has fascinated many men who have gone in stumbling search of a rhythm of creation. The Pythagorean mathematicians, who sought a rational explanation for the phenomenon of beauty in the sixth century BC and decided that the circle was the most beautiful figure and the sphere the most beautiful form, first solved the problem of devising a mathematical basis for the perfect visual proportioning of parts. They discovered how to divide a line into two parts, the ratio of the smaller to the greater being the same as the ratio of the greater to the whole line (roughly .618 to 1). As the Pythagoreans discovered, this proposition leads to absorbingly interesting mathematical consequences. For instance, if the length of the smaller section of the divided line is marked on the larger section, again an extreme and mean ratio is created, for the offcut that remains bears the same ratio to the original small section as the small does to the large, and as the large to the whole. This process may be repeated again and again, but the end of the line—zero—will never be reached, for the parts of the golden proportion are incommensurable, which adds to their fascination and to the aura of mysticism surrounding them for twenty-six centuries. Artists saw in the phenomenon a golden rule of proportions for building, sculpture and painting. Plato saw in it a clue to the secrets of creation, and Aristotle saw in the balanced tension of the long and short parts an analogy for a code of ethics. Developing from the divided line, the aesthetic theory of the Golden Section goes on to state that a rectangle formed of the two parts of the linear division is a plane shape of absolute beauty, a solid rectilinear body based on the proportion is one of the forms of absolute beauty, and a building subdivided in accordance with it will be a building of perfection.

The rule may in fact be traced through the proportions of many famous paintings and buildings, and its 'objective beauty' is occasionally 'proved' by art instructors in simple experiments. If a group of people is asked to select the most pleasing shapes from a range of different lines and rectangles, one is fairly safe in calculating on the majority selecting the figures which approximate to the Golden Section. An experiment even so simple as this supplies substantial evidence supporting the idea of a mathematical formula for beauty. Here, clearly, is the basis of a system of scientific determination of the most popular, satisfying shapes and subdivisions, and eventually an architect might be able to apply this to all the openings and appurtenances of his building.

At the highest pitch of enthusiasm the Golden Section suggests the possibility that the eye can recognize here a microcosm of universal harmony, that the human being somehow senses the progression from zero to infinity of further ratios implicit in the single given ratio, and that somewhere beyond the reach of our present knowledge an understanding of the all-pervading pattern of creation flickers in the soul.

At a lower pitch of excitement the psycho-analyst interprets the mystique of it as a comparatively simple psychological trick. Even when conscientiously applied to the parts of a building, the mathematical simplicity of the proportions of the Golden Section are never obvious. The conscious eye finds nothing offensive yet can find in the lines no apparent mathematical law, but meanwhile the subconscious has perceived the precision hidden in the form relationships, and its secret goading of the surface mind is the seat of the fascination.

At the most prosaic level the 'universal beauty' of the Golden Section may be explained flatly as a matter of compromise. Any pure mathematical form of simple mathematical system is approved by the eye because it is a decisive statement. A line cut in the middle satisfies because there is nothing woolly about the even balance of the halves. In a line cut in the golden proportion of .618 to 1 the ratio of the parts is more subtle but the statement is still clear, for if the cut is moved close to one end of the line, it reduces the shorter section to an inconsequential tag. And if it is not moved far enough from the centre the indecision is disturbing; perhaps the draftsman's hand slipped as he was about to make a central cut. A position in which the cut is far enough from the centre to be clearly no slip of the pen and far enough from the end to give the short section sufficient strength of its own, is the point at which the eye finds a satisfyingly definite statement; this is approximately the point of the Golden Cut. It may not always agree exactly with the mathematician's calculation, but then in practice the eye cannot judge with any accuracy the parts of a building seen in perspective. The golden arithmetical progression may be converted for everyday use from decimals to round figures, say 3, 5, 8, 13, etc., and a board-room may be cut to this pattern with every confidence in its ultimate pleasingness. It will seem neither constrictingly narrow nor oppressively low, and a building on the same pattern will be neither too thin nor too squat. The Golden Mean means neither too much nor too little, but moderation, the comforting average; everything to rest the eye and nothing to concern the mind.

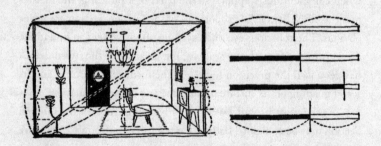

If these are the qualities desired of all buildings irrespective of their site, environment, function and meaning to society, then the Golden Mean should dictate the proportions of everything man makes and *Le Modulor* should be on every drawing-board. But Le Corbusier cannot believe that these qualities are desirable in all buildings, for his own have the expressive range to be expected from a master who can control tons of concrete as few men control a tube of paint. The golden proportions can be discovered in most of his buildings only if they and credulity are stretched to breaking point, and they will relate to almost anything when thus extended. On the other hand they may be sensed like a grid of invisible wires between one's eyes and most of Le Corbusier's paintings, contributing to the singular monotony of his work along this sideline.

Contradicting nearly everything that has gone before, Le Corbusier concluded his first book on *Le Modulor* with a caution: 'Any door that offers an escape is dangerous,' and by quoting Kahnweiler's comment on the Cubist movement—including Le Corbusier's architecture: 'Every one of these artists has attempted to create works of art which have as strong an autonomous existence as possible, to produce objects whose unity is ensured by the force of their rhythm and in which the parts are subordinated to the whole. To each of these objects, fruits of their emotion, they intend by its unique-ness to guarantee complete autonomy.' Could Le Corbusier have discovered a more devastating condemnation of *Le Modulor*'s preten-sions to universal proportioning? How can a work of art have an autonomous existence while it is pulling its forelock to some inviolable rule of proportion? Le Corbusier makes this apparent contradiction because he sees the dimensions on his measuring stick not as an archi-tectural scale like a footrule, but more as a musical scale on which the designer may play freely. But surely language is working some mis-chief here. Le Corbusier's interpretation of playing freely on *Le Modulor* is to ignore it altogether, to change the key, whenever it offers no dimension applicable to a practical task in hand—for instance, in the height of an ordinary doorway. This is the traditional way with systems of architectural proportions. 'The artist is always present beside the geometrician,' said Viollet-le-Duc, 'and will be able, when necessary, to bend the formulas.' [*Dictionnaire raisonne de l'architecture*

francaise du XIe au XVIe siecle: 'Proportion'; 'L'architecture n'est pas
l'esclave d'un systeme hieratique de proportione, mais au contraire peut se
modifier sans cesse et trouver des applications toujour nouvelles.' (p. 534)
'...l'artiste est toujours present a cote du geometre, et sait, au besoin, faire
flechir les formules.' (p. 549)]

Now just what—one may ask in Heaven's name—is bent geom-
etry? It is certainly not geometry, probably it is not the best art, and it
can hardly be the way to the stars.

While scientists are being led into deeper and deeper mysteries,
while the basic theoretical concepts of existence are ever more in
doubt, while scientific writers continually warn against over-simplifi-
cation, while 'all highroads of the intellect, all byways of theory and
conjecture lead ultimately to an abyss that human ingenuity can never
span' (Lincoln Barnett), it is preposterous for artists to play with a
simple formula or two from the mathematician's primers. Many an
artist-architect is a Flash Gordon at heart, but he should not worry
about the cosmic value of his work. Everything he builds must be as
much a part of the universal harmony as he is. The greatest architect
and the meanest speculative builder involuntarily wade, alongside the
vulture and leaf mould, under the ultimate law of the expanding universe. Some artists receive blinding glimpses of what they believe to
be eternity. If you are not by nature the type given to receiving these
messages, mathematics will not increase your capacity. If you are,
translation of the message will not be strengthened but weakened by
dressing it in numbers, by confusing your medium with the elementary mechanics of scientific theory.

But perhaps there is an eternal quality of beauty not discoverable
by numbers or geometry and not mystical, but a self-sufficient object
existing independently of the eyes of the beholder, as C. E. M. Joad
proposed in *Matter, Life and Value.* 'It is a real and unique factor in the
universe,' he wrote. 'When I say that a picture or a piece of music is

beautiful, I am not making a statement about any feeling that I or any other person or body of persons may have or have had…I am making an assertion about a quality or property possessed…' This property, he explained later, is 'the awareness of value'. At a moment of perception the artist, attended by a thrill of excitement, apprehends albeit obscurely the patterns and arrangement of the real world. Recalling their outlines as he works, he reproduces them in his medium.

If this is a correct interpretation, or if there is a single mathematical system behind all creation, and if it is possible for man eventually to discover these secrets and to translate them into buildings; if in an infinitely distant future numbers replace an artist's perception and all buildings repose in sublime harmony, then will architects retire with their logarithms from creative practice? Unless men also are at that time drilled by numbers, the very harmony will be a challenge to some; beauty carried to satiety will goad them into revolt against the codes and numbers and they will find their own satisfaction in some disharmony or, in terms of the canon, ugliness.

But perhaps language is confusing the issue again. Are Professor Joad's 'patterns and arrangements of the real world' necessarily beautiful? How many of Le Corbusier's Cubist painter colleagues would support his search for 'the simple harmony that moves us: beauty'? Nothing stood lower in the Cubist's esteem than the beautiful painting with its oily, introverted composition and its eye-resting, soul-soothing centre of interest. They were not aesthetes searching for beauty. They sought a sharper perception to convey a keener experience of form; perhaps this is Joad's 'awareness of value', and it may be more than beauty. 'Modern Art' may be beautiful to some and ugly to others, but this is irrelevant. Even those who see a painting as 'ugly' may find it intensely stimulating; to this extent it gives them pleasure. Provocative fascination is not, however, what modern architecture means by 'pleasing effect' and 'beauty' when it perseveres today with these terms. Architects still mean the concept of beauty established by the Greeks and maintained throughout the European classical tradition; and it is the adherence to this meaning of beauty and to beauty as an ideal which distinguishes 'Modern Architecture' from the revolutionary art movements of the twentieth century. Generally our architecture has sought to re-create the glory of Greece, in different terms perhaps, but essentially the same sort of glory.

There have been exceptions. Some of the early 'scientific' architects of Central Europe like Hannes Meyer professed no interest in creating beauty, but since they also denied architecture any claim to art and required the architect to suppress any conscious personal expression, their work is not relevant to this discussion. The recent tendency in England towards a revival of early modern architectural morality is more significant. The leaders of this movement hopefully adopted a style-name, 'The New Brutalism', an expression which the Swedish architect Hans Asplund coined ('in a mildly sarcastic way', as he recalled later) in January 1950: a new promise perhaps for the second half of the century. The style was still little more than the mildly sarcastic name when Reyner Banham examined it in the *Architectural Review* of December 1955. Its leaders, Alison and Peter Smithson, could then exhibit one completed building: a large school, and drawings of some unsuccessful entries in competitions. The movement also reached across the Atlantic to claim Louis Kahn's Fine Arts Centre at Yale University. The importance of the movement was not to be found in completed works, however, but in the fact that it was the first consistent assault on the classical conception of beauty, and that it was a hot topic in English architectural circles. Banham defined a New Brutalist building as one having: '1, Memorability as an Image; 2, clear exhibition of structure; and 3, valuation of materials "as found".' These qualities exist to a degree in many modern buildings, especially in Mies van der Rohe's work, but the degree makes all the difference, and in the case of the Smithsons it is the *Nth*. A rugged, heavy, over-strong look in exposed concrete and masonry character-izes their work, and a prominent little detail is the exposure of the mechanical sub-contractors' apparatus: pipes on the ceiling and elec-trical conduits darting up and down the walls to pick up switches. Again, this was hardly an innovation, but the interest lay in their manner of, and reasons for, this exposure. The pipes were not shown simply on the ethical grounds of the scientific school, nor were they rather apologetically aiming to please, as was the ductwork on the ceiling of Markelius's chamber in the United Nations Conference building. And although they looked somewhat like a delinquent youth's pencilled additions to a street poster the pipes were not a destructive but a mildly constructive protest against the reigning con-cept of beauty. The New Brutalists were reaching back half a century to recapture something of the first excitement of the revolution, and they found a string of devoted disciples falling in behind them.

Aesthetic theory has often observed that the abstract arts have not an extensive repertoire of emotional expression. The traditional expressions of great architecture tend to convey either a great sub-limity or a gentle serenity, but here in New Brutalism was a renewed promise of different expressions beyond the aesthetic limitations. The most unfortunate thing about the movement was its catch-phrase name, an only half-ironic conceit which suggested a passing 'cult of ugliness'; little wonder that New Brutalism met with much dark misunderstanding in its own country, was brushed aside in the USA as 'poor man's Mies', and has not yet appeared in Australia. The coarse, crude Anti-Featurism of the Brutalists was too much even for architectural students in the land of the Featurists.

Sir Herbert Read has pointed to the need in art for a new word or a new meaning for the old word of beauty: '...a Greek Aphrodite, a Byzantine Madonna, and a savage idol from New Guinea or the

234 THE AUSTRALIAN UGLINESS

Ivory Coast cannot all belong to this classical concept of beauty. The latter at least, if words are to have any precise meaning, we must confess to be unbeautiful, or ugly.' Here is the point of collapse of the idiom: to be unbeautiful in the classical concept is to be 'ugly'. No one wishes to create more ugliness when so much already abounds; hence all good architects should aspire to nothing but beauty. Any building which does not conform to this idea is reprehensible. The external form of Saarinen's sliced dome at MIT has been criticized on the basis of its not appearing at rest from some angles, and photographers are careful to select the viewpoints from which it appears symmetrical, avoiding the disturbing unbalance from some aspects. Australian architectural criticism is usually confined to discussions of whether a dome looks too low or a tower too high. But there is a rich world of visual stimulation, which already happens to include the savage idol and many arts of other eras and civilizations and much mature modern painting, lying between classical beauty and objectionable ugliness.

A command of the technique of architectural composition, of proportion, balance, rhythm, scale and so on, is of course essential to an architect, but the way of everyday modern architecture, as taught in most schools and practised in most streets, is not to control these elements but to be controlled by them. The student is taught not the method of driving so much as the end to which he must drive. He is taught, under the heading of balance, not the sensorial strength of the various forms of unbalance but only how to achieve even balance; under scale, not the odd power over the emotions of unfamiliar scale but only how to preserve 'perfect scale'; under proportion, not the fascination of the unexpected which Mondrian turned to account, but only how to aim for 'good proportion'; in the sum, how to design for familiarity.

Gropius has said in explanation of his approach to Functionalism: 'The slogan "fitness for purpose equals beauty" is only half true. When do we call a human face beautiful? Every face is fit for purpose in its part, but only perfect proportions and colours in a well-balanced harmony deserve that title of honour: beautiful. Just the same is true of architecture. Only perfect harmony in its technical functions as well as in its proportions can result in beauty.' To carry further this analogy with the human face: whether or not we accept Freud's explanation of the aesthetic feeling here as an extension of sexual excitation or Ehrenenzweig's belief that it is a trick of the subconscious to subdue sexual excitement, in any case beauty in human features cannot occur but in a sound healthy structure formed in the nature of the selected materials of bones, flesh, skin, hair and so on. Facial beauty also requires good proportions, which can only mean in this case proportions obeying a familiar rule, proportions which conform to the average features of our own ethnic division of the human race: nose neither too sharp nor too retroussé, eyes big but not bulbous, far but not too far apart, no feature too square or too round or too small or too prominent; everything just right. Thus the judges might select a Miss Universe. But conformation to 'perfect' proportions may lead only to a vapid prettiness, and ultimately to the demolition of all character down to the perfect mean level: a world of toothpaste models. We do not select our friends by beauty tests; the faces which mean most to most of us are often stern, rugged, noble, perhaps funny faces—but faces of character and as often as not describable as beautiful only if in affection we stretch the word's meaning out of shape. Ugliness of features, on the other hand, is more than the absence of beauty. It requires a positive quality of repulsiveness, perhaps from physical distortion through ill-health or injury or from an expression of evil or some despicable intent.

The analogy between faces and architecture may be pressed a little further, for a positive quality of ugliness is found in building only when the original intention has been frustrated by accidents,

clumsiness, mistakes, incompetence—some ill-health in the execution
of the concept, or in a dissembling style or structure, or when the
concept is in some way despicable, the character of a building pre-
tending to be what it is not or attempting to exalt an unworthy cause
or to prettify a grim or unpleasant function.

This last explanation of a cause of ugliness is not, of course,
accepted by Featurists, eclectics, or many aesthetes. If one believes in
the existence of an independent, eternal quality of beauty one usually
believes that it may turn up anywhere. It may, for instance, be borrowed by a department store from a cathedral round the corner
provided only that the architecture is reproduced well. A building's
'beauty need have no relation to its utility (though we like it today if
it does)', wrote A. S. G. Butler in 1927 during the morning of modern
architecture, 'and an architect may, therefore, possess an unhampered
vehicle for the presentation of any emotional quality which he wishes
to appear in his building.' Indeed it is undeniable that the aesthetic
qualities of attractiveness, repose, balance and those other pleasing
properties of architecture may be transferable; but the beauty so produced—so very easily produced—is cheap. It is not repose so much as
an architectural tranquillizer pill of no lasting value. Even if the
architecture remains unmoved in the transition from cathedral to
department store, the observer's mind will be coloured by the change.
Once he knows that the store is exploiting the other, stealing from the
collection plate as it were, he can never regain his initial pleasure in
the design. The knowledge of the building's function must always,
however lightly, alter the beholder's vision, just as a rat may be
pleasing to the eye, positively beautiful, a little furry friend, to an
innocently fearless child but may look a loathsome plague-carrier and
positively repulsive to an alarmed parent.

In all fairness to beauty it should be admitted here and now that
a beautiful building can be not only enchanting but absolutely right

for the occasion. But the question remains: is every occasion right for it? The vagueness of the word complicates this question; we know there can be many sorts of beauty. Nonetheless, there are times and places when any sort seems inappropriate. Francis Greenway's Hyde Park Barracks in Sydney is beautiful to many people, but every time this famous colonial building of 1817 comes up for public discussion— should it be demolished, restored, preserved?—others state their dislike of it. To these sensitive people the barracks' associations with the brutalities of convict existence overrule any niceties of proportion and mouldings. Indeed the obvious thought and attention given to these trivialities seems offensively incongruous. Beauty which seems out of place is not beauty at all. It is like sentiment out of place: saccharine, inane and self-destructive.

Morality is a personal, very private qualification of beauty. The effect of evil depends largely on how close the evil is to home, to oneself. Consider the remote, beautiful ugliness of Port Arthur, Tasmania. Consider a German concentration camp: Dachau, as it looked shortly after it had been cleaned and opened for public inspection. The leafy courtyard between the dark red brick buildings was a pretty green turning yellow under the gentle autumn sky, and visitors were politely requested by neat signs erected by the American Army not to throw their orange peel, cigarette butts or other trash on the trim new lawns. All was serene, reposeful, restful, and in good proportion. Yet the knowledge of the function of the murder offices and disposal ovens still permeated the court. No building has had a viler function than a Nazi extermination camp; the odium still attached to its architecture was surely strong enough to convince any aesthete who visited of the relevance of the known function to one's total visual experience of a building. In the light of the recent function of this court beauty could exist only in tormented parody, and the normal elements of beautiful surroundings, the same kinds of trees which were beautiful in the open fields beyond the brick wall, were almost obscene in their inappropriateness.

Even in a healthy society, normal concepts of beauty can become in certain circumstances offensively unsuitable, as even Ruskin testily discovered while waiting in a beautified railway station. No one is in temper while waiting, he argued in *Seven Lamps*, and no one wants the symbol of his discomfort beautified. To be appropriate is more blessed than to be beautiful.

The principal distinct functions in the community demand of architecture a distinctive appearance. This was firmly believed by architects through the eclectic era, and to this end the nineteenth century developed a code of styles related to functions. Architects achieved a kind of visual appropriateness by means of the crudest symbolism and association with ancient stylistic periods: Gothic was for churches, impressive columns were for banks, Scottish Baronial was fitting for a clothing magnate's mansion, and so on. The early pioneers of the twentieth century reacted violently against all such conceits and deceits and placed these practices at the head of their black-list. However, in the course of ridding architecture of the association of style, they also tossed out the principle of appropriateness of character. For nearly half a century the *avant-garde* stood for a character so pure and sterilized that it could be applied universally. Moreover, technical developments continuously tended to level all architectural character by leading the motive away from functional planning to structure, and from structure to mechanics. For example, in the tropical areas of north Australia during the nineteenth century comfort was provided by planning devices: the free passage of air under raised buildings, open verandas, breezeways, shaded courts: a pronounced character grew from these distinctive devices. This century has extended to the tropics its sturdier construction, better insulation and mechanical cooling, and comfort now is often accomplished within a building which might have been built in Hobart, except for the somewhat self-conscious louvred concrete sun-shades. Within the foreseeable future the cost of power to operate air-conditioning may drop so low in proportion to building costs that the outer walls of a building may be reduced to the thinnest film while a purring mechanical heart produces halcyon interior conditions in Alice Springs or Marble Bar. But what of the buildings not content to be so impersonal? How can modern architects seek appropriate character for special buildings now that the direct association of functions with ancient stylistic categories is taboo? Even symbolism is now suspect: a cross placed on a factory may advertise that it is serving as a church but will not make the building more appropriate. A genuine quality of pertinence is above symbolism and more subtle than the nineteenth century's demand that a building should 'speak well', as Ruskin put it: advertise by its style and character its function in society. It need not be necessary for the man in the street, before he reads the name above the doors, to know that this building is an apartment block, and that is a hotel, and the third is a sanitarium. It is not necessary for him to be able to tell by a high-pointed roof that the soulful structure across the square is a place of worship or by symbols of solidity that the pompous little edifice is a branch insurance office. These are external and Featurist kinds of appropriateness. A less frivolous approach demands that any architectural sensations should stem from the use of the building, that the occupiers should be presented with a sense of space which is attuned and sympathetic to the activity of the building and its environment and, as an artistic ideal, that the architectural character should heighten the experience of the phase of life being sheltered. If beauty were all there is to architecture, Featurism would be enough. A Featurist building can be as beautiful as one could wish, in a soothing, eye-resting, feeble sort of way. But architecture is more than this. The architect is a portraitist rather than a non-objective abstractionist. He portrays an incident in human life in the medium of its shelter, by the arrangement of the spaces and subdivisions and enclosing forms of structure, and by the nuances of balance, scale, proportion, and the effect upon them of colour, texture and the details of finish. While the forms, spaces, structure and materials may be expressed or expressive in passing, they are important to the building only in their relevance to the character formed in the idea, the motive: whether they support or confuse the issue. The motive, if it is worth anything at all, is everything in the artistic structure of the building. It is the first rule of design, taking charge, superseding all other rules, contradicting the authority of any absolute canon. The technical hints and tips on proportion, scale, balance, and so on are useful only so long as they remain in submission to the motive: the temple's proportions are keyed to the temple's motive; the restaurant's proportions are keyed to the restaurant's motive. The act of architectural creation is the statement of a particular definitive rule, or order, or discipline for the portrait in hand; the proportions which accept the discipline are 'good proportions' for the building, and those which do not support it, though they may be observing some private agreement with a mathematician, are 'bad proportions'.

The beauty, proportions and rules approved by most textbooks are not fundamental or universal things but subjective values accompanying the comfort of familiarity. Expressions like 'beauty' are widely acceptable only while they are allowed to remain enshrouded with mist. As soon as they are analysed and described in concrete terms the sense is narrowed so that all meaning is lost to the poets in the audience. Beauty is a private secret; it cannot be a target. Any attempt to pin it down invariably finishes with some stiflingly inflexible dogma like William Hogarth's 'completely new and harmonious order of architecture': his Rococo rule of maximum variety, which he finally reduced to 'one precise line, properly to be called the line of beauty'. The better the formula, the more fixed is the expression on the pretty face of architecture.

Yet we know architecture can be more than merely pretty. It can be, for instance, infuriating to some people, as witness letters to the editors on the completion of any uncompromising non-Featurist structure. It can be other than reposeful, charming, soothing; the 'Great Spirit' referred to by architecture's great apologists suggests something more than a monumental tranquillizer pill. What, then, is the essence of architecture?

Return to Professor Joad's statement, not for a definition of beauty but to reconsider his remark that in a moment of perception an artist may apprehend, albeit obscurely, the patterns and arrangements of the real world and that his work may reproduce somehow this awareness of true values. The increase of awareness of realities: this seems to be the key. Beauty may result inadvertently, but when beauty is the goal style sets the course and fashion steers: it's a dangerous drive. And if beauty is questionable, the other goals mentioned by Vitruvius ('pleasing appearance') and Wotton ('delight') are even more suspect. At least 'beauty' is capable of personal interpretations and can be stretched to cover things more vital than chocolate-box covers, but 'pleasing appearance' and 'delight' restrict architecture to some fey world of romance and mythology. In this age and in the West they restrict architecture to some sort of reproduction of the quality held by the acknowledged masterpiece of classic art: the Parthenon. There on the acropolis of Western culture is a building which has been held beautiful, off and on, for two thousand four hundred years. There is the classic exception to the rule which warns against the over-eager courting of beauty. The Parthenon was beautiful so consciously that it even deliberately distorted itself to counteract various optical illusions inherent in the images of parallel lines. For instance, its massive columns lean inwards very slightly to

correct an impression of toppling outwards which vertical columns might give to the eye. Again, the horizontal lines are bowed upwards to avoid any impression of sagging. The bow is only about two and a half inches high. It is not seen. The building looks beautifully straight. In other words, the Parthenon was so consciously beautiful that its architects felt the need to improve on God's imperfect work in making the human eye. As a result the Parthenon is a brilliant example—but of what? Not of universal cosmic perfection, as is sometimes suggested. It is a perfect example only of its own remote, majestic, rather pompous kind of beauty.

Modern architecture can be beautiful in this way. It can also be beautiful in the delightful, relaxed, drowsy sense. It can also be frivolous, forbidding, robust, tensed, tough, brutal, gentle, warming, even witty. In short, it can have character. It can reflect real life as well as it can romanticize it and disguise it. It can increase awareness by heightening the experience of each phase of life it shelters, by creating a visual environment appropriate to the occasion. But the Vitruvian concept of pleasingness and the Wottonian one of delight gives licence to every irrational, pretentious, pseudo-artistic act in architecture. Acceptance of the doctrine of delight is the justification of all empty decoration and the vindication of Featurism.

Architecture can flourish only by dismissing the essentially unreal concept of beauty as a sort of detachable glamorising agent and substituting the concept of pertinence, so that every type of building commands its own visual quality. The main task of architecture indeed is to try to rise above pleasingness, to allow the actual circumstances of the most suitable materials available and the human problems of the time and the place to shape every concept, and to allow every concept its own freedom to use a knowledge of proportion and balance and the other technical tricks of the trade, not to serve academic rules, but to suit its own character.

Acceptance of appropriateness to the occasion as the first aim of architecture is no contradiction to the increasing, almost overwhelming tendency of building to adopt impersonal technology. The curtain walls and other standardized space-envelopes can be true to prosaic activities as an individually, painstakingly designed church can be true to the activity of worship. This sort of appropriateness has nothing, of course, to do with fashionable symbols or iconography, and little directly to do with external appearances. The important thing is the appropriateness of the shelter to the job being done, and the psychological effect on the occupant of the space to the shape, scale, proportions, colour, details of the space. The desirable things are that all these relate to and are disciplined by the concept, or motive, in hand, and that this motive is impeccably forthright and unsententious in its acceptance of the realities of the situation, that it does not try to make a silk purse on every occasion, that it is strong enough to accept the naked truth, even when the truth is dull, even when it seems ugly.

Architecture should never have allowed itself to get into the habit of glamorising or glossing over the facts with smooth visual effects. A building can rise to full stature only when it has, firstly, definite and unequivocal form in its masses and its spaces, for without this there is no statement at all; and secondly when the formal statement relates directly to the realities of the problem, for without this every building may as well be done in the image of a fairy castle. To deny the realities consciously for one relaxed moment, in the cause of beauty or expression or religion or commerce, is to start down the slippery road to Featurism and the ultimate ridicule of architecture.

8

THE ETHICS OF ANTI-FEATURISM

By definition Featurism stands for the subordination of the whole and the accentuation of selected separate features, and it is bad enough from Plato's point of view when the conflicting, restless features are necessary functional elements. But in the most common form, the featured features are not required functionally by man or beast. They mean very little and they do absolutely nothing. They are the gratuitous adornments known throughout most of art history as ornament, or, when their lack of meaning is especially obvious, decoration. They take several forms. They may be half-pretending to be real functioning parts of the object to which they adhere, like the stone columns standing in front of the self-sufficient concrete structure of most pre-war bank facades. They may be lies of such Goebbelian proportions that they convince the viewer that they must be true, like the Sydney Harbour Bridge pylons or the tower of Melbourne's Manchester Unity Building. They may be sordidly economic-functional, like the wriggling patterns on plastic table-tops intended to hide the scratches or the vivid marble effects on floor tiles intended to hide the dirt. They may be an involuntary traditional or fashionable habit, like lipstick. Or they may be a very special additional artistic thing given to another thing by someone who loves both of them.

When every scroll or figurine had to be carved by hand, no one questioned their right to exist. But from early in the nineteenth century when the casting, printing, turning, moulding, veneering, spinning and stamping machines first began producing cheap, intricate ornament, the ethics of its use have probably raised more argument than any other topic in design. Righteous antagonism to the mass-produced decoration was in large measure responsible for the revolution that eventually crystallized in the modern idiom of design. As an axiom, the modern movement demanded from the beginning impeccably honourable intentions towards materials. The Europeans were more scrupulous than the Americans, but in general all agreed that there should be no concealment of anything essential to the structure, no dissembling or falsifying, no redundant enlargements to make things 'in good proportion', and no forcing of any material into shapes not entirely sympathetic with its nature. In short, the architect or product-designer should be morally bound by structural and mechanical laws and prepared to forsake all other means of achieving form.

The rules seem simple enough. One must follow the engineer's formulae and the slide rule, and these do not equivocate. Even Oscar Wilde probably would have admitted that nothing much could be said in favour of an architect who, by whim or incompetence, makes the foundations three times as big as required for permanence. By logical extension of this thought, most people will accept in theory the code that the sizes dictated by experience and scientific analysis are the only sizes which can in conscience be used for the visible parts. A column made fatter than its safe, economical size because it thus looks 'in better proportion' and more enchanting to its architect is just as reprehensible, if not as dangerous, as one made beautifully slimmer than safety permits.

The attention paid here to the structural properties of the selected material leads easily to the rule that no material should be twisted into shapes unsympathetic with its nature. The mason's shape of a pointed arch carpentered into the wooden weather-board walls of a mock-Gothic wayside church is now an object of derision to anyone prepared to give it a second thought. Such a fate eventually overtakes any shape contrived purely for stylistic reasons. Some shapes in reinforced concrete and steel which are taken for granted today will be derided ultimately when fashion moves on to some new phase and leaves our predilection for 'floating planes' unsupported. Then posts may be used again where suitable in place of elaborate cantilevers and cables, and buildings may no longer feel obliged to try to look lighter than air. If one twists its hidden bones, concrete will carry heavy loads while allowing itself to be posed in almost any strange position. The ethical code decrees that one should not take unfair advantage of such a compliant nature.

In the past, although 'firmness' was one of the three requisites, a wide woolly fringe area for the operation of artistic licence was allowed on the high side of minimum strength requirements. One criticized an unnecessary classical column which obviously had been added simply for effect, but one did not question a column for being grossly thicker than required provided it looked 'in good proportion' and gave the impression of being wanted. One applauded a redundant Gothic flying buttress provided it looked as if it might be supporting the wall. The new ethics trimmed down the fringe of artistic licence and demanded the operation at all levels, and not merely the semblance, of structural rule. In the backwash of the first wave of success for the modern movement, however, a reaction set in against the code. Exposed concrete and expressed steelwork began to pall on many architects, who looked about for new means of restoring life and amusement. They had no serious thought of returning to the application of moulds and scrolls, but the simplicity won by the pioneer rationalists changed its nature gradually and subtly after the Second World War to be a new rule of taste rather than logic. 'Ethical' shackles on architecture are an arbitrary and ridiculous fallacy, the new aesthetes said. If the result is beautiful, ethics and rules are of little consolation. Mies van de Rohe helped to demolish the dogmas which once he helped develop. He applied false light steel members to the faces of the structural columns in his Lake Shore Drive apartments in Chicago in order to bridge the gaps in the rhythm of vertical window members. The effect of simplicity was now more prized by him than innate simplicity, and beauty was once more its own reward.

The ordinary Australian everyday designer never had much patience with the ethical idea, if he ever heard of it, and these free methods were not new to him. The meanest designer often seeks to give the impression that his building, or at any rate its facade, holds together as a single artistic unit, hoping to indicate to anyone interested that he was able to conjure up the inspiration necessary to interrelate the conflicting demands of the problems. It is not difficult for anyone who has learned a few tricks of a style to give an illusion of unified design to a muddle of thoughts and a tangle of spaces. Every popular style of architecture has its own set of features and disguises, like false moustaches and wigs, which can help a designer escape the emptiness of his thoughts or habits, or the ugly consequences of a misconception. One such device is the symmetry of the Georgian facade and its numerous progeny, often tied like a papier-mache mask in front of an unsightly disarrangement of rooms. Once the entrance hall is fitted behind the central front door—the nose fixing the mask in place—an appearance of competent conception is given to the casual observer. The popular sub-styles of the twentieth century have devices of their own to recommend them to busy commercial designers. Simple Functionalism is sometimes convenient for those who do not attempt to conjure up a motive for a building. The first diagram of functional circulation provides a plan for a series of rectilinear cases, and when rooms refuse to be fitted into a rectilinear case it is only necessary for the architect to complete the box by adding pergolas, posts and beams, like chalk lines in the air, sketching in what is lacking in solid building to make a balanced whole.

More obvious practices of false pretence crowd the lower strata of commercial design. The cubists' plain box with gashes for windows was never a rage in the land of Featurism, but between the wars various compromises with modern architecture were produced by false means. Often in urban buildings a bold effect was given to facades by the simple subterfuge of colouring selected panels between windows a dark hue roughly matching the effect of the glass. The predominating lines of the building could thus be made to run in any direction that the designer wished, according to which sections of the wall he made dark and which he made light. Thus in the mid nineteen-thirties the vertical received a forced stress, as in the Hotel Australia in Martin Place, Sydney. A few years later it was the horizontal, as in the Hotel Australia in Collins Street, Melbourne. Now the fashionable line is the diagonal. Roofs zigzag in parody of engineers' stress diagrams. Walls are carried up yards above the roof to screen machinery and make a cleaner, more uncluttered facade. Grilles of metal, masonry, or plastic mask a multitude of doubts with the convenient excuse of sun-shading. In smaller buildings there are parlour tricks with fieldstone veneer and copper, illusions with mirrors and glass, and harmless but meaningless mockery in many other guises. If one allows any pretence, thereby denying the idea that a satisfactory visual image should be extractable solely from structural and functional logic, then the crassest of vulgar tricks should be acceptable.

Even more abhorrent to the pioneers than the thought of dissembling construction was the very suggestion of any sort of ornament. While no one is likely to defend in principle the cruder fraudulent means of achieving architectural effect, the frank application of adornments is another matter. A tradition of undecorated design for function, older than history, is evident in most primitive housing, military posts, farm structures, silos, bridges, aqueducts, sea walls— wherever building was building and was not confused by self-conscious symbols, conventions, pretensions, or the primitive urge to embellish nature. The Victorian era, which felt this urge more strongly than most and had the means of satisfying it, was hardly under way before reactionaries in its midst began dying for a return to simplicity. Many foresaw the disasters of the decorated jungle ahead and warnings came from near and far.

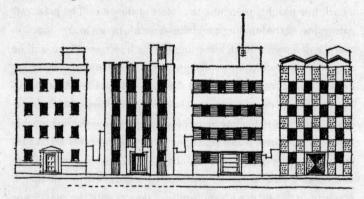

'Beauty, convenience, strength and economy all more or less depend on architecture's cardinal virtue—simplicity,' said *The Australasian*, Melbourne, in 1850, calling for an architecture of organic design in which beauty and utility were one. Horatio Greenough, the American sculptor, was not the first theoretical Functionalist and Anti-Featurist, but of the early ones certainly he was the most eloquent. The aim of the artist, he explained in *Form and Functions* in 1853, is to seek the essential and, 'when the essential hath been found, then, if ever, will be the time to commence embellishment.' The architectural essential was 'external expression of the inward functions... the unflinching adaptation of a building to its position and use.' And he ventured to predict that the essential design, when found, would be complete and that completeness would instantly throw off all irrelevancies, commanding: ' "Thou shalt have no God beside me." ' Greenough saw any ornamentation as evidence of ignorance and incompetence, 'the instinctive effort of infant civilization to disguise its incompleteness', and he was not dismayed when told that his theories would lead to total nakedness. 'In nakedness,' he said, 'I behold the majesty of the essential instead of the trappings of pretension.' The first downward step in architecture's ancient history was the introduction of the first 'inorganic, non-functional element', thought Greenough the sculptor, whose art was so close to architecture in language and so far from it in content.

All warnings against the mechanized multiplication of ornament were lost in the clatter of decorative castings during the second half of the eclectic century. Even architects who professed to agree with ethical theory crowded their buildings with non-functional features. No architect of the time believed that the theorists meant their remarks to be taken quite literally. None could think that a sane man would ask architects to abandon *all* ornament. This understanding was left to the European rebels of the turn of the century, who insisted that a building which could not stand as conceived before the world without cloak or petty titivating was an ignoble object. Ornament on a building was at worst comparable to the slashes of paint on a savage warrior. At best it was a confusion of media, comparable to a written explanation attached to a canvas by a painter who had been eluded by the full pictorial expression he sought. To scrape decoration from the sides of architecture was a simple act of housekeeping after the Victorians' squalid behaviour. Ornament's most bitter adversary was now the Viennese architect Adolf Loos (1870–1933), a sculptor's son who could distinguish between his father's medium and his own. He was the first to practise the plainness of which Greenough and others had dreamed. He saw the elimination of ornament as a cultural crusade: 'Evolution of human culture implies the disappearance of ornament from the object of use.'

When Loos's buildings and those of the other early Functionalists proved unpopular, 'stark, forbidding, unlovable', the psycho-analysts produced a ready explanation: the sexual symbolism of many familiar architectural forms—column, tower, dome, doorway and so on—long-recognized but decently camouflaged by decoration, was now laid bare to the conscious mind. The elements were shocking now that they were stripped of their string courses and acanthus leaves. When the psycho-analysts noted the appearance after the First World War of streamlining and Paris Moderne fashions, they were inclined to misconstrue these cheap commercial styles as heralding the inevitable return of architectural clothing. In fact these styles were not caught in the middle of re-dressing, as it were, but in the middle of undressing. These were merely delaying tactics, part of a transition period between Victorian furbelows and the popular style of today which, though not entirely unadorned, likes to leave its symbols sportively free.

The question of dress or applied ornament was never, however, the cause of many arguments on the higher levels of design discussion. No serious architectural theorist has countenanced the idea of pinning decorative objects on a wall to clothe or enrich a building already artistically complete in itself. The enrichment which is admired is rationalized by its admirers to be an essential element of the building irremovable without artistic calamity, something in an entirely different category from any applied titivation.

Those crafts-lovers who have found enjoyment in ornament, from Ruskin to Wright, have wanted to explain their taste, as if they really recognized deep down that there might be something small-minded about their interest. Ruskin, dedicated to 'war upon affectation, falsehood and prejudice of every kind', insisted that the only ornament which he admired was not applied, extraneous, or superfluous. 'You do not build a temple and then dress it,' he wrote in *The Stones of Venice*. 'You create it in its loveliness, and leave it, as her Maker left Eve. Not unadorned, I believe, but so well adorned as to need no feather crowns. And I use the words ornament and beauty interchangeably, in order that architects may understand this.' Ruskin emphasized that all ornament is relative to the object ornamented. It is not something to be made separately and fastened on. It cannot be good in itself, in the stonemason's yard, or in the ironmonger's shop. Before we can judge it, 'we must know what it is to adorn, and how. As, for instance, a gold ring is a pretty thing; it is good ornament on a woman's finger; not a good ornament hung through her under lip.' Ruskin of course is very old hat. No one could be more scornful of him than a bright modern Featurist who keeps his features up to date. Yet the Featurist, if called upon to explain a liking for some featured ornamentation, will argue in precisely Ruskin's terms. The feature is by no means redundant and superfluous, he will claim; it self-evidently was conceived as an inherent part of the total design.

This most accommodating argument may be stretched to cover the most repulsive piece of superficial prettification ever devised by man. Ruskin's analogy with the gold ring merely argues that the anti-social practice of holing a woman's lips to carry a ring produces deformity, which is ugly *per se*. This has nothing to do with the crucial questions: Why ornament? Why the nervous, savage urge? How could the sensitive Ruskin say a ring is good on a woman's finger when she is already 'so well adorned as to need no feather crowns'? He escaped this issue by likening bodily adornment to a building's furnishings, which are '*not* the *architecture*' (his italics) and no concern of the architect. At another time, in *Seven Lamps*, he showed in one of his moments of pique that he did in his heart view all ornament in the only light which sanity will allow: as a separate entity from the honest solid stuff of the building. It was to be applied or omitted according to taste and appropriateness. He had this thought while waiting for his train: 'There was never a more flagrant nor impertinent folly than the smallest portion of ornament in anything concerned with railroads or near them.'

Despite all pleas of mid nineteenth century critics in America and Australia, the ideological fight against ornament took place almost entirely on the face of European walls. It was a foreign war to America and to Australia almost as remote as any Old World fighting of the time. Even in Chicago, where the sky-scraper and the candid expression of the big building frame were pioneered, ornament clung to the terra cotta. There was one exception: the great, gloomy, powerful Monadnock building by Burnham and Root, which sweeps in an unbroken line from pavement to parapet. But Louis Sullivan, the leader of the Chicago School, was also the first and best of the flamboyant decorators of the new century. 'It is not evident to me,' he once admitted, 'that ornament can intrinsically heighten [architecture's] elemental qualities.' But he could not resist adding it to every building he designed. Frank Lloyd Wright, his pupil, never forsook applied ornament for long, arguing as Ruskin did that every decorative strip of wood or fold of metal, which may appear so unnecessary to some observers, is in fact essential to his motive, conceived in the moment of inspiration, and 'growing like the blossom from the tree'.

The early European expressions of Adolf Loos's creed were in concrete and plaster, steel and glass, and other self-consciously machined materials which in their naked state were attractive for all purposes only while the novelty lasted. The Loos revolution failed. Ornament gradually returned, taking new guises including abstract mural paintings, pierced metals, bas-reliefs and Italian mosaic tiles. The new humanist welcomes this. He has no time for ethical shibboleths and depends upon his taste: If I cannot tell by external examination that a column is redundant, he says, I am not concerned with the engineer's theory that it could be removed without disaster. If it delights me it rises to a plane above the reach of logarithms.

This attitude is a godsend to the tired architect who cannot achieve proportions and emphases which satisfy him by a sensitive arrangement of the essential elements. It permits him to bring in new elements to complete the composition. A line of ornament, whether a cornice borrowed from Greece or a row of louvres from Brazil, may improve the building's apparent proportions. A mural by the entrance will give the desired accent which he could not provide in the motive. Arbitrary features, breaks and bends will relieve the monotony of a dull expanse. But honesty of intent and the abhorrence of misrepresentation are no more than a timeless code of craftsmanship. Whenever a new, stricter, convincing interpretation of that code is understood by a craftsman he cannot allow himself to return to looser methods. The integrity of a building is not divisible. Dissembling of any sort reduces the dignity and meaning of architecture. Without this discipline it is only a semi-paralysed sort of sculpture. Discipline does not condemn architecture to naive functionalism. There is all the scope for poetry which any architect could desire in the interpretation of the reality of the function, and the devising of a form to typify it. But the poetic looseness should cease once the formal motive is adopted.

Observation of the ethics need not imply sanctimony or demand a self-righteous display of every element and the expression of all means to the end. A man may be deemed truthful without his opening his bankbook to everyone he meets. The ethics condemn redundancies and deliberate disguises. But they still permit the sympathetic control of all the essential elements in accordance with the building's motive. The great builders of the world have demonstrated a number of times that it is within the bounds of possibility, economy and even ordinary everyday architectural practice, to create character while observing the natural laws of structure, the practical rules of use, and the code of Adolf Loos. Architecture is simply the manipulation of necessary elements of shelter, and an architect would seem to have missed his vocation if he finds it impossible to achieve the kind of character he seeks within the structural and practical rules.

Nothing is easier for a clever stylist than the designing of an attractive building exterior, redolent of any desired atmosphere, if he separates it entirely from the realities of function and structure. This is done every day for the backdrops of the stage, films and advertisements. With his greater facilities for illusion, a modern architect could go further and, outstripping the Baroque, build beautiful gauze and plastic screens in front of his buildings, permanently coloured in any fetching design he desired. But even the most uncaring or cynical Featurist will guess that this proposal is made in heavy sarcasm, because he knows that underneath every responsible human's apparent insensibility to his shelter there is a desire for some sense of reality in the background of life. The most frivolous Featurist designer, moulding like putty the tastes of a public hypnotized by fashion, acknowledges an instinctive revulsion against blatant counterfeit. Even in the abstract sphere of car design, the fins and dips and chromium strips pretend to be practical. The swept-wing tail fin of useless metal is given a taillight to hold so that it may try to look useful. Arbitrary breaks in the body line are often given little black slots suggestive of a ventilator or perhaps some electronic aid to comfort.

Not all surface adornment is arbitrary, or bolstering some weakness in the basic form. Sometimes the building is strong in itself, but the ornament is added somewhere along the path of design as an unsolicited gift of love from the architect. Much of Walter Burley Griffin's ornament in Australia had this look of a sentimental gift, and it may be accepted in this spirit without our having solemnly to hunt for the significance which the donor saw in the gift. Colour may be an architect's ornamental, irrational gift to a motive. Since something must be applied the architect should be able to select materials which support his motive. So far the ethics are fairly precise: if an element must be included, select the best for the case. But what of murals, mosaics, sculptural pieces, or symbolic or iconic objects like the cross on the church?

At this point the ethical rules change, as it were, into small type on the back of the sheet. The introduction of other arts and crafts by sub-commissioned painters and carvers may be a helpful type of feature to an irresolute architect, allowing him to dispense with some descriptive lettering and freeing him from the moral and economic responsibility of adding a feature of his own invention to a weak spot in his composition. Painting and sculpture can add their own descriptive and symbolic overtones to the architectural range of expression, projecting currents which could never be started by architecture's own abstract means, but these emotional overtones have nothing to do with architecture. And, in any case, the 'free' arts seldom are invited to add their own messages; usually they are no more than decoration by proxy, the painter or sculptor being used by the architect to escape with clear conscience, within the accepted terms of modern architecture, from the drabness of his creation.

There are, in short, three kinds of architectural ornamental feature. One is a gift from the architect's heart, and one is descriptive extrinsic art or symbol. But the third and most common type is the architect's admission of his own indecision. For a little of each sort no better example could be found anywhere than Wilson Hall, the ceremonial hall of the University of Melbourne and the crowning jewel of Australian Featurism. The circumstances of this building and the character of its undoubted beauty are worthy of examination as a record of the highest level of Australian public taste in the mid nineteen-fifties, and the highest levels to which Featurism and sensitive creative ornamentation can aspire.

The building is named after Sir Samuel Wilson, who gave £30,000 for the erection in 1879 of the first hall to the design of Joseph Reed, who chose for this special occasion 'Tudor Perpendicular'. In 1952 it was gutted by fire, and the ashes of its oak-faced oregon beams were hardly cold before a discussion was raging on the style of the building required immediately to replace the burnt one. The division was more complicated than in the usual traditional-versus-modern argument, for the bulk of the Hawkesbury sandstone walls remained upright, and a third school of thought advocated that these be left as a comparatively genuine Gothic ruin, grassed within, and that a new, uncompromising modern building be erected elsewhere. No matter what was to be done, the choice of architect was a foregone conclusion: Bates, Smart and McCutcheon, the firm Joseph Reed founded, was still one of the biggest and the most distinguished in Australia. No doubt the university authorities had in mind also that this office would still possess the original drawings, and reconstruction would be for it a simple task. Mr Osborn McCutcheon, the principal of the firm, succeeded, however, in convincing his clients that neither a reconstruction nor a ruin would be economic or efficient or architecturally satisfactory. Eventually the stone remains were removed, and a great square hall of cream bricks and heat-absorbing glass took their place. This was counted as an unquestionable victory for modernism.

The new hall was opened on 22 March 1956. The praise for it was hardly qualified, except by a lone cry in the Sydney *Bulletin* from the Jorgensen art colony which lives in a Gothicky stone chateau at Eltham, Victoria, made from pieces of wreckers' salvage including bits of the old Wilson Hall. Several prominent men from the university, and outside, who had been strong advocates of reviving the Gothic Revival went so far as to admit their mistake and to acclaim the new building not only for being practical but for being beautiful, impressive, and dignified as well, for which qualities modern architecture was not well-known at the time. The new hall was a personal triumph for Osborn McCutcheon, for without his persuasive advocacy it would not have existed except as rehashed Gothic, and without his masterly diplomacy it might have been far less of a popular success. When introducing his design to the university authorities, McCutcheon announced 'it will be a box', and went on to explain what means he had in mind for relieving the severity of the box. This is the spirit, then, in which the architects offered it—and let us remember that at the same time they were engaged in building the unrelieved non-Featurist ICI buildings in Sydney and Melbourne.

The box is long: a hundred and seventy feet, and sixty-three feet high. The only dimension at all restrained is the width, which is forty-eight feet, and this is compensated by a transparent side wall: five thousand square feet of glass on the east, through which the enclosed hall looks sideways to a planted terrace. The entrance is at the north and through a glazed foyer fitted underneath the hall's balcony. The foyer ceiling is a fine curve of spaced wooden battens sweeping down low overhead, and the visitor experiences a notable spatial sensation as he passes through this bottleneck into the great airy volume of the hall, the beautifully fitted jewel-box, clear space but for a line of globular feature light pendants strung off-centre to the left; the right wall and ceiling are sheeted as one, as if made from one huge board smoothed by some giant fist to an easy curve at the cornice, the whole using a third of an acre of Swedish birch panelling. Ahead is the square dais and above it, dominating everything, is the principal feature: a giant mural by Australia's most distinguished decorative artist, Douglas Annand. The central figure of the mural represents humanity with arms raised to the sun, his legs still bogged down in an unpleasant tangle of ignorance. Annand designed the piece; Tom Bass, sculptor, carved it in position in the wall's thick blocks of plaster, and Annand painted it. The result is quite the largest but not one of the most impressive of Douglas Annand's works. His sensitivity and his subtle taste bring dignity to the rather pedestrian theme and his superb craftsmanship somehow manages to maintain an attractive delicacy over hundreds of square feet of wall area. Not even the bog of ignorance looks really strongly repulsive. As Annand himself joked, it looks perhaps like the remains of an elegant lobster salad rather than raw ugliness. Like all Annand's murals, its interest changes and develops as you approach it, and finally it will reward the most minute inspection as strange little unexpected intricacies show up even in the depths of the bog. The attention to detail here reflects the nature of the building, the numerous, carefully selected means of relieving the severity of the box: beautiful black Italian marble on the columns freestanding inside the glass wall (its grain, a white tracery of lines, might have been designed by Douglas Annand), a glass mosaic screen that was designed by Annand, fragments of stone salvaged from the first Wilson Hall and built into the creamy-pink brickwork, plain battens, ribbed battens, perforated metal, a rococo sweep of organ pipes, more sculpture, and bronze reliefs by Tom Bass round the outside.

All these things, selected with utmost care and cultivated taste, relieve the severity and transform the box into a glowing space. The new building was a success, but not as modern architecture. In some ways it was more akin to the Gothic Revival building it replaced than to the unadorned modernism which theoretically challenged the Gothic in the stylistic argument that preceded its conception. As in Gothic Revival, and more than in most other carefully stylized work, this building frankly elevates features to the major emotional role. All its ornament—including the giant mural, which was always a commissioned feature and never could have been, under the circumstances, a strongly felt expression—is truly contemporary to the nineteen-fifties, when it was built. It is ornament applied with imagination and skill and in many cases with such sophistication that few people viewing it recognize it as ornament. They are deluded into thinking they are looking at the bland empty box they expected but for some unaccountable reason are enjoying the experience.

Thus modern architecture fought the battle of the Wilson Hall, won it, and was popularly acclaimed the victor; but in the process it had jettisoned most of what was once considered essential to modern architecture.

Acceptance of the structural and functional ethics restricts the range of architectural expression, and this is exactly what is intended. Even without the physical disciplines architecture is stiff and inarticulate compared with the freer 'fine' arts. But within the discipline it enters a field of contact and participation with humanity which the others can never attain. The very physical limitations of architecture are its strength when they are translated into motive. Comparisons with other arts, usually intended to increase understanding, generally depreciate architecture. The English architectural advocates Clough and Anabel Williams-Ellis, amiably disagreeing with the notion that building beauty is better unadorned, say that it is 'equivalent to demanding that the lyrics…should be cut out of a play by Shakespeare or the epigrams out of *The Importance of Being Earnest*.' This nice analogy holds only when the architectural ornament is as expressive as the lyrics or as witty and succinct as the epigrams. On this ground no architecture has ever approached the standards of Shakespeare or Wilde. But judged on architecture's ground, on the strength of theme rather than the niceties of execution and the nuances of interpretation, even a plush Victorian theatre may leave the play on its stage standing. The theme in music, painting, literature, may be no more than a peg to hang thoughts on. Loquacious media have the prerogative of unfolding a slim theme by circumfluent action, introducing contrasts and contradictions, and views from many sides. Each new impression may even be more significant than the sum. Henry James tells in his preface to *The Spoils of Poynton* how the theme for the book came to him during a Christmas Eve dinner as the lady beside him dropped an item of gossip into the conversation: 'a small single seed…a mere floating particle in the stream of talk.' It touched some nerve in his imagination and years later he built a novel on the situation evoked by 'the stray suggestion, the wandering word'.

The good architect is as restrained as, but no more restricted than, other artists who voluntarily accept the sharpest disciplines of their media. As they refine their means of expression, eliminating all that is inessential to communication, they are obliged to concern themselves more with the idea to be communicated, and to focus it clearly before they attempt to convey it. For the early impressionist painters all was in the execution: the industrious pursuit over a busy canvas of a frail, elusive quality of light. But for Henri Matisse, after years of whittling away at inessentials, 'all is in the conception. I must have a clear vision of the whole composition from the very beginning.'

The argument that architectural ornament supports the central theme, like minor figures on a canvas, or dialogue in a novel, is only another example of the confusion that usually accompanies analogies between architecture and the other arts. The dialogue is a part of the very form of a novel; without it the theme may not be elucidated.

Each brush stroke is a brick of the painting's structure. But architectural ornament is always separable from the form of the building. That is not to say that every material and detailed shape must be austere, barren and steely cold; this was merely the taste of most of the pioneer modernists in their reaction to Victorian elaboration. The twentieth-century architect has wide scope to build up emphasis, punctuation, contrasts as he selects from the groaning larder of modern materials and finishes, but there is a difference between sensitively selected elements which strengthen the motive, and featured colours, textures, or patterns which are deliberately made insistent enough to captivate the eye. These are in the same class as the emptiest ornament and since they cannot be regarded separately, as Ruskin insisted, and have no meaning of their own, they must be parasitic. They must draw their subsistence from the forms they ride, inevitably detracting from the motive. Thus the second objection to features, on top of the ethical issue, is that they weaken the reality and the strength of architecture. At best a feature is inconsequential and at worst it is distracting. It is never an addition but always a subtraction.

Forms and spaces can be a delight in themselves without any observer feeling any need for features. Architecture makes a statement in its motive, but it cannot pursue a stray suggestion or a wandering word. It will not elucidate. Hence the importance of clarity and strength in the form, which is in a finely conceived building a kind of portrait in building materials emphasising the realities of the human activities being sheltered. If it is clear and incisive it will heighten the experience of these activities by all who come within its range.

Very often a building of this century, of this country, can be most appropriate simply by being objectively scientific, by encouraging the hesitant advance of building technology, and by refraining from emotional comments or bright small talk. But there are times when a building, because of its position and function, is called upon to say something positive, and then it must be emotionally constructive without being irrelevant.

A building of this century makes a constructive, appropriate statement in the same fundamental architectural language as that used by the Greeks and the Goths. To be real it should be based on a motive which recognizes all the practical and psychological problems connected with the building and synthesizes the solutions to all of them in a single driving architectural theme. After all this the building may not have the same visual attraction for the viewer as it has for the architect. It may not seem elevating or inspiring or reposeful. It may not even appear beautiful. A capacity to appreciate the unbeautiful is a quality which no Featurist would envy and few would be interested in cultivating; yet this is the key to depth in appreciation of architecture and all the useful arts. To be free from the sirens of beauty, pleasingness, delight, is to be free to create and to appreciate the real thing, the whole thing.

To the Featurist, architectural appreciation exists only on a plane of trivia. A popular symbol or a personal association invests a certain memorable combination of colours or textures or proportions with some significance, and the visual reaction to them wherever they are repeated is transferred into an emotion of delight or distaste.

Man builds up through the ages and races habitual patterns of visual reception which amount to an evolving aesthetic instinct. At one time and place a satisfaction with symmetry is bred into the eye, and at another a certain arbitrary distribution of the proportions of an object, received as a block impression by the unanalytical eye, may set off the involuntary emotional reaction. Interpreters of architecture have often sought and are still seeking formulas to explain the nature of architectural delight and to tie up all the loose ends of appreciation. This task is all the more fascinating and perplexing in the complex architectural scene of the twentieth century. Perhaps one day, reliable, mathematically precise codes and criteria of modern Western beauty may be calculated. If and when that happens it will be a great day in the factories which are mass-producing the space-envelopes, but the discovery will be irrelevant to the creative architect. To try to find laws of beauty in the works of the great creators is a flat adventure, leading, if relatively successful, only to a sort of gilded prison for the spirit. But the search for the realities of design for everyday use is one of the most consequential activities in the cultural life of a nation.

Even with the highest zeal and best intentions, the visual arts cannot rid the world of evil and ugliness, and they should not be interested in applying pleasing cosmetics to the face of the sick patient. They are doing well if they can portray, honestly, richly and vividly, the world as it is, as distinct from the way it is represented by the paid or honorary purveyors of Featurism.

The universal visual art: the art of shaping the human environment, is an intellectual, ethical, and emotional exercise as well as a means of expression. It involves the strange sort of possessive love with which people have always regarded their shelters. The Australian ugliness begins with fear of reality, denial of the need for the everyday environment to reflect the heart of the human problem, satisfaction with veneer and cosmetic effects. It ends in betrayal of the element of love and a chill near the root of national self-respect.

AFTERWORD

John Denton, Philip Goad & Geoffrey London

Fifty years on, Robin Boyd's *The Australian Ugliness* still reads as a beautifully written rage against visual squalor in this country. And the very last phrase of his diatribe rings as true as ever. There are ugly aspects of our built environment and ugly aspects of our visual culture that, in Boyd's words, leave 'a chill near the root of national self-respect'. Has anything really changed? There are still philistines in the street but also philistines across the corridors of power, whether in government, industry or commerce, whose design sensibility remains rooted in the eighteenth century, ingloriously timid about innovation or in ignorant thrall to shallow glamour. How rare is it to win generous government and industry support for design and the arts that is institutionalised and ongoing, and embraces more than just the blockbuster or the rolling out of national clichés? Boyd wanted to wake us from the slumber of complacency. It was a pioneering call and remains so.

At the same time, there's absolutely no doubt that the Australian built environment has evolved since Boyd's vivid and satirical portrait of 1960. We've successfully remade our cities to possess a cosmopolitanism of which Boyd could not have conceived. A huge influx of population from Asia starting in the 1970s brought with it massive apartment investment and an intense consumer culture that has acclimatised us to a dense urban condition which will not change. Italian, Greek and Lebanese migrants took up the suburban house from the 1950s and with alacrity in the 1960s and made it their own. Boyd was on the cusp of this, unaware that cappuccino, falafel and souvlaki would become part of daily fare, unaware that the highs and lows and gritty reality of suburban culture would be examined and lionised, however darkly, by artists and architects like Howard Arkley, Mia Schoen and Peter Corrigan, writers like Christopher Koch (*The Boys in the Island*, revised 1974), Melina Marchetta (*Looking for Alibrandi*, 1992) and Christos Tsiolkas (*The Slap*, 2008), and filmmakers like Geoffrey Wright (*Lover Boy*, 1989, and *Romper Stomper*, 1992) and Jane Campion (*Sweetie*, 1989), as central to the productive, sometimes tense multiculturalism that would characterise Australia at least by the 1970s and definitively by the end of the century.

Yet Boyd was absolutely spot-on about design and the suburbs. The look of the suburbs hasn't changed. They have just moved further and further out and the scale of the roads, highways and intersections has ballooned. Nothing has really changed. Developers have offered nothing more. Block sizes have reduced, roof eaves have shrunk and houses—along with their mortgages—have grown larger and larger, justly earning the label of 'McMansions' and now officially recognised as the largest freestanding dwellings in the world. And, paradoxically, this has happened as household sizes have shrunk. The same building materials are being used as were used in Boyd's day but they are lighter, flimsier, with more steel roof sheeting rather than terracotta tiles. There are now windowless central rooms that are 'media rooms', faceless double rather than single garages, walled front yards that create private fortresses and 'al fresco' entertainment zones, functionalised outdoor living spaces designed like cemeteries that have spelt the death knell of the art of suburban gardening.

'Arboraphobia', Boyd's term for the hatred and fear of trees, is rampant. It has continued unabated for fifty years, as has the fear and loathing of Australian native trees and shrubs in the suburban landscape. What is remarkable and disappointing is that the example set by the 1960s project houses of Pettit and Sevitt (New South Wales), Corser Homes (Western Australia), Merchant Builders (Victoria) and a host of others, all productive collaborations between architects and builders, was not taken up by speculative builders and developers. These project houses held subtle lessons about the benefits of appropriate solar orientation, efficient planning and effective integration of house and garden. The assimilation of their ideas into the common housing market remains an unfinished project in itself. But the housing industry and associated agencies remain doggedly conservative, supported by almost medieval techniques of building, resistant to alternative housing types and sustaining the values that lock everyday Australians into unrealistic expectations of space and energy use and reliance on cars.

The parody of Surfers Paradise as 'a fibro-cement paradise under a rainbow of plastic paint' is one of the sections of *The Australian Ugliness* where Boyd revels in highlighting a physical site as 'a musical comedy of modern Australia come to life'. Surfers, he claims, is the capital of 'Austerica', the epitome of Australia's habit of cheaply imitating the worst aspects of American commercial culture. Yet Surfers, like the suburbs, has also endured and developed, been celebrated and hence accepted within the annals of culture in films like *Muriel's Wedding* (1994) and Matthew Condon's novel *A Night at the Pink Poodle* (1995). Surfers, like its model, Miami, is also a type of place now recognisable across the world as a precursor to the visual gymnastics of a Dubai or Las Vegas. It's a place not especially Australian, part of a global rather than a local phenomenon.

It might be argued that Boyd's fear of a dominant American

visual culture was a deliberate caricature and that the late-twentieth-century universalisation of culture has since leavened such influence. The American built environment today provides very few visual models for the Australian setting. But American legacies persist and include the ultimately conservative concept of gated communities, the mawkishly retrograde pleasantries of 'new urbanism' and the shopping mall behemoths that through their very scale seem to deny any sense of design ambition. Boyd would be alarmed and disturbed by this shift in scale and more so by the now unrestrained consumption of American culture, apparent even in the accents of young Australians shifting in response to much-watched American sitcoms.

Is Australian ugliness any worse than ugliness elsewhere? Probably not, but Boyd saw it as *our* ugliness and something for which we should take responsibility. And, since Boyd's time, there are new forms of Australian ugliness. There are the scores of poorly designed and poorly built apartment blocks in the inner suburbs and inner city, especially Sydney and Melbourne's Southbank, often the work of the same developers who had earlier plastered their cities with six-pack walk-up flats. These will be the weeping sores of Australian cities of the future. We build now with a new sense of bigness at the edges of our cities, with shopping malls, factory outlets and huge barn-like structures to buy a few screws and a doormat. Eye-catching fast-food outlets are accepted as the norm and even Boyd himself was guilty of designing one of those: his controversial Fishbowl Takeaway Food Restaurant (1969) was a polygonal glazed kiosk topped by a giant blue fibreglass ball. It's now not 'a humble of Holdens' but a larger, faster and menacing force of 4WDs, all soon to be called SUVs, emulating the American acronym and the streamlining of their global marketing. We scar the coast with suburban developments on the edge of ecologically vulnerable sand dunes, north and south of Perth and endlessly from Brisbane, and with unstinting arboraphobic zeal. The desecration of the natural environment is now well understood to be harmful and yet still we don't back off. More—though crude—tools have been put in place to enable local government to manage and even resist change, but often these agencies simply don't have the skills or the will, and hence continue to be unable to resist, let alone limit, the perpetuation of ugliness.

Boyd's messages in *The Australian Ugliness* thus continue to resonate. One way of dealing with the dilemma of the 'ugly' would be to resort to the relativism of 'anything goes' and the maxim that 'everything has value'. But that would be to avoid highlighting moments of artistic, architectural or design beauty; in effect, such a position asks us to suspend judgement. Impossible. Part Three of Boyd's book is, in many respects, a rather old-fashioned way of attempting to impart to the reader some fundamental rules about the production of a 'pleasing' building design through proportion, clarity of idea and the honest use of structure and materials. This was a valiant attempt but doomed to failure because of changing notions of the canonic in architecture and what constituted art in the 1960s. While Boyd's definition of good design was resolutely modernist and soon to be challenged by the widespread international disillusion with late modernism, behind his rhetoric lies a perceptive observation of a continuing problem within Australian culture, especially in the design of the built environment: a perpetual scorn for theory and ideas.

While the 'nervous architectural chattering' (of which Boyd himself was an eager participant) still goes on in today's cities, Boyd would be immensely gratified that contemporary Australian architecture is now highly regarded and visible in world terms. He would be gratified also by the level of design culture in most Australian cities and gratified that climate change and sustainability will, by necessity, force new focus on those aspects he identified in 1960, especially the nature and form of the typical suburban home. And, most especially, the value of trees, with their ability to soften city and suburban streets, as bearers of shade and as climatic mediators. When Boyd was writing, Australians were planting extensive areas of buffalo grass lawns and dumping uncounted litres of water on them daily. Now, no more. Our exotic gardens, especially our botanical gardens, are at serious risk. Water is scarce and our houses, suburbs and cities all have to readjust. The effect on the look of our cities will be dramatic. But the big question is: will Australians change? Will the culture change or will the ugly side of Australia win out? As a rare and early public intellectual for the Australian built environment, Boyd pricked our conscience and his concerns remain vital and relevant.

Today, he would regret that such portents of change in our culture have been forced upon Australia as a reflection of changes in the world rather than of our own volition. Boyd's strategy was to focus on the word 'ugliness'—an idea that almost all Australians would agree on, or at the very least have a strong opinion about. If he'd called the book *The Australian Beauty*, his project of critique would almost certainly have been a flop. As it was, his literary ploy was clever and is still clever. By the time Boyd died, in 1971, *The Australian Ugliness* had been reprinted four times and had become a national bestseller. There hasn't been a book like it since.

At the heart of Boyd's concept of 'featurism' is a history of unwillingness on the part of Australians and Australian governments to spend appropriate money on the built environment, almost as if there was a deep suspicion of it, an ongoing spartan belief in the make-do mentality of early European settlement. No better example of this was the folly and fortune of the Sydney Opera House, under construction at the time of Boyd's writing, an ambitious building that aesthetically and economically has more than paid back its construction costs in tourism, urbanity and national identity. In the end, what Boyd is asking for in *The Australian Ugliness* is not that we make everything aesthetically palatable but that we increase our awareness of the impact of the built environment, that it becomes a pervasive issue in our national consciousness, that the values and benefits of good design are brought to the attention of—and made available to—all Australians. His book exhorts us to take a considered position about aesthetics and to celebrate our exemplary buildings and places. Boyd was a champion of his own definition of good design. Our definitions have expanded but our responsibilities and our capabilities are greater. The risk is that without the kind of vigilance Boyd provided, we might create an even greater Australian ugliness.

INDEX

Tom Ugly's Point, Sydney 101
Toorak, Melbourne 19, 100, 103, 105
Torrens, River, Adelaide 127
Town Hall, Melbourne 54
Trades Hall, Melbourne 54
Tree Society of WA 126
Trees: attitude to 32, 93–99, 125–126
Trollope, Anthony 74
Tucker, Albert 158

Unilever building, Sydney 132, 137, 144
Union Lane, Adelaide 118
United Nations buildings 132, 143, 233
United States Embassy, Canberra 27–28
University House, Canberra 30
University of Melbourne 258, 259

Van Diemen's Land *Monthly Magazine* 60
Vaucluse, Sydney 19, 100
Verdon, Sir George 62
Verge, John (architect) l03, 161
Villawood, Sydney 101, 102
Viollet-le-Duc 229
Vitruvius 202, 206, 216–219, 221, 241

Wahroonga, Sydney 173
'Wanstead', Tasmania 161
Wardell, William (architect) 62
War Memorial, National 214, 215
'Werndew', Melbourne 103
Wesley Church, Melbourne 54
West German Embassy, Canberra 29
Williams-Ellis, C. & E. 261
Wilmot, Chester 158
Wilson Hall, Melbourne University 54, 258–261
Wilson, Hardy (architect) 72, 119, 120, 122
Wittkower, Rudolph 217, 222, 223
Wollongong, Sydney 100
Woolmers, Tasmania 161
Wotton, Sir Henry 202–204, 241
Wren, Sir Christopher (architect) 138
Wright, Frank Lloyd (architect) 20, 23, 26, 136, 141, 144, 150, 198, 201, 206, 253

Yallourn, Victoria 78, 127
Yamasaki (architect) 150
Yass, NSW 78
Yuncken, Freeman (architects) 197

UNDERSTANDING DESIGN:
THE ROBIN BOYD FOUNDATION

Sir John Betjeman, in his foreword to Penguin's 1963 edition of *The Australian Ugliness*, saw the book as a 'symbolic unremitting biography of Australian tastes and fears in visible form'. Robin Boyd was discussing how patterned veneers, plastic facsimiles and borrowed ideas—colonial, unworldly, amateur—were all too evident in the public realm. But it was deeper than that; more profound issues had to be grappled with, as Betjeman alluded to.

Australians, victimised by two world wars and the Great Depression, needed to grasp their post-war opportunities with confidence. In belief and temperament Australia was a second-hand show, Boyd asserted, an imperialist Edwardian affectation fast-forwarded to a Hollywood-derived ersatz Americana. The veneer was the mimetic Austerican sensibility, where 'not too bad' also meant 'not too good'—and housing developments were matched accordingly. *The Australian Ugliness* was about this lack of ideas: about how best to occupy a stimulating cultural landscape where buildings and land come together with greater presence and identity.

Desperate to get Australia out of its inferiority rut, Boyd challenged the cultural lag. He wanted Australians to experience success on their own terms; to lead rather than follow in designing and planning the newly expanding cities; to write their own agenda, distancing the patronising cult of derived urban mediocrity.

Aesthetic intention and universal imagination—vision followed by sensible action—were fundamental to the process, as were progressive education and politics. Government conservatism, whichever the party, was stultifying: ideas went missing.

The Australian Ugliness took aim, with exceptional wit and irony, at culpable public ignorance at one level, and the overbearing pomposity of officialdom at another. Both were sins of carelessness, and subverted research and knowledge instead of fostering an informed community consciousness from which sound urban and environmental judgements could emerge.

Boyd interpreted modernism not as a style but as a way of thinking, advancing a proposition: design was a composite affair. He sought ways of building a city, suburb or house that were expressive and sustaining. Social history, urban design, economic form, city planning and geographic dependency—not just architectural monuments—were equally important to him in developing a unifying idea underpinning Australian architecture and culture. This was the starting point for his imagination, and was soon to be complemented by a movement to create original Australian music, films and literature.

*

As a rare public intellectual Boyd was concerned with both public and professional education. He created the Royal Victorian Institute of Architects Small Homes Service with Melbourne's *Age* newspaper in 1947 and was its founding director. His professional critiques were published regularly in the UK, US and Australia, and read widely for their perceptive observations about the importance of culturally significant architecture that expressed modern, progressive identity and serious individual authorship.

As a patriot Boyd challenged orthodoxies, and despaired that Australian initiatives were gagged unless tested elsewhere. He believed that an independent stance in the arts and sciences, in the city and its suburbs, was essential. His preoccupations as a critic went beyond architecture or design to strike at the public consciousness— the connections that bind, that structure the way we educate ourselves to build, and in turn define, the urban form.

Today, Boyd's desire for a more confident Australia is somewhat assuaged, yet remains relevant. The significant gains in educational and social opportunity achieved in the 1970s and '80s Boyd would value, but he would be disappointed by the unresolved plight of outback Aboriginal Australia, and by the form and character of the Australian suburb, its awkward, anti-urban town centres where shopping is the principal aspiration.

*

This fiftieth-anniversary edition of *The Australian Ugliness* is a collaboration between Text Publishing and the Robin Boyd Foundation, which is based at 290 Walsh Street, the house in South Yarra, Melbourne, that Boyd designed for himself and his family in 1958.

The Foundation was created in 2005 in co-operation with Robin Boyd's family to celebrate Boyd's unique analysis of Australian progress—the establishment and evolution of the urban conditions that now house eighty per cent of the country's population. It conducts exhibitions, seminars and open houses for the public and for professional designers, planners and architects.

The Foundation solicits membership that appreciates Robin Boyd's original, inspirational ideas as a purposeful way of thinking about urban life, a continually expanding consciousness at every level of public and private endeavour. Informed architects and planners, government agencies and development professionals are involved. So too are individuals who want their cities and suburbs to be significant, to nurture the aspiration for a civilising, healthy society where care and safety are paramount.

The Robin Boyd Foundation exists ultimately to promote the importance and benefits of design education in Australian society.

Daryl Jackson
Robin Boyd Foundation Director

Daryl Jackson, AO, is a Melbourne-based architect with offices in Sydney, Canberra, Brisbane and Perth. Internationally he works in India, China and the UK. He is a Gold Medallist of the AIA, a Professor at the University of Melbourne and at Deakin University, and was awarded an Honorary Doctorate from the University of Ballarat.

For more information about the Robin Boyd Foundation go to www.robinboyd.org.au.

Text Classics

textclassics.com.au